Praise for *The Justice Demand*

Ronald Wong, a gifted young Christian thinker in Singapore, has written a remarkable book that is deeply illuminating and challenging. Ronald is relentless in his pursuit of biblical truth, passionate in his call to Christians and churches to live out the gospel with social responsibility, and well-versed with historical and current examples of Christian social justice ministries, especially in Singapore. *The Justice Demand's* pages are drenched with the grace and love of a holy God and urge us to reach out to those who suffer in the cold shadows of societies infected with the sinful habits of selfishness, greed and exploitation, and to engage in the public square on their behalf. This is a book that must be read by pastors, church leaders and those who seek to follow Christ faithfully, because there is more that can and should be done.

Bishop Emeritus Robert Solomon
Bishop Emeritus of the Methodist Church, Singapore

The Justice Demand is a journey that is as informative as it is introspective. Ronald Wong takes a good look at social justice in the Singaporean Church context, addressing it not only comprehensively and clearly—but also with a personal touch that gently moves readers to see the importance of social justice, as well as its integral place in the Gospel of Jesus Christ.

Rev Ezekiel Tan
General Secretary, The Bible Society of Singapore
Executive Director, ETHOS Institute for Public Christianity

The Justice Demand chronicles the journey of a passionate young man seeking to discover the source, motivation and purpose of social justice. Ronald studied the Bible, held interviews with practitioners and Christian leaders, conducted surveys among Christians and considered the laws of the land. With this wide range of research data, he reflected on contemporary issues relating to social justice. He clearly defined his understanding of social justice away from the social gospel. He considered the important partnership between social justice, evangelism and discipleship. He also makes practical recommendations on how the church can get involved in community outreach. This is a textbook-worthy contribution about social justice to the Christian community at large.

Rick Toh
Lead Pastor, Yio Chu Kang Chapel

In Singapore, it is rare to find anyone preaching on weighty subjects like justice and righteousness, not to mention seeing someone, even one who is theologically trained, accepting the challenge of writing a book on such a subject. But every once in awhile, we have a courageous soul who decides that something should be said, and the church should be rallied to address social justice issues. I am pleased and encouraged by the effort of a young friend, Ronald JJ Wong, who has now written this comprehensive book that surveys biblical and theological teachings, deals with social problems, and argues for Christians to be more concerned about social justice. *The Justice Demand* is made richer with the inclusion of some interviews offering perspectives from Christians of diverse backgrounds. Ronald is a lawyer by training. Though not a graduate of any theological school, he is nonetheless well-read as the literature which he cited would attest. This is a book worth reading, reflecting on, and would be an excellent book for use in group discussion.

Rev Dr Daniel Koh Kah Soon
Chairperson, Methodist Welfare Services
Pastor, Christalite Methodist Chapel
Lecturer, Trinity Theological College

In *The Justice Demand*, Ronald puts forth a compelling argument for us contemporary Christians to fully engage with our hearts, souls and minds the entire spectrum of biblical social justice. And he does it elegantly with real stories woven into the fabric of biblical and academic scholarship, extending from a local Singaporean context into the global arena. Brilliant!

Dr Goh Wei-Leong
Chairman, HealthServe
Chairman, LinkingHands

The Justice Demand comes at a critical time for us. The demands for justice today are as great as ever, and the witness of the church demands that she respond. What I enjoy about the book is that the medium is as kaleidoscopic as its topic. At times it reads like an academic monograph with its intellectual rigour—that would satisfy those so inclined. But the reader will also find scattered throughout the book anecdotes from Ronald's personal local experiences and interviews with other local church leaders. It keeps the book grounded and contextually relevant for the Singaporean Christian.

It takes hard work to engage in understanding what justice fully means as God has revealed and mandated it. And with those answers to live out more faithfully what it means to be in the kingdom of God here and now. Reading *The Justice Demand* would be a good start. I would love to see this book spark many a thoughtful conversation in the local churches, and in gatherings of Christians in school and at work.

To the end that the gospel may be wholly lived out by the church in this generation, I heartily recommend *The Justice Demand*!

Ng Zhiwen
Ministry Staff Intern, Zion Bishan Bible-Presbyterian Church

The Justice Demand is a brilliant and unique interweaving of theology and firsthand narratives of justice and mercy from practitioners on the ground. Ronald Wong demonstrates both maturity of thought and maturity of writing in this book. The tome's "one big idea" is that the Singapore church as God's Kingdom community should reclaim biblical social justice as an integral facet of living the Gospel and manifesting God's Kingdom. This is an idea whose time has come. May we the body of Christ in Singapore hear and heed the author's clarion call.

Gregory Vijayendran
Chairman, Law Christian Fellowship
Honorary Secretary, Global Council, Advocates International

In *The Justice Demand*, Ronald provides a biblical-theological framework for a dimension of the Good News which is only beginning to find traction in Singapore churches. His thorough and thoughtful exploration of this under-emphasised facet of the Gospel provides timely fodder for Singapore churches to chew on.

The difficult subject he tries to surface for the church in Singapore is made so much more relatable by incorporating the voice and experience of key church leaders, thinkers and practitioners.

Dr Calvin Chong
Associate Professor in Educational Ministries,- Singapore Bible College
Council Member, Evangelical Fellowship of Singapore

As Christians celebrate the 500th year of the Protestant Reformation in 2017, we are reminded of the spirit of Martin Luther who gave a calm and reasoned plea for what is true and right, for which he will stand and not recant. I see in Ronald Wong a spirit of Luther. In his book *The Justice Demand*, he has provided a good account for his studied conviction on a Christian perspective of Justice based on a return to the original message of Christ, proclaiming the arrival of the Kingdom of God and its implications. Ronald perhaps represents the emerging generation of young leaders of our times which sees the signs of our times and are seeking to make things happen, one person at a time. We need to pay attention to this bold but necessary attempt by Ronald Wong to address the social responsibility demanded of the church in order to reveal the glorious gospel of our Lord Jesus Christ, our Saviour and King.

Lawrence Ko
National Director, Singapore Centre for Global Missions
Director, Asia Evangelical Alliance Mission Commission

THE
JUSTICE DEMAND

SOCIAL JUSTICE & THE SINGAPORE CHURCH

THE
JUSTICE DEMAND

SOCIAL JUSTICE & THE SINGAPORE CHURCH

• • •

RONALD JJ WONG

GRACEW♡RKS

The Justice Demand: Social Justice & The Singapore Church
Copyright © 2024 Ronald JJ Wong

Originally published in 2016 by Armour Publishing Pte Ltd.
(ISBN: 978-981-47-6518-3)

All rights reserved. No part of this publication may be reproduced, stored in a retrieval system, or transmitted, in any form or by any means, electronic, mechanical, photocopying, recording or otherwise, without the prior written permission of the authors, except in the case of brief quotations embodied in critical articles and reviews.

Published by Graceworks Private Limited
22 Sin Ming Lane, #04-76 Midview City, Singapore 573969
+65 67523403 • enquiries@graceworks.com.sg • www.graceworks.com.sg

All Scripture quotations, unless otherwise noted, are taken from The Holy Bible, English Standard Version. Copyright © 2000; 2001 by Crossway Bibles, a division of Good News Publishers. Used by permission. All rights reserved.

Scripture quotations marked "NIV" are taken from The Holy Bible, New International Version®, NIV ®, copyright © 1973, 1978, 1984, 2011 by Biblica, Inc.™ Used by permission. All rights reserved worldwide.

Scripture quotations marked "NLT" are taken from the Holy Bible, New Living Translation, copyright © 1996, 2004, 2007 by Tyndale House Foundation. Used by permission of Tyndale House Publishers, Inc., Carol Stream, Illinois 60188. All rights reserved.

Scripture quotations marked "MSG" are taken from The Message. Copyright © 1993, 1994, 1995, 1996, 2000, 2001, 2002. Used by permission of NavPress Publishing Group.

Cover design by Michael Hu You Ren.

Paperback ISBN : 978-981-18-9334-6
eBook ISBN   : 978-981-18-9333-9

1 2 3 4 5 6 • 27 26 25 24

National Library Board, Singapore Cataloguing in Publication Data

Name(s)	: Wong, Ronald J.J.
Title	: The justice demand : social justice & the Singapore Church / Ronald JJ Wong.
Description	: Singapore : Graceworks Private Limited, [2024]	Originally published in 2016 by Armour Publishing Armour Publishing Pte Ltd.
Identifier(s)	: ISBN 978-981-18-9334-6 (paperback)	978-981-18-9333-9 (eBook)
Subject(s) :	LCSH: Social justice--Biblical teaching.	Social justice--Religious aspects--Christianity.	Church and social problems--Singapore.
Classification	: DDC 261.8--dc23

CONTENTS

Acknowledgments	xvii
1. Stirrings of a Journey: Introduction	1
The Gospel, Discipleship and Justice in God's School	2
Underdogs	3
The Big Picture	5
Who This Book is for and What it's About	8
Outline of This Book	10
2. What's Social Justice Got to do with God's Story? The Gospel of the Kingdom Of God	15
A. *Jesus Preached the Gospel of the Kingdom*	17
B. *The Narrative of God's Kingdom*	21
Kingdom Original	21
Kingdom Fallen	22
Kingdom Promised	24
Kingdom Through Israel	25
Kingdom Prophesied	26
Kingdom Now (And Not Yet)	28
Kingdom Consummated	32
Summary of the Kingdom Gospel	33
C. *Implications of the Gospel of God's Kingdom*	35
Meditation 1: The Mission to Manifest God's Kingdom	37
Meditation 2: Social Justice in the Kingdom Gospel	38
Meditation 3: The Church as God's Kingdom Community	39
Significance of a Holistic Kingdom Gospel	40

Conclusion	43
Discussion Questions	45
Interview: Bishop Emeritus Robert Solomon	46
3. How did Social Justice Evolve Through the Bible? Justice, Mercy and Righteousness in the Old Testament	50
A. *After The Fall*	52
B. *Justice, Mercy and Righteousness Pre-Israel*	53
Abraham Learns God's Justice and Righteousness	53
Chesed: Mercy, Kindness and Steadfast Love	54
Exodus: Freedom from Oppression into a Worship Community	54
C. *Justice, Mercy and Righteousness in the Laws for Israel*	58
Relevance of the Mosaic Law to Us	58
Justice, Mercy and Righteousness in the Mosaic Law	62
Jubilee Law	63
Jubilee Law and land	64
Jubilee Law and socioeconomic justice	67
Jubilee Law and the Sabbath	74
Reflections on the Jubilee Law	78
Gleaning laws	78
Tithing laws	80
Intended beneficiaries of socioeconomic justice laws	81
Treatment of foreigners	83
Treatment of workers, orphans, widows and the poor	87
Mercy in the Mosaic Law	90
D. *Justice, Mercy and Righteousness Beyond the Mosaic Law*	91
Injustice and Unrighteousness are a Sin Issue	91
Justice, Mercy and Righteousness is True Worship	94
God's Judgment on Sins of Injustice and Unrighteousness	96

Justice and Righteousness Expected Universally in Governance	98
God's Favour on the Poor	99
Chesed as Covenantal Faithfulness	100
E. *Reflections on Justice, Mercy and Righteousness in the Old Testament*	100
Discussion Questions	103
Interview: Dr Goh Wei-Leong	104
4. How did Social Justice Evolve Through the Bible? Justice, Mercy and Righteousness in the New Testament	112
A. *The Model of Jesus*	113
Jesus and the Jubilee	113
Mary's Magnificat	116
The Cross: Cosmic Justice, Social Justice	120
Jesus' Life and Ministry	121
Parable of the Good Samaritan	124
Matthew 25: Two Parables and the Final Judgment	127
Parable of the Ten Virgins and Parable of the Talents	128
The Final Judgment: Of Sheep and Goats	130
B. *The Model of the Church*	132
C. *Reflections on New Testament Survey*	138
The Church as a Community of Justice and Righteousness	138
The Church's community life	138
Justice only within the Church?	140
The Church's witness to the world	143
Justice and Righteousness and the Ethics of Love and Good Works	144
Discussion Questions	147
Interview: Joshua Tan Kuan	148

5. What does Social Justice Mean to Me? Social Justice, the Micah Mandate and Covenantal Faithfulness — 152

    A. *Social Justice: In Search of Meaning* — 153

    B. *Imperative of the Micah Mandate: Covenantal Faithfulness* — 154

    C. *The Micah Mandate for the Christian* — 157

        Discussion Questions — 165

Interview: Michael Chiam — 166

Interview: Timothy Weerasekera — 171

6. Discovering Justice and Mercy Ministers in Singapore: Social Justice and Evangelism — 174

    A. *My Journey Discovering Justice and Mercy Ministers in Singapore* — 175

    B. *The Relationship Between Social Justice and Evangelism* — 186

        Social Justice and Evangelism are Both Expressions of Christian Faith — 186

        Social Justice and Evangelism Need Not Always Go Together — 187

        Social Justice and Evangelism May be Expressed in Different Ways and to Different Extents for Each Individual — 188

        Evangelism and Discipleship are Paramount in Priority — 189

        Social Justice is the Result and Purpose of Evangelism and Discipleship — 190

        Social Justice is the Bridge to Evangelism and Discipleship — 190

        Social Justice and Evangelism are Partners: They are the Demonstration and Proclamation of the Gospel of the Kingdom of God — 192

    C. *Is This the Social Gospel or Liberation Theology?* — 193

    D. *Social Justice Through Church Ministry or Church Members?* — 195

    E. *How to Pursue Social Justice and Evangelism in Church Ministry* — 198

The Goal of Church Community Ministries	199
Which Communities to Serve?	200
God's Invitation to the Needy	201
Case Studies	203
Service to What Extent?—The Power of Passion	205
What Type of Justice and Mercy Work Should a Local Church Do?	206
Where Does Evangelism Come in?	206
Discussion Questions	209
Interview: Crystal Goh	210
Interview: Melissa Ong	215
7. What's Distinctive About the Christian View of Justice: Principles of Biblical Justice	224
A. *Causes of Injustice and Suffering*	225
B. *Didn't God Allow the Suffering?*	229
C. *Principles of Biblical Justice*	233
Justice as Rights	233
Justice is Justly Seeking Moral Good	239
Justice is Personal Care	240
Justice Prohibits Exploitation and Protects Livelihood	241
Justice is Generous Giving	242
Justice is Dignifying and Responsible	244
Justice is Relational and Empathetic	250
Justice is Restorative and Reconciliatory	254
Justice is Deliverance: It Destroys the Tools and Systems of Oppression	256
Justice is Advocacy: Being a Voice for the Voiceless	258
Justice is Responsible Stewardship of Creation	260
Justice is Practical Wisdom and Virtue	265

D. Biblical Justice and Contemporary Theories of Justice	266
Discussion Questions	268

Interview: Associate Professor Irene YH Ng — 269

8. Should Our Ideas of Social Justice be Brought into Society? Justice and Righteousness in the Public Square — 273

- A. The Anti-Trafficking Advocacy Experience — 274
- B. Salt and Light in the Public Square — 277
- C. What is the Public Square? — 281
- D. The Christian's Mandate: Express God's Love and Truth Through Word and Deed in the Public Square to the Glory of God — 282
  - A Platform to Love by Communicating the Gospel — 283
  - A Platform to Love Neighbours and Love Ourselves by Shaping Public Matters Informed by God's Loving Truth — 284
    - Loving neighbours as ourselves — 284
    - Public matters informed by God's loving truth — 285
    - Christ and culture, God's Kingdom and earthly kingdoms — 285
    - Individual and societal impact of presenting our Christian worldview in the public square — 295
  - A Platform for Loving Neighbours in Deed — 296
- E. What is Civil Dialogue and Why Participate in It? — 296
- F. Application in Singapore — 301
- Discussion Questions — 304

Interview: Rev Dr Daniel Koh — 305

Interview: Dr David LT Yap — 315

Interview: Lawrence Ko — 323

9. What's the State of Social Justice in the Singapore Church Today? Challenges and Opportunities for the Singapore Church — 330

   A. *Where are We Now?* — 331

   B. *Empirical Survey* — 332

      Demographics of Respondents — 333

      Attitudes and Views on Social Justice and the Local Church — 335

      Attitudes and Views on Civil Society — 339

      Attitudes and Views on How Non-Christians View Christians in Singapore — 340

   C. *Trends in the Survey* — 341

   D. *Reflections and Lessons from the Survey* — 343

      A Challenge to Church Leaders — 344

      Engage Your Local Church — 347

      Opportunity for Witness, Discipleship and Gospel — 348

   E. *Some Justice Issues in Singapore* — 349

   F. *Need for Catalyst and Community* — 350

      Discussion Questions — 353

Interview: Eunice Lim — 354

10. Journey's End—or What's the Point of All This? — 370

   A. *Returning to the First Things* — 371

   B. *The End and Always is Being with* — 375

   C. *The Joy of the Just* — 378

ACKNOWLEDGEMENTS

This book is purely the result of the grace of God. Thanks and glory be to God. Of course, all errors are mine.

Thanks to the following persons for their tremendous support in this book project: Bishop Emeritus Robert Solomon, Eunice Lim, James Seow, Crystal Goh, David Yap, Goh Wei-Leong, Gerard Seow, Joshua Tan Kuan, Timothy Weerasekera, Michael Chiam, Melissa Ong, Irene Ng, Lawrence Ko, Juay Wei Tian, Leow Zhixian, Ng Zhiwen, Divinia Lynn Tan, Rick Toh, Daniel Koh, Gregory Vijayendran, Calvin Chong, Shirley Lee, Dominique Choy, Dev Menon, Adrian Ow, Abraham Yeo, Lim Ker Sheon, Jonathan Cho, Joel Keh, Dawn Fung, Cindy Lee, Ruth Wan and the staff of Graceworks Publishing.

Thanks also to my family, faith communities (Page Se7en, the Ninjas, TeamZero, Micah Singapore, Yio Chu Kang Chapel, etc.) and fellow pilgrims in the journey of justice (especial shout out to Tang Shinyong, Vincent Law, Jacqueline Tan and Shih Shu-Hui).

And to my beloved wife, Ethel.

1

Stirrings of a Journey: Introduction

Not all those who wander are lost.

—John Ronald Reuel Tolkien

The Gospel, Discipleship and Justice in God's School

In law school, I thought that if I could study what God says about justice in the Bible, I would ace all my exams and become the smartest lawyer in the whole wide world. So I searched the Bible for every instance the words "justice" and "law" were used. I expected to discover principles of private law, constitutional law norms and so on. What I found surprised me. There were only a few passages on those topics. Instead, what I found were many passages in which God rebuked and judged His people for failing to do right to marginalised persons, such as widows, orphans, migrants and the poor.

Wait a minute, I thought. The omission to seek justice and to do right by marginalised people is a *sin*? God actually punished Israel for that? I had never heard that before! Not in my church. Not in any Christian conference I'd attended. Not in any Christian books I'd read up until that time. Where on earth did this come from? And how did these passages I found in the Bible relate to the Gospel of Jesus Christ?

When I first started going to church, people shared the gospel with me. Four spiritual laws; no mention of justice there. Or, another set of four—the four stages in the Biblical story: Creation, Fall, Redemption, Consummation. Again, no justice there. Not only was justice absent from what I was taught, there was almost nothing about what goes on in the world outside the local church.

After I became a Christian, I was taught that Jesus' Great Commission[1] was a command for evangelism. Every Christian around me said the same thing: That Jesus commissioned all Christians to evangelise, in the sense of proselytization or conversion or preaching "the Gospel" to non-Christians.

Then somewhere along the line, there was a lot of talk in Christian circles about "discipleship". This is because the call in the Great Commission was to "make disciples". Every Christian is to be a disciple! Every disciple is to disciple others! All our church activities must be to make disciples! The problem was, there was so much talk about discipling others and making disciples, but so little substantive discussion and understanding of what exactly disciples are supposed to be. Isn't discipleship just another buzzword for evangelism? Isn't discipleship just about doing our quiet time regularly? And serving in some church ministry actively? If so, then where on earth is *justice* in this whole discipleship thing?

So I went back again and again to discover for myself what the Bible meant by the words "*discipleship*", "*gospel*" and "*justice*".

> **Where on earth is *justice* in this whole discipleship thing?**

Underdogs

As I was exploring the Bible to learn more about God's justice and righteousness, as well as Jesus' Great Commission on discipling and

---

1   Matthew 28:18-20; Mark 16:15-16.

proclaiming the Gospel, I was increasingly made aware of people in Singapore who suffer injustice and marginalisation.

I have always had a strong predisposition towards rooting for the underdog. Someone once suggested that it must have been because I was bullied when I was in school. Perhaps she was right.

I was bullied in my latter years in primary school. I had transferred to a different primary school in Primary 5 because my family moved from Jurong to Toa Payoh. It wasn't easy fitting in at the start. A few classmates harassed me and beat me for no reason. I was again bullied in my early secondary school years. The bully was actually quite small in size, as I was. Perhaps I was one of the few whom he could easily pick on. And I was never really in the "cool gang" in school. Even in my later years in secondary school and junior college, I was flitting around, always in the margins and in between social groups. Whatever it was, I knew what it was like to be bullied, and to be marginalised. I guess that's why I relate to the underdog. Because I was the underdog. The weaker football team or characters in literature and movies who had to face off against powerful enemies—I rooted for them.

In Singapore society, I was sensitised to the plight of the low-income and the elderly. When I was a young child, I observed how my mother would give loose change to the elderly or handicapped who sat along the streets. Where I stayed when I was growing up in Toa Payoh, there were a few blocks of rented one- and two-room flats nearby. I saw the difference in living standards between those living there and myself. Also, I often encountered elderly persons who appeared to be in their 80s, frail and malnourished, and who would earn a living picking metal cans and cardboard boxes, pushing heavy-laden trolleys with great effort on the road. There were also physically or mentally disabled persons who would sit on the dusty pavements and sell tissue packets at Toa Payoh Central. All these are common encounters for most Singaporeans.

Unfortunately, when I was growing up, I was a timid and reserved boy who did not have the courage to reach out and befriend them. At most, I would buy the tissue packets. I once bought a drink for an elderly man at a petrol kiosk and offered it to him without much explanation. He looked at me with a doubtful stare as though I had shoplifted the drink and was offering him stolen goods!

Then in law school, I began to learn about issues of injustice which certain groups of people face. One of which is human trafficking and migration. I found out that Singapore is listed under the US State Department's Trafficking-in-Persons report as a country which has unaddressed problems of human trafficking. I began to do more research.

A friend of mine brought me to a church ministry in Geylang where volunteers would walk the streets, give out home-baked cookies to the sex workers plying the streets, and offer to pray for them. I was scared at first. I had never been to Geylang other than to eat frog porridge or dim sum. In my teenage and National Service days, I had heard all sorts of stories about Geylang. What if I were to be tempted? Nevertheless, I had to see for myself what Geylang was like. So I went. And I discovered human trafficking in Singapore's backyard. I heard stories of deceit, exploitation, oppression, social and economic needs, loneliness and so on. And I couldn't help but ask myself, apart from this particular Geylang church doing street walks, where were the other churches in all this when there are so many churches located in Geylang?

The Big Picture

As I was searching for answers on what the Bible says about Gospel, discipleship and justice, I reflected on my own faith journey up to that point and realised that one of the books which has changed my life during my spiritual formative years is Vaughan Roberts' *God's Big Picture*.[2] It is a simple book based on Graeme Goldsworthy's *Gospel and Kingdom* (first published in 1981) which explains the biblical narrative through the lens of God's Kingdom in history.

It was paradigm-shifting for me because prior to that, I had been taught that the Gospel is simply the forgiveness of our individual sins by God upon our belief in Jesus Christ as Lord and Saviour. I recall that years before, I had prayed the sinner's prayer. Yet, my life remained unchanged after that prayer. It was after I understood the magnitude of the gospel of the Kingdom of God that something significant happened. What I had previously understood as discrete parts of the Bible and separate doctrines of the faith began to cohere, culminating in a heightened understanding of Jesus Christ as King of God's Kingdom. I recall when it first all made sense to me, my heart ached to burst in worship. And then when I re-discovered this Kingdom Gospel, I realised that biblical justice was right there in that Gospel.

> **When I re-discovered this Kingdom Gospel, I realised that biblical justice was right there in that Gospel.**

What was this Gospel of the Kingdom of God? Perhaps this question should be preceded by another one: Is there really such a gospel? Isn't the Gospel set out in 1 Corinthians 15:1-5? The passage states:

> Now I would remind you, brothers, of the gospel I preached to you, which you received, in which you stand, and by which

---

2   Vaughan Roberts, *God's Big Picture: Tracing the Big Storyline of the Bible* (Nottingham, IVP: 2009).

you are being saved, if you hold fast to the word I preached to you—unless you believed in vain. For I delivered to you as of first importance what I also received: that Christ died for our sins in accordance with the Scriptures, that he was buried, that he was raised on the third day in accordance with the Scriptures, and that he appeared to Cephas, then to the twelve.

Indeed, it is the Gospel. But it is not the complete picture. It is certainly not the full Gospel which Jesus preached. The Apostle Paul's recital of the Gospel in 1 Corinthians 15 was made in the context of addressing a heresy in the Corinthian church that there was no such thing as the resurrection of the dead. Paul rebutted this heresy by pointing out in 1 Corinthians 15:16-17 that the very foundation of the faith requires the resurrection of the dead: "For if the dead are not raised, not even Christ has been raised. And if Christ has not been raised, your faith is futile and you are still in your sins."

Yet, when I turned to the gospel narratives, I noticed something striking. When Jesus went around preaching the Gospel, He was said to have been preaching the gospel of the *Kingdom of Heaven* or the *Kingdom of God*.[3] Where did the Kingdom go in 1 Corinthians 15? It could not have disappeared! I realised from the context that it was just not the focus. The focus in 1 Corinthians 15 was the death and resurrection of Christ and the resulting forgiveness of sins. But the Kingdom of God is both the context to, and the ultimate end of, the death and resurrection of Christ and the forgiveness of sins. Without that context and end, the conception of the Gospel set out in 1 Corinthians 15 is insufficient for faith. I had so many other questions left unanswered. Who is Christ?

---

3 Matthew 4:23; 9:35; Mark 1:14-15; Luke 4:43; Luke 8:1; Luke 16:16-17; John 3:3.

Why did He have to die? Why did He have to be resurrected? What is sin? Why do we have to be forgiven of our sin? What did "in accordance with the Scriptures" mean?

And I realised that each of those questions relates to biblical *justice*.

Who This Book is for and What it's About
Through my exploration of the Bible on the gospel and justice, and my discovery of the social, economic and political issues around me, I eventually became convicted that I had a blind spot, that there was a hole, in my understanding of the Gospel (to borrow the title of Richard Stearn's *The Hole in Our Gospel*).

Where in *my Gospel* was justice? Where in *the Church* was justice? I became not only puzzled, but also disappointed. Why wasn't anyone talking about it? Why didn't church leaders care about it?

I talked to people about it. I met people who were struggling with the same issue I was struggling with. I met people who were doing good works in justice and mercy ministries. And they too continued to grapple with those issues. I realised then that in fact, God had already been leading many Christians in Singapore to discover and pursue social justice.

You may be one of the above types of people. You may have many questions about what social justice means and where it's found in the Bible. You may have experienced disappointment or doubt about why your local church is not talking about social justice issues. You may be out there doing good works serving people in justice and mercy ministries but feel alone and wonder what the point of your ministry is. You may struggle with how best to pursue biblical justice. Or, you may be a church leader, a pastor, an elder or a deacon who has no idea why there are people in your church doing these things, talking about these things, or expressing disappointment or even frustration that your church is not actively involved in them.

INTRODUCTION

If you fall into any of the above categories, this book is for you. It is especially targeted at: (i) Youth and young adult Christians; and (ii) Church leaders. Why? Because I have observed a chasm between these two groups. The young are wandering in search for answers on this issue. Some even leave their churches. The old are wondering why the young are in that state. This book aims to bridge that chasm.

This book is about how I discovered the justice and righteousness of God and what that meant for me as a disciple of Jesus. During the course of my journey, I discovered also how the Singapore Church has a massive blind spot in which biblical social justice is hidden from her consciousness, theology and practice.

It is from a conviction and burden that I have to address this blind spot that I decided to take up the challenging task of writing this book. If this book has any one big idea, it is this: *The Singapore Church being God's Kingdom community must reclaim biblical social justice, which is the enabling of every person to freely and fully participate in community, as an integral facet of living the Gospel and manifesting God's Kingdom.*

I believe that every Christian must embrace biblical social justice as an integral part of his or her faith. And that is why I hope all Singapore Christians will read this book. Whether or not one ultimately accepts everything or even most of what I say here, I believe that this book will challenge Christians to question their core beliefs and assumptions about their faith, and help them to consider ways to express a holistic faith which fulfils God's intent for His Kingdom people.

In the rest of this book, I describe my journey in this discovery and exploration. It is not a journey that is meant to be universalised. It is merely a convenient structure and narrative through which I can draw out perspectives from both the scriptural and the pastoral, the theoretical and the practice, and highlight experiences in which those tensions are lived out—not just mine but that of many others who have gone before me, and many others who are still walking the journey.

For that reason, I have included in this book interviews with different individuals on the theme of biblical social justice. I believe I do not have all the answers, and that my views are not definitive of what the Bible says on biblical social justice. Further, some issues are not a matter of doctrine but of wisdom and discernment. Hence, I believe these personal interviews and stories will help you appreciate the range of views and experiences which other Christians have on this topic. I have interspersed the interviews between substantive chapters to serve as variety in the flow of text. Also, insights from the interviewees may serve as a juxtaposition to my own views, for your consideration.

Outline of This Book

The rest of this book adopts a structure based on an exploratory journey of the topic. In Chapters 2 to 5, I will explore what the Bible says about social justice and the Gospel. In Chapter 2, I will start by unrolling an important map—that is, to elucidate the Gospel of the Kingdom of God. Why? Because the Gospel must be the distinctive foundation for a Christian's worldview and roadmap for his life.

It may seem at first like the map has little relation to social justice. So in Chapters 3 and 4, I will use a magnifying glass to zoom in on specific details arising from the roadmap. I will course through the Old and New Testaments respectively to non-exhaustively highlight the key passages and themes on social justice from the Bible.

Then in Chapter 5, I will zoom out again and integrate the different points arising in Chapters 2 to 4. I will offer my perspective on how the Gospel and biblical social justice are intertwined. I will suggest that social justice is an essential part of a Christian's and the Church's faith, discipleship and witness.

After attempting to establish that proposition, the question which will inevitably be asked of me is whether social justice or evangelism is the most important task for the Christian and the Church. So in Chapter 6, I seek to address this question. I will also go into a discussion on how practically local churches can pursue both tasks.

Assuming that by the end of Chapter 6, you are with me on the need for Christians and churches to pursue biblical social justice, I will then try to delineate in Chapter 7 what is distinctive about biblical justice as opposed to how the rest of the world understands social justice. This is important because it gives us both the philosophical foundation and practical guidelines on how to pursue social justice.

> **The Gospel must be the distinctive foundation for a Christian's worldview and roadmap for his life.**

Then in Chapter 8, having in mind the principles of a distinctively biblical social justice, I will seek to explain what I think is a suitable process, posture and point in pursuing social justice in the public sphere (as opposed to just limiting it to a private inter-personal affair).

In Chapter 9, I will present a survey through the history of the universal Church and the Singapore Church to glean lessons from how Christians in the past have gone about pursuing justice. It will also show that social justice is not some modern fad.

We will then look critically at the Singapore Church in Chapter 10 in the light of what we have learnt about biblical social justice and the Church's historical practices. I will consider the findings of an empirical survey of Christians in Singapore on their views about their local churches' attitudes and practices regarding social justice. The findings and trends will reveal to us challenges and opportunities for the Singapore Church on the issue of biblical social justice.

Finally in Chapter 11, I will round up by attempting to answer a question of final things: What is the ultimate point of all the justice-seeking that we do, especially in the light of the end to come.

I wish to make five other comments. First, if you are not a Christian, I thank you for giving this book a try. And I'd encourage you to read this book assuming one fundamental premise: That the Holy Bible states the truth of the only true God. May you discover Truth which transforms your heart, mind and soul.

My second comment is that I have deliberately chosen to not begin by expressly defining "social justice". I will discuss this at some point—although you'd be disappointed to know that I will not offer a universal, abstract and non-contextual definition of the term. I have chosen to avoid discussing a definition at the start because, as you will see in the first few chapters, the starting point is what the Bible says about justice, righteousness and mercy, rather than the term "social justice", which is not found anywhere in the Bible. But this does not mean that the Bible has nothing to say about "social justice", just as the fact that the Bible does not expressly refer to the Holy Trinity does not mean that the Bible does not speak of a Trinitarian God.

Third, there are already good books available on biblical social justice, so why did I write this one? The distinctive about this book is the Singapore, and to some extent Southeast Asian, contextualisation. Throughout the book, I will raise examples and issues which are specific to Singapore or Southeast Asia. In the historical survey of the Church's practice of biblical social justice found in a chapter on the book's website (see below), there is a section on the Singapore Church. In Chapter 9, I will discuss specifically the challenges and opportunities for the Singapore Church with reference to an empirical survey I conducted on the generational differences in attitudes of Christians in Singapore. The various interviews with Singaporean Christians on different issues included in this book will further flesh out local perspectives on this matter. The hope is that while the biblical principles I have mined on this matter may be universal, their particular application in the Singapore context will challenge you if you are a Singaporean reader, or help give you local insight if you are not.

Fourth, as you progress through the book, you may notice footnotes directing you to visit the book's website for elaboration on points in that section or other additional material. I have removed portions of the book manuscript and placed them on the book's website instead. These portions were informative but not necessary to the book's main message. Putting these portions online help to make the book more readable. You will also find an additional chapter on the website titled "Is Social Justice Just a New Fad? Social Justice in the History of the Church". The chapter on social justice in the history of the universal and Singapore Church highlights various influential Christian individuals throughout history who have lived justly and shown mercy in accordance with God's Kingdom and the God-given Micah Mandate.

When we examine the practice of the Church's history in social justice, it reminds us of the heritage we have in doing likewise. We learn that the modern Christian's engagement in social justice is neither radical nor unorthodox. Instead, it has always been a norm. The neglect or failure to pursue social justice is the anomaly. You may also find other online materials, e.g., updates and additional interviews on the website. You may access the book's website at http://www.ronaldjjwong.com/the-justice-demand.

Finally, you may have many questions after reading this book. In particular, the "so what should I do now?" question. You should know that this book is not meant to be prescriptive. As I will elaborate in the subsequent chapters, there can be no static or one-size-fits-all approach to the question of what to do now. Each of us must discover first who we are before God and then His calling on our life. We must let a deep and holistic understanding of the Gospel permeate and transform our lives and behaviour from the inside out rather than from the outside in. Truth be told, this book isn't going to be enough for that to happen. That is why I, along with others who share the same burden, am committed to helping you continue the journey after reading this book through the ministry of Micah Singapore, a catalyst community group which envisions the Singapore Church embracing integral mission, especially biblical social justice, as a core aspect of the Christian faith. More information can be found in the last chapter.

My hope is that this book will enrich you in your faith journey, in discovering God's heartbeat and will for you, as it has for me.

Soli Deo Gloria.

2

What's Social Justice Got to Do with God's Story? The Gospel of the Kingdom Of God

Then Pilate said to him, "So you are a king?" Jesus answered, "You say that I am a king. For this purpose I was born and for this purpose I have come into the world—to bear witness to the truth. Everyone who is of the truth listens to my voice."

—John 18:37

*But what are kings, when regiment is gone,
But perfect shadows in a sunshine day?*

—Christopher Marlowe

The Gospel is central to the Christian faith because it is the central narrative in God's revealed word. If social justice is absent from the Gospel, it cannot be important. Further, the conception of one's Gospel, either too narrow or too wide, will affect the place of social justice in one's faith. So I shall begin with discussing what I think the Gospel is.

Reflecting on my journey thus far, I realised that before I could discover the biblical meaning of justice, I had to first understand the Gospel of the Kingdom of God. A Kingdom paradigm was a necessary overarching narrative by which everything else could make sense. It is also the framework which allows me to make sense of the purported tensions between the Old

> **The Kingdom Gospel is the story of God establishing His Kingdom by gathering His people under His rule on earth and in heaven through the perfect King, Jesus Christ.**

Testament and the New Testament.[4] It is the central narrative of the entire Bible. The Kingdom Gospel is the story of God establishing His Kingdom by gathering His people under His rule on earth and in heaven through the perfect King, Jesus Christ. The consequence of this Kingdom Gospel is that the Church as God's Kingdom community must manifest the Kingdom Gospel by living a life of integral discipleship, which includes practising biblical social justice.

In this chapter, I will sketch out a broad outline of the Gospel that I understand the Bible's main thrust to be. Then I will elucidate the implications of the Gospel followed by meditations on social justice and the Gospel. These meditations are only preliminary and will be fleshed out in the subsequent chapters. So what is the Gospel?

A. Jesus Preached the Gospel of the Kingdom

Perhaps we should start with the four gospels, traditionally known to be the Gospels *of Jesus Christ* as told respectively by Matthew, Mark, Luke and John (like how one event could be covered by *The Straits Times*, *Channel NewsAsia* and *TODAY*). In the gospels, Jesus was described to have preached the Gospel of the Kingdom of God or the Kingdom

---

4   The hermeneutical approach undergirding this Biblical Theology (which adopts a historical approach based on the structural unity of the theology expressed across, and from, the whole Bible itself) as opposed to Systematic Theology (which is logical, systematic, didactic and apologetic in its focus): See John Bright, *The Authority of the Old Testament* (Baker Book House, 1975); Grant Osborne, *The Hermeneutical Spiral: A Comprehensive Introduction to Biblical Interpretation* (IVP Academic, 2006) at pp 347-373; Graeme Goldsworthy, *Gospel and Kingdom* (Paternoster Press, 1998), 22-43. Kingdom theology is not the only way to read the Bible. But in the way that the subplots of a story do not detract from the main plot, this does not undermine the Kingdom narrative. There are also other ways to read the Old and New Testaments in unity, e.g., covenant theology. (See e.g., Andreas J Köstenberger and Richard D Patterson, *Invitation to Biblical Interpretation* (Kregel, 2011) at 174-187.) I do not think that Kingdom theology is inconsistent with covenant theology. Without the benefit of space for elaboration, it appears to me that the latter is a subset of the former.

of Heaven.[5] What was this Gospel? Why didn't the gospel writers, who purported to tell the Gospel, expressly and specifically spell it out?

But they did! They each purported to tell the Gospel, each with their own unique characteristics and emphases, but all telling the same Gospel. Upon closer study of the four gospels, we would realise that the Gospel is not only 1 Corinthians 15:1-5. Why else would the gospel writers record so many things about Jesus' birth, genealogy, teachings, miracles, acts and relationships? John expressly summarised the Gospel thus:[6]

> Now Jesus did many other signs in the presence of the disciples, which are not written in this book; but these are written so that you may believe that Jesus is the Christ, the Son of God, and that by believing you may have life in his name.

Jesus is the Christ, the Son of God. It sounds trite to us. That's because we have come to take for granted that Jesus is the Christ. (Some people may even think that Christ is Jesus' surname!) The original readers of Matthew, Mark, Luke and John would have been floored by the news that the Christ (the Messiah) has come!

What about the "Son of God"? Studies reveal that the original audience of the gospel writers would have identified the parallels between on the one hand, the Roman Caesars as self-declared 'Lords', emperors or 'sons of god' and the *euangelion* (meaning gospel, good news) of their victories and ascendency to power, and on the other hand, Jesus as a humble servant King.

---

5   Matthew 4:23; 9:35; 13; Mark 1:14-15; Mark 4; Luke 4:43; 8:1, 14-15; 16:16-17; 21:29-33; John 3:3.
6   John 20:30-31.

At that time, pervasive propaganda promoted Caesar as a saviour who would bring civilisation, peace and justice (*Pax Romana*) to the whole world. Archaeological findings and other historical literature reveal that Octavian a.k.a. Augustus Tiberian Caesar relied on oracles and myths which told of his adopted father Julius Caesar becoming a god to assert himself as a 'son of god'. It's been suggested that when Jesus picked up a denarius coin and declared "render unto Caesar the things that are Caesar's and to God the things that are God's", the coin was likely to have been inscribed with the phrase "Caesar Augustus Tiberius, son of the Divine Augustus".[7] By Jesus specifically qualifying His answer with "render unto... God the things that are God's", He was asserting that people could certainly pay taxes to Caesar as they rightfully should because Caesar was authorised by God to rule in the first place.[8] But God alone is worthy of total worship. By referring to Jesus as Son of God, the gospel writers were not only declaring Jesus' deity. They were declaring Him to be the true Saviour of the World, the real King, declaring that "Jesus is Lord [and] Caesar is not".[9]

The 'euangelion'[10] that the gospel writers were telling us about is that Jesus is established as the King of God's Kingdom! This is where the

---

[7] See Paul Barnett, "Jesus, Paul and Peter and the Roman State" in *Pilgrims and Citizens: Christian Social Engagement in East Asia Today*, ed. Michael Nai-Chiu Poon (ATF Press, 2006), 68.

[8] Romans 13:1-7; 1 Peter 2:13-17.

[9] See Scot McKnight and Joseph B Modica, eds., *Jesus is Lord Caesar is Not: Evaluating Empire in New Testament Studies* (InterVarsity Press, 2013).

[10] Judith A Diehl, "Anti-Imperial Rhetoric in the New Testament" in Scot McKnight and Joseph B Modica, eds., *Jesus is Lord Caesar is Not: Evaluating Empire in New Testament Studies* (InterVarsity Press, 2013) at pp 48-49. Diehl notes that specific events in Mark's gospel bear striking similarity to the stories and myths of Emperor Vespasian. For instance, certain contemporary Roman historians wrote that Vespasian healed with spittle, paralleling the account in Mark 7:32-37; 8:22-26, but whereas Vespasian did it in full view of an amazed crowd to prove his power, Jesus instructed people not to tell anyone about the healing. In another anecdote, when Vespasian defeated Vitellius and the latter was led to his execution, it was recorded that one of the emperor's supporters actually cut off an ear of a solider guarding him. This would be a striking parallel to the account in Mark 14:47. The point then is that the Gospels contained these subtle subtexts which sought to juxtapose Jesus and Caesar, but ultimately exalt Jesus as the true king worthy of worship.

Old Testament Scriptures come in. We must understand the person of Christ as revealed by God in both the Old Testament and New Testament. It's like how one cannot only read the third book in the Lord of the Rings trilogy and expect to comprehend the whole plot!

Luke 24:13-35 emphasises this. Two former disciples of Jesus had just left Jerusalem and were on a road to Emmaus. There, they encountered a stranger who asked them why they looked downcast. They explained that their master, Jesus, had been crucified. The stranger then explained everything to them. Luke 24:25-27 describes it:

> And he said to them, "O foolish ones, and slow of heart to believe all that the prophets have spoken! Was it not necessary that the Christ should suffer these things and enter into his glory?" *And beginning with Moses and all the Prophets, he interpreted to them in all the Scriptures* the things concerning himself. (Emphasis added)

By the time the stranger finished his course, it was evening. The two disciples urged the stranger to stay the night with them. When the stranger gave thanks and broke bread at supper, the spiritual eyes of the two men were opened and they realised that the stranger was none other than Jesus! Then Jesus disappeared. And somehow they finally understood the Gospel! Immediately, they got up and dashed back to Jerusalem to tell the other disciples of what had transpired.

Luke 24 shows us that understanding the Gospel—and indeed, knowing Jesus—requires a proper understanding of the Old

Testament Scriptures.[11] The whole Bible is witness to this Gospel![12]

I will now attempt to briefly sketch out my understanding of the biblical narrative of God's Kingdom here because it is integral to my understanding of biblical social justice and Christian discipleship.

B. The Narrative of God's Kingdom

Kingdom Original

The biblical narrative begins in Genesis 1-2 with God creating humanity to be His people and the Garden of Eden to be the place where He would dwell with humanity. Humanity is represented by the first man and woman, Adam and Eve. God looked at His entire creation and said it was "very good".[13] The Hebrew word translated as "good" is "*towb*", which is associated with "beautiful", "pleasing" and "agreeable". So the way things were at the beginning was good, beautiful and pleasing to God.

God then bestowed on humanity an important duty of stewardship over the earth: To be kings and queens of the earth under God's ultimate Kingship.[14] This necessarily included the physical and the intangible, the

---

11 While Luke 24:27 refers only to the Law of Moses, i.e., Genesis to Deuteronomy, and the Prophets (Joshua, Judges, 1 Samuel to 2 Kings and the prophets excluding Daniel, which is included in "the Writings" under the Jewish Scriptures), in contrast to the three categories in Luke 24:44, it is likely that the reference to "all the Scriptures" includes all the Jewish Scriptures, i.e., the Old Testament: see Carson, et. al., *New Bible Commentary* (IVP, 1994), 1019.

12 On this I would recommend several books: Vaughan Roberts' *God's Big Picture*; Graeme Goldsworthy's *Gospel and Kingdom*; NT Wright's *How God Became King: The Forgotten Story of the Gospels*. See also C René Padilla, *Mission Between the Times* (Langham Monographs, 2010) at 83-102; Scot McKnight, *Kingdom Conspiracy: Returning to the Radical Mission of the Local Church* (Brazos Press, 2014); Kevin DeYoung & Greg Gilbert, *What Is the Mission of the Church? Making Sense of Social Justice, Shalom and the Great Commission* (Crossway, 2011), 67-90.

13 Genesis 1:31.

14 Genesis 1:28; 2:15.

natural and the cultural.[15] Thus began God's Kingdom on earth: The relationships between God, humanity and creation were as God intended them to be. God's Word was given and treasured, to which Adam and Eve submitted. We can glean from this the Pattern of the Kingdom: God's people, God's dwelling place, and God's rule and blessing.[16]

God's People	Adam and Eve
God's Place	Eden
God's Rule	God's word Direct relationship with God in His visible presence

Kingdom Fallen

Then the Fall happened. The essential wrong committed by Adam and Eve was that they were not satisfied with being kings under God's Kingship; they wanted to be "like God";[17] they wanted to take God's place and become ultimate Kings.

Because of the Fall, God's people were banished from the presence of God.[18] And instead of God's rule and blessings, there were curses.[19] The consequence of the Fall was three-fold. Disruptions in the relationships: (i) Between God and humanity; (ii) within humanity; and (iii) between humanity and creation.[20]

The first is evident in the banishment from God's presence. This consequence is referred to in the Bible as death. It's clear the Bible is not

---

15 TM Moore, *Culture Matters: A Call for Consensus on Christian Cultural Engagement* (BrazoPress, 2007), 104.
16 See also Graeme Goldsworthy, *Gospel and Kingdom* (Paternoster Press, 1998), 46.
17 Genesis 3:5.
18 Genesis 3:24.
19 Genesis 3:16-19, 23.
20 Vaughan Roberts' *God's Big Picture* (IVP, 2009) at 39-41.

only talking about physical death but eternal spiritual death. That is an eternal separation from God. Genesis poetically refers to the Tree of Life in Eden. Banishment from Eden post-Fall was banishment from eternal life. The Bible conversely contemplates eternal death. Verses referring to hell suggest an eternal state of eviction from God's Kingdom full of suffering and darkness.[21] Perhaps one way to imagine it would be simply the worst state of the world in despair.

The second consequence was first evident in the relationship between Adam and Eve,[22] and later in the events which followed (e.g., Abel's murder). The third is evident in God's declaration that creation would rebel against, and cause pain to, humanity.[23] Elsewhere in the Bible, we also see that the sin of humanity is interwoven with the bondage and suffering of creation.[24] Yet, God expressed grace and mercy to humanity. Already in Genesis 3:15, God promised that the offspring of Eve would bruise or "crush" (NIV) the serpent's head. This promise is traditionally deemed by scholars as the "first gospel" or "protevangelion" in that it is the first hint of a saviour for humanity.[25]

God could have, but did not, destroy humanity there. Instead, He had to sacrifice the life of animals in order to cover the 'shame' of humanity.[26] He preserved the image of Himself in humanity[27] and consequentially decreed order in human society.[28]

Before Adam and Eve consumed the fruit of the knowledge of good and evil, they were naked but unashamed of it. The moment

---

21 Revelation 19:20; Revelation 20:13-14; Revelation 21:8; Matthew 25:46; 2 Thessalonians 1:9; Matthew 13:42, 50; Matthew 25:41; Mark 9:43; Jude 1:7.
22 Genesis 3:12, 16.
23 Genesis 3:17-19.
24 Romans 8:19-23.
25 Carson, et. al., New Bible Commentary (IVP, 1994) at 63; Victor P. Hamilton, Handbook on the Pentateuch, 2nd edn. (Baker Academic, 2005) at 44-46.
26 Genesis 3:21.
27 Genesis 5:1-3.
28 Genesis 9:6.

they consumed the fruit, they became ashamed of it.[29] God immediately connected their self-perception of nakedness to violating His command not to eat the fruit.[30] This suggests to me that human morality—what humanity considers to be good and evil—is a matter of perception and relativism. What God created to be good, beautiful and pleasing—divine morality—is objective. It does not matter whether I believe that as a human being, I can fly by jumping off the top of a building. God made gravity. And this is an objective fact. Humanity chose to see what God sees to be good, beautiful and pleasing as shameful. Thus humanity's sin was and is that they choose to be the ultimate when only God is and can be: Ultimate kings of their lives and of the world—ultimate arbiters of morality.

Where human morality deviates from God's way of right relationships, of good and evil, negative consequences ensue. Because people live in a way which is divorced from the objective moral facts of what is good and right, people live apart from the ultimate Kingship of God. In the Genesis 3 narrative, the consequence of humanity's wrongdoing was shame, escapism, suffering and mortality.

God's People	No one
God's Place	No place
God's Rule	Humanity rejected God's rule

Kingdom Promised

Following Adam and Eve's banishment from Eden, the next significant milestone is the Abrahamic Covenant. God promised Abram (later

---

29 Genesis 3:7.
30 Genesis 3:11.

named Abraham) that He would bless Abram, restore His Kingdom through Abram, and bless the whole world through Abram's descendants.[31] Yet, God's promises made in the Abrahamic Covenant were later only partially fulfilled in the nation of Israel. The complete fulfilment of the Abrahamic Covenant was in Jesus Christ. Indeed, Jesus is Abraham's descendant through whom the whole world is blessed. It is no coincidence that the narrative of Jesus being God's Son, a sacrifice for the sins of the world, is parallel to the nerve-wrecking episode of Abraham almost sacrificing his son Isaac:[32] God Himself will provide the sacrifice for worship[33] and it is by faith that we may obtain the blessings of that sacrificial worship.[34] The Abrahamic Covenant reveals that God promised to establish His Kingdom in relation to the whole world. The entrance ticket to God's Kingdom extended to Gentiles was not an afterthought.

God's People	Abraham's descendants
God's Place	Canaan
God's Rule	Abrahamic Covenant

Kingdom Through Israel

The next milestone is the formation of the nation of Israel. During this stage, God made a covenant with Israel (what Christians today would refer to as the Old or Mosaic Covenant) and made the Israelites His people.[35] During the desert years, God made the nation of Israel and the Tabernacle

---

31 Genesis 12:1-3, 7; 15.
32 Genesis 22.
33 Genesis 22:14.
34 Hebrews 11:17-19; Genesis 22:17-18.
35 Exodus 19:6.

the place in which He would dwell with His people.[36] When Israel entered into Canaan and then later set up capital in Jerusalem, the Temple became God's dwelling place. It was during this stage that God delivered the Mosaic Law to Israel. The Law was meant to set out God's justice and righteousness, which we will explore in a later chapter.

God's People	Old Testament Israel
God's Place	Canaan and Jerusalem; Tabernacle and Temple
God's Rule	The Mosaic Law

Kingdom Prophesied

Yet, time and again, Israel could not live up to God's justice and righteousness expressed in the Law. After the time of Moses and Joshua was the time of the judges, a violent and lawless chapter in Israel's history. A key line which repeats several times in the book of Judges, like a refrain in a folk song, is this: "In those days *there was no king in Israel*. Everyone did what was right in his own eyes" (emphasis added).[37] Because Israel had abandoned the rule of God as King, injustice, unrighteousness, violence and lawlessness flourished.

But Israel kept 'looking for answers in all the wrong places'. They demanded the prophet Samuel ask God for a human king to rule over them, just like how all the other nations had human kings.[38] God said to Samuel that by this, Israel had "rejected [Him] from being king over them".[39] Yet,

---

36   Exodus 29:44-46; Psalm 114:2.
37   Judges 17:6; 18:1; 19:1; 21:25.
38   1 Samuel 8.
39   1 Samuel 8:7.

God gave Israel a king: King Saul. Things were fine at the start with King Saul but when he started messing up and God decided to appoint David to the throne, it soon descended into a theatre of politicking, betrayal, violence and so on. Even after King David took the throne, things were rough (David's rape of Bathsheba and murder of her husband, the sins and rebellion of David's son Absalom, among other events).

Yet, even in the nadir of God's Kingdom, there was hope. In 2 Samuel 7, David decided to build a house for God since he was living in a lavish palace while God was still living in a tent. God refused David his plan and instead told David a prophecy of the Messiah or Christ. In 2 Samuel 7:12-16, God declares:

> When your days are fulfilled and you lie down with your fathers, I will raise up your offspring after you, who shall come from your body, and I will establish his kingdom. He shall build a house for my name, and I will establish the throne of his kingdom forever. I will be to him a father, and he shall be to me a son. When he commits iniquity, I will discipline him with the rod of men, with the stripes of the sons of men, but my steadfast love will not depart from him, as I took it from Saul, whom I put away from before you. And your house and your kingdom shall be made sure forever before me. Your throne shall be established forever.

This promise made to David is known as the Davidic Covenant. It is widely regarded as one of the most important passages and promises in the Old Testament. Walter Brueggemann considers this passage to be "one of the most crucial texts in the Old Testament for evangelical faith", and this promise to be the "taproot of the messianic idea in ancient Israel".[40]

It may appear that David's son, Solomon, fulfilled this prophecy. But that was only a partial fulfilment. King David's descendants later reigned on the throne of Judah for only about four centuries before Judah was extinguished. After King Solomon's demise, Israel was a broken kingdom. Civil war erupted. Kings came and went. Yet, God did not forsake His people. God's Kingdom was in ruins.

But through His prophets, both the exilic and post-exilic prophets, God reiterated to His people the prophecy of redemption and the establishment of an everlasting Kingdom in the future.[41] As late as the last prophet Malachi in around 4th Century BC, the Davidic Covenant had still not been fulfilled. Then came 400 years of silence. God's Kingdom was in shambles. Until the Christ, the Messiah, broke into the world to fulfil the Davidic Covenant.

God's People	Nation of Israel; Later, remnant of Israel
God's Place	Temple; New temple during post-exilic period
God's Rule	Earthly king; Mosaic Law; Promise of a future Kingdom

Kingdom Now (And Not Yet)

Then the long awaited King arrived. In Luke 1:31-33, God's angels declared to Mary:

---

40 Walter Brueggemann, *First and Second Samuel* (Louisville: John Knox Press, 1990) at 253, 257.
41 Jeremiah 23:5-6; 31:31-34; Isaiah 9:6-7; 11.

> And behold, you will conceive in your womb and bear a son, and *you shall call his name Jesus*. He will be great and will be called the Son of the Most High. And the Lord God will give to him *the throne of his father David*, and *he will reign over the house of Jacob forever, and of his kingdom there will be no end*. (Emphasis added)

When Jesus commenced His public ministry, He declared "[t]he time is fulfilled, and the kingdom of God is at hand; repent and believe in the gospel".[42] All the 'hints' in the Old Testament led to that "time":[43] Jesus is the fulfilment of God's promises concerning the Messiah and the Kingdom of God.[44]

Under the New Covenant, the people of God's Kingdom constitute all who are in Christ—the Church.[45] In this sense, the Kingdom establishes the Church. And the Church is a part, and is representative, of the Kingdom.[46]

---

42 Mark 1:15.
43 E.g., Genesis 3:15: the 'protevangelion' of the offspring of Eve bruising or crushing the Serpent's offspring; Abrahamic covenant in Genesis 12, 15; Genesis 22: Abraham sacrificing Isaac on the altar only to be stopped by God's angels, whereupon God Himself provided the sacrifice; the Passover in Exodus as model of Jesus as the Christian's Passover; the golden serpent which Israelites looked upon and lived: Numbers 21:8-9; John 3:14; the sacrificial system and the Day of Atonement: Hebrews 10:1-14; the promise of a Davidic everlasting King in 2 Samuel 7:12-16, Isaiah 9:6-7; Isaiah 42:1-9; 49:5-7; Daniel 7:27 fulfilled in Luke 1:32-33; Jesus as the Suffering Servant in Isaiah 53; promise of the New Covenant in Jeremiah 31:33-34; herald of the one who comes in the name of the Lord in Malachi 3:1 and Isaiah 40:3 fulfilled in Mark 1:2-3 and 3:2-3; Psalms 22; 69; 110 (see Matthew 22:41-46; Mark 12:35-37); prophecy of the Messiah would atone for sins and bring everlasting righteousness in Daniel 9:24-27; in Acts 13:16-41, apostle Paul gave a concise sermon stretching from Abraham, Israel in Egypt to Jesus as the Christ fulfilling the promises of God made throughout Israel's history; every covenantal promise by God is fulfilled, finds its 'amen', in Christ: 2 Corinthians 1:20: see Warren W Wiersbe, *The Bible Exposition Commentary*, Vol. 1 (Victor Books, 1989) at 279; Vaughan Roberts' *God's Big Picture* (IVP, 2009) at 113-128; C René Padilla, *Mission Between the Times* (Langham Monographs, 2010) at 91-94.
44 C René Padilla, *Mission Between the Times* (Langham Monographs, 2010) at 86-91.
45 1 Peter 1:3-2:10.
46 But the Kingdom is not equivalent to the Church; the Kingdom is much larger than the Church: John F Balchin, *I Want To Know What The Bible Says About The Church* (Kingsway Publications, 1979) at 20-21.

> **Jesus is the fulfilment of God's promises concerning the Messiah and the Kingdom of God.**

Jesus is the place of God's presence: He is the tabernacle and temple of God itself.[47] God's rule and blessings are found within a New Covenant established by Jesus' work on the Cross,[48] sealed by His blood and open to all peoples and nations, not just Israel.[49] It is by Jesus' work as the mediator of the New Covenant that all who are found under this covenant are free from their sins and entitled to the eternal inheritance of the Kingdom of God.[50] It is important to recognise that while the forgiveness of sins is an important aspect of the New Covenant, it is not the be all and end all.

It is a means to a larger end: Entrance into the Kingdom of God in which believers become a people of God[51] and can draw near to the presence of God.[52]

Jesus Christ—the King of God's Kingdom, the King over all human kings and rulers, the King who created the whole universe—carried my sins and the consequences of all my sins—my shame, guilt, brokenness, suffering—onto the Cross, and paid the price of my sin, that is, death, so that I can be made whole, good and beautiful. So that I can have a right relationship with God, right relationships with other people and right relationships with creation. So that I can become a citizen of the Kingdom of God, along with all the Christians past, present and future, that is the Church, the family of God.

---

47   John 1:14; 2:13-22.
48   See generally John Stott, *The Cross of Christ* (IVP Books, 2006).
49   Jeremiah 31:31-34; Isaiah 42:6; Luke 22:20; 1 Corinthians 11:25; Hebrews 8-10.
50   Hebrews 9:15; Colossians 1:12-13.
51   1 Peter 2:9-10.
52   Hebrews 10:19-22.

And now this King is picking up all the broken pieces. He is reconciling all things to Himself.[53] He is rebuilding and restoring the Kingdom of God. This King is reconciling all of us to enter into His Kingdom. And the entrance into the Kingdom of God is at the Cross of the King.

The Cross is the means by which the new form of God's Kingdom is inaugurated. The Cross is central to, and shapes the ethos of, this Kingdom. God's King establishes His Lordship as a humble suffering servant who took up the Cross rather than the sword,[54] and who for that reason was exalted to the status of King *over all earthly Kings*.[55]

The utter failure of God's Kingdom on earth preceding Jesus was not because God messed up His plan. In His sovereign will, He destined that humanity would descend into darkness and silence for it to be ready for the ultimate King. Jesus entered the world as the Suffering Servant who would live, die and rise again in order to establish God's Kingdom on earth. NT Wright in *How God Became King: The Forgotten Story of the Gospels* summarises the message of the four gospels as "the story of Jesus [being] the story of how Israel's God became king" of the whole world.[56]

The Gospel of the Kingdom is not only about the death and resurrection of Jesus, as though His earthly life was merely the byproduct of a divine plan. The earthly life and public ministry of Jesus was meant to show us what Kingdom life would look like; what the nation of Israel was supposed to be; how the people of God are supposed to live; the last Adam,[57] the true Man. *Jesus' life showed us God's way of being human.*

---

53   Colossians 1:19-20.
54   Jesus refused at many points to take up power as an earthly king or wield violence or earthly forms of power: John 6:15; Luke 4:5-8; Matthew 4:8-11; Luke 22:49-51.
55   Philippians 2:5-11; 1 Timothy 6:13-16; Hebrews 12:2; Revelation 4-5; 19:16. See also John Howard Yoder, *The Politics of Jesus* (Eeerdmans, 1994), 51, and Elizabeth Phillips, *Political Theology: A Guide for the Perplexed* (T&T Clark International, 2012), 79.
56   NT Wright, *How God Became King: The Forgotten Story of the Gospels* (HarperOne, 2012), 38.
57   1 Corinthians 15:45.

God's People	All who are in Christ, i.e., the Church
God's Place	Jesus Christ as the true Tabernacle and Temple
God's Rule	New Covenant in Christ

Kingdom Consummated

Yet, Jesus' work during His Incarnation brought about a mysterious state of God's Kingdom: It is now and not yet; present yet future; fulfilled but not yet consummated.[58] While Jesus had done all that was necessary to restore God's Kingdom on earth, He expressly stated that the restoration would not be completed in His time on earth; there was work to be done.[59] Instead, He declared that He would return one day and only then would the restoration and establishment of God's Kingdom be complete,[60] would "[t]he kingdom of the world... become *the kingdom of our Lord and of his Christ, and he shall reign forever and ever*" (emphasis added).[61]

The epistles constantly refer to this hope.[62] Revelation 21 shows us a glimpse of what the future-consummated Kingdom would be like. There, God would dwell directly with His people[63] comprising people of all races, nations and languages whose names are in Jesus's Book of Life[64] in the Holy City of God, the New Jerusalem.[65] There'd be no more brokenness and suffering.[66] The tree of life in the Edenic Kingdom shows up again in

---

58 Graeme Goldsworthy, *Gospel and Kingdom* (Paternoster Press, 1998), 95-96; John Piper, "Is the Kingdom Present or Future?" (4 Feb 1990).
59 Acts 1:6-8.
60 Matthew 26:29; John 14:1-4; Luke 17:22-37; 19:11-12.
61 Revelation 11:15.
62 1 Corinthians 13:9-12; Colossians 3:4; 2 Peter 3:3-10.
63 Revelation 21:3.
64 Revelation 21:24, 27.
65 Revelation 21:2.
66 Revelation 21:4.

the consummated Kingdom.[67] This is important for our discussion on social justice. Without having the end in mind, we may lose our perspective of the present. I discuss this in a later chapter.

God's People	All found in Christ, whose names are in the Book of Life
God's Place	New Heaven and New Earth; New Jerusalem; God the Father and God the Son are the temple
God's Rule	Direct relationship with God in His visible presence

Summary of the Kingdom Gospel

How then would I explain in one sentence what this Gospel is? To me, *the Kingdom Gospel is the good news that God is establishing His Kingdom by gathering His people under His rule on earth and in heaven through Jesus, the long-awaited Christ.*

This three-fold framework of God's Kingdom as God's people, God's place and God's rule is helpful for us in understanding the Gospel. It helps us to remember that the Gospel is not only about individuals but also entire communities; the Gospel is about both tangible and intangible places; the Gospel is about God's kingly rule.

God's Kingdom is like people living in a country who left their land desolate for a long time. One day, a gardener comes to teach the people how to tend their land. As people become captivated by this gardener, those parts of the land they live in become filled with beautiful trees, plants and creatures. God's Kingdom reign expands as more people are

---

67   Revelation 22:2.

captivated by the beauty of the gardener's work and also take up the joyful task of tending their own land. In CS Lewis' *The Lion, The Witch and The Wardrobe*, the White Witch's spell over Narnia caused a 100-year long winter. But the winter curse broke as Aslan returned to Narnia and roamed the land. Indeed, this beautiful image helps us remember that the Gospel is about the reign of God's Kingdom.

A summary of the progression of God's Kingdom as recorded in the biblical narrative is set out in this graphical chart.

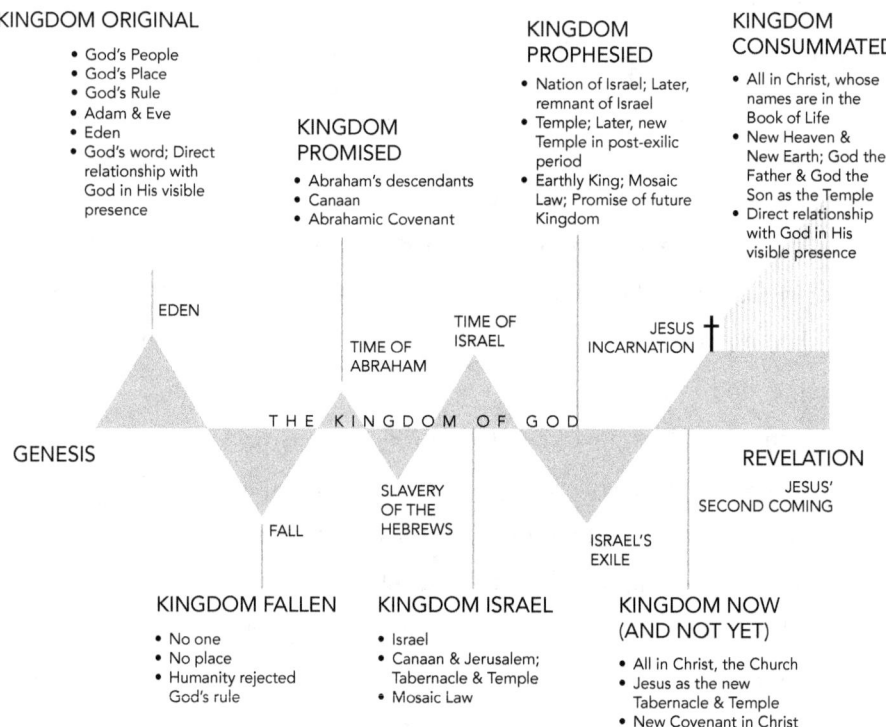

C. Implications of the Gospel of God's Kingdom

The Gospel of the Kingdom of God has profound implications on how we as God's people ought to live today. I think there are four main implications to this Gospel which concern the concept of "salvation", a word many of us toss around without understanding its biblical meaning.[68] And I have three meditations on social justice and the Kingdom Gospel.

a. Individual reconciliation with God: Justification, or the satisfaction of the just—the forgiveness of our sins because of Jesus' work on the Cross so that we may have a relationship with a holy and just God.[69]

b. Individual transformation in the Holy Spirit: Our ongoing sanctification,[70] and confession of, and repentance from, sins; learning to do as Jesus teaches us to do;[71] our faith working through love and good works.[72]

c. Membership in the Church as the community of God's Kingdom people: While we are being transformed, we are to live according to the way of God's Kingdom instead of the world's systems and values;[73] God's Kingdom being established on earth, as against the world's kingdoms;[74] Christians and the Church going out into the world to seek

---

68 See C René Padilla, *Mission Between the Times* (Langham Monographs, 2010) at 96-99; Kevin DeYoung & Greg Gilbert, *What Is the Mission of the Church? Making Sense of Social Justice, Shalom and the Great Commission* (Crossway, 2011) at 118-139.
69 Romans 5:1-2; Ephesians 2:5; Titus 3:5.
70 1 Corinthians 1:18; 2 Corinthians 2:15.
71 Matthew 28:20; John 15:10.
72 Galatians 5:6.
73 John 15:18-21; Romans 12:2; James 4:4; 1 John 2:15-17.
74 See Shane Claiborne and Chris Haw, *Jesus for President* (Zondervan, 2008), 65-137.

reconciliation of people to God,[75] inviting people into the Kingdom of God, thereby transforming the world, individual by individual, each from the inside out.[76]

d. **Shalom**: "*Shalom*" is often translated as "peace" but its biblical usage suggests something much deeper: "[It] is the human being dwelling at peace in all his or her relationships with God, with self, with fellows, with nature... *Shalom* at its highest is *enjoyment* in one's relationship".[77] As the Westminster Shorter Catechism instructs us, the chief end of man is to "glorify God, and to *enjoy* Him forever". It is in Christ that *shalom* can be brought about.[78] The Gospel of God's Kingdom is the Gospel of *shalom*.[79] Nicholas Wolterstorff says that "[s]halom is both God's cause in the world and our human calling".[80] At the same time, it is clear that complete *shalom* will only be realised in the future consummated Kingdom where our sanctification will be complete and we will be glorified.[81] What we enjoy now is a foretaste of *shalom* in God's consummated Kingdom. The individual Christian's role then is to proclaim and demonstrate the Gospel of *shalom* so that others too may enter into *shalom* in Christ.

> **The Gospel of God's Kingdom is the Gospel of shalom.**

---

75 Colossians 1:15-20; 2 Corinthians 5:18-21.
76 Matthew 28:19-20.
77 Nicholas Wolterstorff, *Until Justice and Peace Embrace* (William B Eerdmans Publishing, 1983); cf., Kevin DeYoung & Greg Gilbert, *What Is the Mission of the Church? Making Sense of Social Justice, Shalom and the Great Commission* (Crossway, 2011) at 197-213.
78 Isaiah 9:6; Luke 1:79; 2:24, 29.
79 Acts 10:36; Ephesians 2:17. C. René Padilla, *Mission Between the Times* (Langham Monographs, 2010) at 94-96.
80 Nicholas Wolterstorff, *Until Justice and Peace Embrace* (William B Eerdmans Publishing, 1983).
81 Romans 8:18-25; Philippians 1:6, 2:10-11, 3:21; Revelation 21; 1 Peter 1:5; 2 Peter 3:13.

Meditation 1: The Mission to Manifest God's Kingdom

Through His life, Jesus showed us what Kingdom life on earth, what God's mission (*missio Dei*), looks like. His work was to 'manifest' the name of God and His Kingdom, and He sent His disciples out into the world to do likewise.[82] He showed us that the *manifestation* of the Gospel is the *proclamation* of the Gospel and the *demonstration* of the Gospel. When He declared that the Kingdom of God was at hand,[83] I think He was not saying that the Kingdom was *'akan datang'* or 'coming soon'. He was saying that the Kingdom was right there. He was revealing the Kingdom itself. That is why in Luke 17:20-21, when asked by the Pharisees when the Kingdom would come, Jesus replied, "The kingdom of God is not coming in ways that can be observed, nor will they say, 'Look, here it is!' or 'There!' for behold, the kingdom of God is in the midst of you".

And I don't think He said that only because He was *the King* of the Kingdom. I think He meant that, as someone who perfectly lived out the righteousness of God, He was perfectly manifesting the Kingdom for people to see, hear, touch, smell and taste. He is the way by which people can taste and see that the Lord is good![84]

Jesus specifically instructed His disciples to proclaim the Gospel of the Kingdom[85] and do the things He did[86]—actually, even greater things than He did. Hence, the role of *manifesting* God's Kingdom by proclamation and demonstration is not exclusively for Him as the Christ, but indeed for *all* His disciples, and for *all* of God's people. This mission of God which Jesus fulfilled is the mission which Jesus sends

---

82 John 17:4-6, 18, 26. Cf., Kevin DeYoung & Greg Gilbert, *What Is the Mission of the Church? Making Sense of Social Justice, Shalom and the Great Commission* (Crossway, 2011) at 53-59.
83 Matthew 3:2; 4:17; 10:7; Mark 1:5.
84 Psalm 34:8.
85 Matthew 10:7; Luke 9:2.
86 John 14:12.

His followers out on. The very mission we as Christians are called to embark on. *Jesus' life is the perfect expression of God's Kingdom. And He calls us to live that life too.*

Meditation 2: Social Justice in the Kingdom Gospel

What has social justice got to do with the Gospel of the Kingdom of God? First, as we will see later, social justice is an aspect of righteousness which God's Kingdom people were supposed to live out but consistently failed to. Such failure is sin. In other words, our failure to pursue social justice is sin.

Second, social justice is the right way of relationships within God's Kingdom: Right by God, by people and by God's creation. Importantly, God desires for His Kingdom to be in *shalom*, and justice is necessary for *shalom* because "*shalom* is an *ethical* community... the responsible community in which God's laws for the multifaceted existence of his creatures are obeyed".[87] According to Yoder, God's justice is a response to the lack of *shalom* in order to create the conditions of *shalom*.[88] It follows then that the pursuit of *shalom* entails the pursuit of justice. And God's Kingdom will not be God's Kingdom without social justice. Imagine heaven was devoid of right relationships between people. Imagine in heaven, people treated one another in heaven with hostility or indifference or unfairly. If you cannot accept this version of heaven, then the necessary inference is that God's Kingdom community on earth *today* cannot also be as such.

Thus, social justice is an integral aspect of the Kingdom Gospel because it is a facet of God's righteousness which we are to live by but fail, thus

---

[87] Nicholas Wolterstorff, *Until Justice and Peace Embrace* (William B Eerdmans Publishing, 1983).
[88] Perry B Yoder, *Shalom: The Bible's Word for Salvation, Justice, and Peace* (Faith & Life Press, 1977), 34.

requiring the grace of the Cross; it is also the right way of relationships which God's Kingdom people on earth, i.e., the Church, and in heaven are supposed to live by. In short, *social justice is integral to the Kingdom Gospel because it is why we fall short, what we are saved for and what we are saved to.*

Meditation 3: The Church as God's Kingdom Community

The Church is God's community founded on the Kingship of Christ. However, the Church is not to be equated with the Kingdom. The Kingdom is all of God's people living under God's rule. *The Church is the community of the Kingdom.* The Kingdom is the rule of God; the church is a society of men.[89]

The Church is empowered by the Holy Spirit to be one united body of Christ,[90] to love one another and seek the common good of all in the Church,[91] and to be a missionary community.[92] The Church's acts of love and good works are a manifestation of the Kingdom. The Church is the "primary arena God has chosen to make his redemptive reign over his people visible".[93]

The Church without the Holy Spirit is merely a human earthly community. The Church led by the Spirit is then an expression of God's Kingdom because God Himself indwells the community. Lesslie Newbigin explains it this way:[94]

> It is the community which has begun to taste (even only in foretaste) the reality of the kingdom which alone can provide

---

89   C René Padilla, *Mission Between the Times* (Langham Monographs, 2010), 203.
90   Ephesians 4:1-6.
91   1 Corinthians 12:4-7.
92   Acts 1:6-8.
93   Kevin DeYoung and Greg Gilbert, *What Is the Mission of the Church? Making Sense of Social Justice, Shalom and the Great Commission* (Crossway, 2011), 127.
94   Lesslie Newbigin, *Sign of the Kingdom* (Grand Rapids: Eerdmans, 1980), 19, cited in C René Padilla, *Mission Between the Times* (Langham Monographs, 2010), 205.

the hermeneutic of the message... Without the hermeneutic of such a living community, the message of the kingdom can only become an ideology and a programme; it will not be a gospel.

However, Christians and non-Christians have often been disappointed by other Christians, churches and perhaps the universal Church. Two things have to be borne in mind. First, the Church is a community of individuals who are works-in-progress. Hence, grace is so important. Grace through faith justifies us. Grace empowers us to be transformed in sanctification. Grace helps us forgive the failures of others inflicted upon us, as God forgives us. Grace helps us tolerate, even love, the irksome in our community. The second point is that, as the Protestant Reformers would tell us, there are true Christians and there are professing but not true Christians.[95]

> **The Church led by the Spirit is an expression of God's Kingdom because God Himself indwells the community.**

Significance of a Holistic Kingdom Gospel

Understanding this holistic Kingdom Gospel is critical. A missionary recounted to me how a pastoral staff told her that he felt his church was losing focus. He felt that the church, in embracing justice and mercy in its core values and activities, was going off on a tangent because justice and mercy are secondary to the Gospel. To him, the Gospel was simply that Christ forgave our sins so that we can be saved from eternal damnation. The missionary was surprised by his comment. How could justice and mercy be secondary to the Gospel? Such a narrow view of the Gospel

---

95   Matthew 13:24-30.

gives us liberty to tear out every other page in the Bible except Genesis 3 and 1 Corinthians 15; perhaps throw in Romans 3. Why did God bother with giving us so many other texts in the Bible?

Unlike that pastoral staff's narrow view of the Gospel, which many Singaporean Christians hold to, the Kingdom Gospel fully accounts for many important truths revealed by God to us in His Word. It explains how justice, mercy and righteousness are primary to the Gospel. Indeed, they are the way of life by which we fell short and thus sinned. They are what Christ has *saved us to*.

A friend recently mentioned how she once got her campus ministry cell group to conduct a social experiment: They were to ask their non-Christian friends what these friends thought of Christians. The frequently mentioned view was this: "Christians stand *against* many things. But no one knows what they stand *for*."

This is humbling and dismal. Christ stood for many things. How is it that we lost the plot along the way? It occurred to me that the narrow Gospel probably accounts for this. If the Gospel's focus is on sin, forgiveness of sin, and a ticket to eternal life, the outworking of such a Gospel in a Christian's life is necessarily on what we stand against (sin) and belief in Jesus to be saved (forgiveness and eternal life).

But this narrow Gospel is a *negative* view of God's Word. A positive view of God's Word would be a holistic Gospel of God's Kingdom. It would be about the good and right which God desires for the world, which is the justice and righteousness of God. Those are what we should *stand for*. Our failure to live up to them is what we *stand against*.

A holistic appreciation of the Kingdom Gospel also helps us reconcile the tension between 'social action Christianity' on one hand and on the other hand, saving-souls-for-heaven Christianity (which I elaborate on in a later chapter).

The Kingdom Gospel also profoundly impacts how we 'do' Church and live in the tension between the Kingdom of God and the Kingdom of the world.⁹⁶ The Church, constituting Jews and Gentile believers, is the new Israel. And God's Kingdom and its citizens will inevitably stand against the Kingdom of the world: In but not of the world.⁹⁷ It is unsurprising that throughout the biblical narrative, the theme of God and His people coming up against the world's kingdom and powers constantly surfaces: Egypt, Babylon, Assyria, Persia, Greeks, the Roman Empire, etc.⁹⁸ There were good kings and bad kings among these foreign empires. Yet, Jesus is the one true King who would bring perfect peace, justice and righteousness to, and become the Saviour of, the whole world.

At different points in Israel's history, Israel had to negotiate between the elusive hope of her own everlasting king coming to power on the one hand, and the extant reality of an earthly king who could momentarily provide conditions of order, justice and righteousness on the other hand.⁹⁹ As mentioned earlier in the book, during the time of the New Testament, the Roman Caesars adopted for themselves titles and narratives which

---

96 NT Wright, *How God Became King: The Forgotten Story of the Gospels* (HarperOne, 2012) at 196-209.
97 John 17:14-18.
98 Daniel's interpretation of Nebuchadnezzar's dream in Daniel 2 prophetically suggests that the Israel would be subject to different successive earthly kingdoms before the eternal king would be established.
99 Daniel's interpretation of Nebuchadnezzar's dream in Daniel 4, and in particular Daniel 4:20-22, suggests that earthly pagan kingdoms could be a means by which God provides His blessings of peace and order to the world: Andy Crouch, "Foreword" in Scot McKnight and Joseph B. Modica, eds., *Jesus is Lord Caesar is Not: Evaluating Empire in New Testament Studies* (InterVarsity Press, 2013), 12. However, it is important that these earthly kings do not become conceited and take credit where it belongs to God, or they will be brought low. That was the case for Nebuchadnezzar in Daniel 4 and arguably every earthly king which came subsequently. See also Paul Barnett, "Jesus, Paul and Peter and the Roman State" in Michael Nai-Chiu Poon, ed., *Pilgrims and Citizens: Christian Social Engagement in East Asia Today* (ATF Press, 2006), 68. The Caesar during the time of the Book of Revelation was precisely out of place by declaring himself to be 'Dominus et Deus'. For that reason, the apostle John, through striking prophetic imagery, criticized the emperor as the beast in Revelation 13.

promoted themselves as saviours who could bring *Pax Romana* to the whole world. The New Testament writers subverted this propaganda by declaring Jesus as Son of God, the Saviour of the World. The Roman imperial cult, i.e., the public and private worship of Caesar through temples, propaganda, etc., became prevalent and dominant within the first few decades of the New Testament Church's establishment. Hence, in various passages, the New Testament writers exhorted the Church to direct their allegiance and worship to the true King rather than Caesar.[100] This is as applicable to us today as it was for the early Church. And a holistic Kingdom Gospel helps us appreciate this. A narrow Gospel does not.

Conclusion

In the light of these points of meditation on the Kingdom Gospel, I think we can synthesise them into a broader theological truth: When we as a Church community live out God's righteousness by living justly, we will fulfil God's mission for us to manifest His Kingdom. In other words, *by living a life of integral discipleship, which includes practising biblical social justice, the Church as God's Kingdom community can manifest the Gospel of God's Kingdom.* It is important to note that the consequences of the Kingdom Gospel is not limited to social justice but also relate to other aspects of the Christian faith and Christian living. However, for the purposes of this book, we focus particularly on social justice.

So how exactly is social justice linked to the Kingdom of God? We turn next to examine the biblical passages which I have found to illuminate features of God's Kingdom: God's justice, mercy and righteousness. These help us to understand God's intent for biblical social justice in His Kingdom.

---

100   NT Wright, "Paul's Gospel and Caesar's Empire", Centre of Theological Inquiry.

Chapter Summary

- The Kingdom Gospel is the good news that God is establishing His Kingdom by gathering His people under His rule on earth and in heaven through Jesus, the long-awaited Christ.
- The entrance into the Kingdom of God is at the Cross of the King.
- The four implications of the Kingdom Gospel is that those who truly believe in Jesus Christ may enjoy reconciliation with God, transformation in the Holy Spirit, membership in the Church as the community of God's Kingdom and a foretaste of *shalom* in God's Kingdom.
- Jesus' life is the perfect expression of God's Kingdom. And He calls us to live that life too.
- Social justice is integral to the Kingdom Gospel because it is why we fall short, what we are saved for and what we are saved to.
- The Church is the community of the Kingdom.
- By living a life of integral discipleship, which includes practising biblical social justice, the Church as God's Kingdom community can manifest the Gospel of God's Kingdom.

Discussion Questions

1. Which aspect(s) of the biblical narrative of the Kingdom of God particularly strike you? Why? What practical implications on your life would these aspect(s) have?
2. How does your life manifest the Kingdom of God now? Do you feel that any facet of this manifestation is missing?
3. How is your faith community expressing the Kingdom of God?
4. How do you think *shalom* can be expressed in your life and your faith community?

INTERVIEW: Bishop Emeritus Robert Solomon

• • •

Bishop Emeritus Robert Solomon served as Bishop of The Methodist Church in Singapore from 2000-2012. He had served previously as a medical doctor, church pastor, principal of Trinity Theological College and president of the National Council of Churches of Singapore. Dr Solomon has degrees in medicine, theology, intercultural studies, and a PhD in pastoral theology from the University of Edinburgh. He has contributed many articles to books, theological dictionaries and journals, and authored more than 20 books, including *The Race, The Conscience, The Enduring Word, The Virtuous Life, The Sermon of Jesus, Apprenticed to Jesus* and *The Trinity and the Christian Life* (Armour Publishing). He now has an active itinerant ministry of preaching and teaching in Singapore and abroad.

1. Do you think that social justice is a key expression of Christian discipleship and witness? Why or why not?

Social justice is an essential part of Christian discipleship because we worship God, who is described in Scripture as just and merciful, righteous and compassionate. He is one who cares about the helpless in society: The orphans, widows and aliens. The prophets in the Bible often spoke against idolatry and socially unjust practices, covering all our relationships, both vertical and horizontal.

2. What do you think is the local church's role in relation to social justice? How do you think the Singapore local churches have fared historically and recently?

The local church can reach out to the underprivileged in its neighbourhood and try to alleviate the sufferings of the poor and the needy. Being good neighbours would be an expression of its life in Christ and its vocation as salt and light, witness and servant. Historically, the local churches have attempted to do some of this, though more can be done with greater understanding of the issues and challenges. The local church itself should be inspired to be a microcosm of a just society—in the same way that the early church was, where resources were radically shared so that there were no needy persons among them (Acts 4:34). The church can seek to be exemplary in the way, for example, individual members treat their domestic helpers or bosses treat their workers.

3. The Methodists have always had a concern for the less well-off in society, and a passion for social action, since the Wesleys. (I understand some people have criticised George Whitefield for lacking in this department.)

How has the Methodist Church in Singapore expressed this since it was established here?
For a long time, the Methodists have been involved in education, having built many schools. In its history, the Methodist Church has also sought to bring healthcare and other services to the needy. Helping the poor has taken many expressions, the most recent being the raising of $1.8 million to help more than 1000 families in chronic poverty in 2010 and the GOOD (Getting Out Of Poverty) project this year to help families get out of crippling debt.

4. What is the relationship between the local church and the individual Christian in relation to justice and mercy?
The church is only as strong as its individual members. Collective projects to help the weak and powerless are only as strong as individual lifestyles that reflect the same. The church must educate its members about the Bible's teaching on social righteousness and encourage them to practise it in their own spheres of life and influence.

5. How can Singapore local churches disciple and empower believers in relation to justice and mercy? How has the Methodist Church done this?
Teaching, mentoring, exposure to already existing ministries, praying for the challenges and needs and many more. The MCS has done some of these through its local church programmes, but also through its agencies such as the Methodist Welfare Services and the Methodist Missions Society, which encourage overseas trips for members where they can be personally involved in missions work, which often includes social ministries.

6. What do you think is the relationship between social justice and evangelism?

They are to be seen as an integrated whole, like two wings of a bird. It is difficult to share the Gospel without also caring for the physical and social needs of the person(s) we are trying to reach and help. It is also difficult to meet these needs without thinking of the spiritual needs of the person and doing something about it. To reduce the person to a single dimension is not helpful and does not reflect God's concerns and the way we are made. Individuals are part of society and larger systems. Their wellbeing depends on many factors related to the larger spheres, and if these are unrighteous or unjust, one cannot ignore these.

7. How does the tension (if any) between social justice and evangelism play out in a local church?

Sometimes the champions for each see their work in competition—which is unfortunate. A good test is in the range of sermons in the pulpit, what the church prays for, the budgetary allocations, and the number of volunteers in the various ministries.

8. What do you observe about the Singapore Church in relation to social justice?

The church has some blind spots. While members are rightly concerned about moral issues such as sexuality and threats to family, there is often a lack of similar concern about the plight of the poor or the exploitation of the weak, economic issues and the need for policies to protect the powerless and to help those who are left behind by prosperity.

Bishop Emeritus Solomon recently authored a book on social justice, Jesus Our Jubilee *(Discovery House, 2015).*

3

How did Social Justice Evolve Through the Bible? Justice, Mercy and Righteousness in the Old Testament

> *Instead let there be a flood of justice*
> *An endless procession of righteous living, living*
> *Instead let there be a flood of justice*
> *Instead of a show*
>
> –Jon Foreman, "Instead of a Show" (2008)

So what does the Bible really have to say about social justice? In this chapter, I will journey through the biblical narrative of God's Kingdom to draw out what I believe to be God's intent in terms of social justice for His Kingdom by looking at three biblical concepts: Justice, mercy and righteousness.

In the Old Testament (OT), the Hebrew words for justice is *"mishpat"* (often translated as "justice" or "judgment") or *"tsadaq"*, *"tzedek"* or *"tsadaqah"* (sometimes translated as "righteousness"). The Hebrew word for mercy is *"chesed"*, more often translated as "kindness", "lovingkindness" or "steadfast love". Another word for mercy is *"racham"*, sometimes translated as "compassionate". Let's consider these concepts throughout the OT.

A. After the Fall

The first thing which occurred after the Fall was Cain committing murder.[101] God judged him and cursed him to be a fugitive and wanderer away from the presence of the Lord.[102] But even in meting out justice, God took mercy on Cain by ensuring his protection from violence.[103]

After that episode, humanity descended into such evil that God regretted creating humankind[104] and wanted to blot them out. But God had mercy on Noah because God saw him as "*tsaddiyq*", i.e., "just" or "righteous", as he walked with God.[105] This appears to be the first mention of righteousness. The text doesn't reveal the sins of the people or Noah's righteousness. However, it is described that the earth was "corrupt in God's sight" and filled with "violence".[106] God declared that He would execute judgment on humanity because of their "*chamac*" or "violence".[107] The Hebrew word "*chamac*" is translated elsewhere as "injustice", "oppressor" and "unrighteous". Indeed, violence and injustice are inextricably bound. In the course of my work, I have come across many stories of migrant workers and foreign domestic workers (FDWs) who are victims of violence. The violence is often coupled with other forms of injustice and oppression, e.g., malnourishment, emotional and psychological manipulation, deprivation of rest and unfair employment terms. In Genesis 6, we see the first glimpse of what God considers as justice and injustice, and the gravity with which He views them.

---

101 Genesis 4.
102 Genesis 4:16.
103 Genesis 4:15-16.
104 Genesis 6:6.
105 Genesis 6:9.
106 Genesis 6:11.
107 Genesis 6:13.

B. Justice, Mercy and Righteousness Pre-Israel

Abraham Learns God's Justice and Righteousness

In the next milestone of God's Kingdom, the Abrahamic Covenant or the Kingdom Promised, justice and righteousness appear in an important event: Genesis 18-19, when God taught Abraham His justice and righteousness.

In Genesis 18, God visited Abraham and informed him that He was going to judge, convict and punish Sodom and Gomorrah. Before that, God declared in verses 17-19:

> The Lord said, "Shall I hide from Abraham what I am about to do, seeing that Abraham shall surely become a great and mighty nation, and all the nations of the earth shall be blessed in him? For I have chosen him, that he may command his children and his household after him *to keep the way of the Lord by doing righteousness and justice*, so that the Lord may bring to Abraham what he has promised him." (Emphasis added)

And what was "the way of the Lord", the "righteousness and justice", which was expected of Abraham? Subsequent biblical passages stated that the sin of Sodom and Gomorrah were: (i) Sexual immorality, lust and unnatural sex;[108] (ii) hedonism and pride;[109] and (iii) the failure to help the poor and needy despite being prosperous.[110] So "justice and righteousness" is about right living and includes right sexual ethics, character ethics and socioeconomic ethics.

108　Genesis 19:4; Jude 1:7; 2 Peter 2:6-10.
109　Ezekiel 16:49; 2 Peter 2:10.
110　Ezekiel 16:49.

Chesed: Mercy, Kindness and Steadfast Love

Chesed—"mercy", "kindness" or "steadfast love"—surfaced in biblical passages written during the pre-Israel period. *Chesed* was used in the context of inter-personal relations. *Chesed* means compassion and faithfulness to one's obligations, as well as to relatives, friends and slaves, and can be in the form of good deeds to another person.[111] This is evident in the following instances where the word *chesed* is used.

When the Lord was about to judge Sodom and Gomorrah in Genesis 19, His angels went to Lot beforehand to take him away from the coming wrath. Lot expressed profuse gratitude for the angels' "great kindness [*chesed*]".[112] This suggests that *chesed* can be an act of kindness and not obligation or covenant.

> **To have *chesed* is to be faithful to one's covenant.**

In Genesis 20-21, Abraham sojourned in Gerar and took refuge with Abimelech, King of Gerar. Abraham recounted that he had requested Sarah to do "kindness" to him by pretending that they were siblings, for the sake of their lives.[113] Then in Genesis 21:23, Abimelech requested that Abraham swear to deal "kindly", and not "falsely", with him as he had done to Abraham. This reveals the association of *chesed* with covenant: To have *chesed* is to be faithful to one's covenant.[114]

Exodus: Freedom from Oppression into a Worship Community

The Exodus story of God liberating the Hebrews from slavery and oppression in Egypt highlights an important motif that appears

---

111 *Holman Illustrated Pocket Bible Dictionary* (B&H Publishing, 2007), 206.
112 Genesis 19:19.
113 Genesis 20:13.
114 See also Genesis 24:12,14, 27, 49; 32:10; 39:21; 40:14; 47:29.

throughout the biblical narrative of God's Kingdom. This motif is a prism through which we can understand God's *salvation* and God's *justice*.[115]

The backdrop to the story is this. Joseph had been appointed Egypt's Prime Minister and consequently, Joseph's family, i.e., Jacob's/Israel's family, became refugees in Egypt. The descendants of Israel multiplied quickly and Egypt was soon filled with them.[116] Fast-forward 430 years. The Pharaoh at this time did not know of Joseph.[117] He became insecure about the Hebrew people. He feared that they would grow strong and attack Egypt along with Egypt's enemies. So he put them to forced labour and even committed the infanticide/genocide of their male children.[118]

Just pausing here for a brief observation, it is unfortunate that such sinful behaviour and thinking still exist today. Whenever a distinct minority of ethnic, linguistic, cultural or religious difference grows in strength or power within a majority-dominated polity, the sinful human response seems to be insecurity, tribalism of "us" versus "them" and the fear of the 'Other', resulting in some unjust assertions of power.

The Hebrew people couldn't bear the slavery. "Their cry for rescue from slavery came up to God. God heard their groaning, and God remembered his covenant with Abraham, with Isaac, and with Jacob. God saw the people of Israel—and God knew".[119]

God appointed Moses to lead the Hebrew people out of oppression. God told Moses that He had "seen [the] affliction of [His] people who

---

115 See generally, in juxtaposition with liberation theology, Steven Harris, "Biblical Theology and Liberation", *9marks* (20 August 2014): <http://9marks.org/article/biblical-theology-and-liberation/>; John Coffey, "'To release the oppressed': Reclaiming a biblical theology of liberation", *Jubilee Centre* <http://www.jubilee-centre.org/to-release-the-oppressed-reclaiming-a-biblical-theology-of-liberation-byjohn-coffey/>.
116 Exodus 1:7.
117 Exodus 12:40.
118 Exodus 1:10-22.
119 Exodus 2:23-25.

are in Egypt and [had] heard their cry because of their taskmasters. [He knew] their sufferings, and [He had gone] down to deliver them out of the hand of the Egyptians".[120] In Exodus 6:6-8, God declared to the Hebrews. "I am the Lord, and I will bring you out from under the burdens of the Egyptians, and I will deliver you from slavery to them, and I will redeem you with an outstretched arm and with great acts of judgment. I will take you to be my people, and I will be your God, and you shall know that I am the Lord your God, who has brought you out from under the burdens of the Egyptians. I will bring you into the land that I swore to give to Abraham, to Isaac, and to Jacob. I will give it to you for a possession. I am the Lord". Yet the people of Israel did not listen "because of their broken spirit and harsh slavery".[121]

God declared through Moses to the sinful heart-hardened Pharaoh, "Let my people go, that they may serve me in the wilderness".[122] But the Pharaoh refused, even after nine supernatural plagues. The final plague was catastrophic. Every firstborn of human and animal in Egypt would die.[123] This would have included the firstborn of the Hebrew people. But God was merciful to the Hebrews. He had already prepared for them a means by which they would be spared this tragic execution—the Passover. They were to sacrifice a lamb without blemish and spread its blood over the doorposts and lintel of the houses in which the Hebrews lived in, and they were to have a meal (a meal amidst all that death!)—unleavened bread, bitter herbs and the flesh of the sacrificed lamb. They were to eat the meal in haste, possessions in hand, ready to depart at any moment. God would pass through the land of Egypt and strike all the firstborn in Egypt, but He would *pass over* the Hebrew people in their homes with

---

120   Exodus 3:7-10.
121   Exodus 6:9.
122   Exodus 7:16.
123   Exodus 11:5.

the blood of the lamb spread over the doors.[124] This happened and the Hebrew people made their escape from Egypt, crossing the Red Sea supernaturally and into safety.

The Exodus narrative reveals several significant truths about God, His Kingdom and His justice, mercy and righteousness. First, the Bible emphatically states that "God knew" the cries of the oppressed Hebrews.[125] When a child has been bullied in school, her father knows. He would not take it lying down. God knows the cries of the oppressed. As God's agents on earth, do we know the cries of the oppressed around us, just as He knows?

Second, God was moved into personal action. He was so moved by compassion that He declared "I have come down to deliver them out of the hand of the Egyptians".[126] The Bible portrays God *descending* to where the Hebrew people were. God did not stand aloof nor did he merely strategise an escape route from afar. He got His hands dirty. When we see injustice and oppression, do we stand far off or do we go to where the people are to empathise and to take personal action?

Third, God *delivered* and *redeemed* the Hebrew people from slavery and oppression.[127] Where there is suffering, injustice or oppression, do we merely apply plasters and prescribe Panadol to those who are hurt? Or, do we work to deliver those who are suffering from the chains which enslave them?

Fourth, God's purpose for the Hebrew people's deliverance was that they would become *His covenant people*: "I will take you to be my people, and I will be your God".[128] So that they could "serve" Him.[129] Delivering

---

124 Exodus 12:1-13.
125 Exodus 2:25.
126 Exodus 3:8.
127 Exodus 6:6.
128 Exodus 6:7.
129 Exodus 7:16.

people from oppression *per se* does not go far enough. Deliverance must lead to identity, community and purpose. In a sinful and broken world, delivering people from oppression may mean they become enslaved by some other oppressive evil. True deliverance must lead to identity in, community with, and purpose of, God.

This theme of deliverance, redemption, liberation and freedom from oppression so as to be brought into God's covenant community recurs throughout the biblical narrative of God's Kingdom people. First, the Hebrews in Egypt. Freedom of slaves under the Mosaic Law (which we will examine shortly). The Jews in Babylon and Assyria and their subsequent return to Jerusalem. Then the whole world through Jesus. The Exodus narrative is important because it foreshadows the true and complete liberation which can only be obtained through Christ. But we shall save this for the next chapter. Suffice to say, we learn from the Exodus narrative important truths about God's justice, especially the social dimensions of His justice, His mercy and His compassion.

C. Justice, Mercy and Righteousness in the Laws for Israel

We fast-forward to the next milestone in the Kingdom narrative: Israel. At this stage, Israel as God's people had the benefit of receiving God's Law, also known as the Mosaic Law since it was given through the prophet Moses.

Relevance of the Mosaic Law to Us

It's important to realise the significance of the Mosaic Law for God's people, both for OT Israel and for modern-day Christians. Some dispensationalists go so far as to suggest that the Mosaic Law is completely irrelevant to Christians, who are not parties to the Old Covenant.[130] Indeed, the Mosaic Law is not a set of laws which Christians are bound by. Some Old Covenant laws may be specifically excluded from the New Covenant, and some may be expressly and specifically included.[131] But this legalistic construction is missing a few important points.

First, the Mosaic Law is not presented as an abstract, timeless universal code but as part of a historical-theological narrative in relation to a specific group of people.[132]

Second, the Mosaic Law is nevertheless God's revelation to His people as a reflection of His character and standards of what is good, beautiful, pleasing and right. These standards continue to hold true today because God's character is unchanging.[133] It is useful to consider the declarations of God's character of justice, mercy and righteousness in the OT: [134]

- With righteousness he will judge the needy, with justice he will give decisions for the poor of the earth. (Isaiah 11:4, NIV)
- Let him who boasts boast in this; that he understands and knows me, that I am the Lord, who exercises kindness, justice and righteousness on earth, for in these I delight. (Jeremiah 9:23)

---

130   The distinction between Covenant and Law may be simplistically seen as such: The Covenant creates a new relationship whereas the Law regulates the terms of the relationship. See e.g., Victor P. Hamilton, *Handbook on the Pentateuch*, 2nd edn. (Baker Academic, 2005), 189.
131   Gordon Fee and Douglas Stuart, *How To Read the Bible For All Its Worth*, 2nd edn (Zondervan,1993), 166-168.
132   Andreas J Köstenberger and Richard D Patterson, *Invitation to Biblical Interpretation* (Kregel, 2011), 164.
133   Timothy Keller, *Generous Justice: How God's Grace Makes Us Just* (Hodder & Stoughton, 2010) at 19-24; Andreas J Köstenberger and Richard D Patterson, *Invitation to Biblical Interpretation* (Kregel, 2011) at 164; Malachi 3:6; Hebrews 13:8.
134   See also Deuteronomy 32:4; Isaiah 30:18; Job 37:23; Zephaniah 3:5; Psalm 99:4.

- But the Lord sits enthroned forever; he has established his throne for justice, and he judges the world with righteousness; he judges the peoples with uprightness. The Lord is a stronghold for the oppressed, a stronghold in times of trouble. (Psalm 9:7-9)
- Righteousness and justice are the foundation of your throne; steadfast love and faithfulness go before you. (Psalm 89:14)
- I know that the Lord will maintain the cause of the afflicted, and will execute justice for the needy. (Psalm 140:12)

These declarations indicate that God's character of justice and righteousness are universal and timeless. They reveal an especial concern for the poor, needy, afflicted and oppressed. So what if God's character is just and righteous? In a conversation I had with some young parents, we discussed possible names for their children. I realised how important it was for them to choose names that reflect the character they hope their children would have. How much more our Heavenly Father, who desires that His children grow into the likeness of His character? As our Heavenly Father is just and righteous, He desires us to be just and righteous; to have our hearts resonate with His.

Third, the ethical laws in the Mosaic Law inform the two New Covenant laws which Christians today are to live by:[135]

> You shall love the Lord your God with all your heart and with all your soul and with all your mind. This is the great and first commandment. And a second is like it: You shall love your neighbor as yourself. On these two commandments depend all the Law and the Prophets.

---

135 Matthew 22:37-40.

This was also how OT Israel understood the Mosaic Law. The Psalmist in Psalm 119 equates meditating on, and living according to the Law, with loving God.

Fourth, principles of the Mosaic Law set out a vision of what is good and right for all of humanity, not just Israel.[136] Deuteronomy 4:6-8 says:

> Keep [God's Law] and do them, for that will be your wisdom and your understanding in the sight of the peoples, who, when they hear all these statutes, will say, "Surely this great nation is a wise and understanding people." For what great nation is there that has a god so near to it as the Lord our God is to us, whenever we call upon him? And what great nation is there, that has statutes and rules so righteous as all this law that I set before you today?

Indeed, by obeying the Law, Israel was supposed to be "a people of God whose life shall draw nations to inquire after Yahweh".[137] Christians today share the same responsibility.

---

136 Jonathan Burnside, *God, Justice and Society* (Oxford University Press, 2011) at 466-470.

137 See Exodus 19:6; Isaiah 49:6; Jonathan Burnside, *God, Justice and Society* (Oxford University Press, 2011) at 476; Michael A Grisanti, "Israel's Mission To The Nations In Isaiah 40–55: An Update", *The Master's Seminar Journal* 9/1 (Spring 1998) 39, p. 62. Nevertheless, it should be noted that the Mosaic Law was not entirely unique during its time. Various legal codes of other nations in the ancient Middle East also existed around the time, the most famous of which is the Code of Hammurabi: See Victor P Hamilton, *Handbook on the Pentateuch*, 2nd edn (Baker Academic, 2005), 201. However, under the Hebrew Scriptures and worldview, social justice is ordained by, and divinely revealed by, God as an ethical obligation whereas in other nations in the Near East, justice was ordained by the king to obtain favour from his people, notwithstanding that the king may not live up to the standards of justice himself; laws of justice and equity were monumental rather than enforced or lived: Moshe Weinfeld, *Social Justice in Ancient Israel and in the Ancient Near East* (Fortress Press, Minneapolis, 2000), 10; Jonathan Burnside, *God, Justice and Society* (Oxford University Press, 2011), 8-10.

Justice, Mercy and Righteousness in the Mosaic Law

There are many facets of justice in the Mosaic Law which I would categorise broadly under two types: Socioeconomic and legal-adjudicative.[138]

Legal-adjudicative justice relates to procedural justice in legal proceedings, constitutional law, substantive private law as well as criminal law, and includes corrective and retributive justice.[139] Another type of justice envisaged in the Mosaic Law is commutative justice, i.e., honest weights and measures in order to facilitate fair and equitable transactions.[140]

Yet, the majority of verses in the Bible about justice and righteousness are not about legal-adjudicative justice. Instead, they are about socioeconomic justice. A survey of the Mosaic Law suggests that *God's justice is about His desire for egalitarian inclusion of all persons to freely and fully participate within His community and their enjoyment of His gracious provision.* Injustice, on the other hand, is social, economic or political segregation and the exploitation of power inequality.[141] God's righteousness on the other hand is about right relationships and fulfilment of covenants: Between God and humanity,[142] between people,[143] and between humanity and creation.[144]

---

138   I note that there are many other possible classifications: E.g., formal justice, substantive justice, retributive justice, distributive justice, etc. See e.g., Daniel Koh, "Justice: A Christian Social Ethical Perspective" in Daniel Koh and Kwa Kiem-Kiok, *Issues of Law and Justice in Singapore* (Armour Publishing, 2009) at 11-13.

139   E.g., Exodus 20:16; 22; 23:2-3; 23:8; Deuteronomy 1:16; 19:15 (see John 8:17-18); Leviticus 6:1-7; 19:15; 24:22 (see similarity with Article 12(1) of the Constitution of the Republic of Singapore).

140   Leviticus 19:36, 25:15; see also Job 31:6, Ezekiel 45:10.

141   Trent C Butler, ed., *Holman Bible Dictionary* (Holman Bible Publishers, 1991), 827-829; Stephen Mott and Ronald Sider, "Economic justice: a biblical paradigm", *Transformation* (2000) 17:2, 50-63 at pp. 55-56.

142   See 1 Chronicles 12:6; Daniel 9:14; Psalm 71:2, 24.

143   See Genesis 38:26; 1 Samuel 24:17; Job 31:3-40.

144   Trent C Butler, ed., *Holman Bible Dictionary* (Holman Bible Publishers, 1991) at 1194-1195; Timothy Keller, *Generous Justice: How God's Grace Makes Us Just* (Hodder & Stoughton, 2010) at 10-15.

As there are many legal stipulations in the Mosaic Law on socioeconomic justice, I shall begin by focusing on the Jubilee Law, which provides a framework to understand several related socioeconomic justice laws. [145]

Jubilee Law [146]

Imagine this. You have been working tirelessly as a dishwasher in a coffee shop for the past 15 years, earning less than enough to support your family. You were just released from an imprisonment sentence for assisting loan sharks. Well, you did not have a choice. You owed those loan sharks just a few hundred dollars. You still do. Now and then they harass you to work for them. You do not have any viable alternative source of income. You never completed your primary school education. You have no other skill. (This scenario is actually based on the real story of a *pro bono* client of mine who was charged for assisting loan sharks.)

Imagine today, you receive a letter. The letter reads like a scam but is endorsed with an official Government stamp. It declares that the outstanding mortgage payments for your HDB apartment is henceforth fully paid. In addition, you have been given—yes, a gift—a new house around Brighton Crescent, near Serangoon Gardens—a large semi-detached house. Your extended family will also move to that area. (At this point, you vaguely recall your father talking about his extended family living in that area in the past.) The letter continues: You are released from all your debts to the loan sharks. You are also given a cash gift of $100,000 that is meant specifically for you and your children to start a business or receive further education or skills upgrading.

---

145 See Moshe Weinfeld, *Social Justice in Ancient Israel and in the Ancient Near East* (Fortress Press, Minneapolis, 2000); Hemchand Gossai, *Social Critique by Israel's Eighth-Century Prophets: Justice and Righteousness in Context* (Wipf & Stock Publishers, 1993).
146 See generally Robert M Solomon, *Jesus Our Jubilee* (Discovery House, 2015).

The above narrative is fictional. It is an illustration of how applying the Jubilee Law might look like in modern Singapore. The Jubilee Law is a piece of legislation found in Leviticus 25. It is also the origin of the term, "Jubilee", i.e., the celebration of a 50-year anniversary.

In brief, the Jubilee Law returned land, which had otherwise been 'sold' to others in times of financial hardship, to the families who were bestowed as stewards of that land; it reunited families and clans at their ancestral hometowns; it obliged the people of Israel to release their fellow citizens of all monetary debts; and it emancipated all Israelite slaves from debt slavery. This happens every 49th/50th year of Israel's covenant with their God since the time Israel obtained their Promised Land. The Jubilee Year climaxes in the Day of Atonement (Yom Kippur) and its commencement is signalled by the blowing of ram's horns throughout the country, which symbolises the proclamation of liberty. Indeed, the word "jubilee" is etymologically derived from the Hebrew word, "*jobel*", which refers to the ram's horn trumpet that is blown when the Jubilee Year was proclaimed.

Jubilee Law and land

The Jubilee Law is a complex legislation rooted in a specific social, cultural and historical context. Appreciating that context is crucial to understanding the Jubilee Law.

Land in OT Israel is intertwined with the Jubilee Law. This is because the Law provides that all Israelites were to return to their respective ancestral land, which had been allotted as 'inheritance' to their forefathers according to their tribes.[147] Land has multiple meanings

---

147   Leviticus 25:10, 28.

for the Israelite: (i) Land is a tangible testament of Israel's covenant[148] with God; (ii) land is the physical embodiment of Israel's national identity; (iii) land is the locus of deep historical kinship; and (iv) land is the foundation of Israel's national economy.

First: Land and God's covenant with Israel. God's relationship with His people has always been made through covenants. As mentioned in the previous chapter, one of these was the Abrahamic Covenant, in which God promised Abraham that his descendants would receive land stretching from the Euphrates to the river of Egypt. This was known to the Israelites as the Promised Land. God forewarned that Abraham's descendants would be enslaved and given the Promised Land only in the 4th generation from Abraham. The Israelites' eventual reception of the Promised Land was the fulfilment of God's covenant with Abraham.[149] The underlying imperative for the Jubilee Law was God's covenantal faithfulness: God had been faithful to them; they were to reciprocate and observe this law. Therefore, do not hoard. Instead, release the land to the ancestral tribes.

Second: Land and OT Israel's national identity. OT Israel's identity was grounded in being descendants of Abraham. Israel was thus said to have received the Promised Land as an inheritance from God.[150] In the time of Moses, God entered into a covenant with the nation of Israel, i.e., the Mosaic Covenant. Central to both covenants was the Promised Land. Under the Mosaic Covenant, the Israelites' fulfilment of their obligations would determine their continued prosperous existence in the Promised Land. OT Israel's deliverance from slavery under Egypt to the Promised Land was the impetus for Israel's faithful participation in the Covenant. Israel's identity as the descendants of Abraham and of Jacob

---

148 Genesis 15.
149 Joshua 21.
150 Leviticus 20:24.

was thus embodied in the Promised Land.[151] Hence, replete in the Bible are references to the "God of Abraham, Isaac and Jacob".[152] Again, the theme of covenantal faithfulness strongly emerges.

Third, land is the locus of deep historical kinship. When God's promise was fulfilled during the time of Joshua, the son of Nun, and the Promised Land was mostly delivered to Israel, the Israelites were allotted various parcels of land according to their tribes. Within the tribes, parcels of land were further allotted to respective clans.[153] So when the Israelites first settled in the Promised Land, they built their homes alongside their extended family. Throughout subsequent generations, it remained that the various parts of geographical Israel were identified with the Israelites' forefathers. Hence, Joseph, the earthly father of Jesus, being a descendent of David, had to return to Bethlehem in Judah, i.e., the City of David, during the census commanded by Augustus Caesar.[154]

The Jubilee Law therefore posited the basic family unit and the wider family clan as being of great importance. By requiring families to return to their ancestral homes, it made families seek relational restoration. This should cause us to wonder: Are we making our lives, our workplaces, our country, conducive for thriving familial relationships and reconciliation? The Jubilee Law also supports the view that the family is the basic socioeconomic unit, followed by the extended family, and finally the whole community. This gives us fodder to consider the role of state welfarism as opposed to the principle of devolution of responsibility.

Fourth, land is the foundation of Israel's national economy. OT Israel was an agrarian society. God made it clear that He owned the land. The Israelites were merely tenants or stewards of the land bestowed

---

151   Deuteronomy 6.
152   E.g., Exodus 3:6, Matthew 22:32.
153   See Joshua 15.
154   Luke 2.

upon them as a gift.[155] They were however free to work the land for their livelihood. Moreover, the Israelites were merely "strangers" or "sojourners" in God's land.[156] This was to ground the Israelites' paradigm for observing the Jubilee Law. They weren't to hoard the land because it was not theirs to begin with! They would be ultimately held accountable by the landowner.

Jubilee Law and socioeconomic justice
First, the Jubilee Law was intended to ensure intergenerational equity. Because every Israelite family had been bestowed an equitable portion of land, every Israelite had an equitable opportunity to economic prosperity and to thereby pursue the 'good' life. Each new generation is brought to an equitable starting point and given level opportunities to harness the resources equitably distributed to them for development and for making good their lives. Your parents might have been poor or even debt slaves. But under the Jubilee Law, you would not be visited with a debt cycle that was almost impossible to be emancipated from. This enables meritocracy of opportunity and social mobility. Because how you turn out in life depends on how effectively you harness the land and other capital given to you at the start of each Jubilee cycle.

The issue of social mobility has been an increasing source of worry in Singapore. In 2011, the issue surfaced in the public media. It was noted that intergenerational economic mobility was low in Singapore.[157] Then Minister Mentor Lee Kuan Yew also observed this in regard to the make-up of the student population in Raffles Institution.[158] It has been explained

---

155 Leviticus 25:23; see Deuteronomy 15:4; Psalm 24:1.
156 Leviticus 25:23.
157 Irene Ng, "Singapore's Education System; Growing worry of social immobility", *The Straits Times* (16 February 2011), A25.
158 Rachel Chang, "RI honours MM with new award", *The Straits Times* (14 January 2011).

that "low intergenerational mobility implies that those whose parents were at the bottom tend to also remain at the bottom, while those whose parents were at the top tend to stay there" and "the type of education system has an impact on mobility"; these are noted to be explained by the fact that "entry into the more prestigious primary schools is not based on merit, but on factors such as the location of the family home and parents' connections to the school... [and] education in Singapore is differentiated and increasingly so".[159]

Social mobility issues don't just start at formal education. They begin in the family that a child is born into. In 1995, US psychologists Betty Hart and Todd Risley conducted a study of the number of words spoken to young children from 42 families at three different socioeconomic levels: (1) Welfare homes, (2) working-class homes, and (3) professionals' homes.[160] To their astonishment, it was found that children in professionals' homes were exposed to an average of more than 1,500 more spoken words per hour than children in welfare homes. In one year, that amounted to a difference of nearly 8 million words. By the time the children are four years old, there was a total gap of 32 million words. They also found a significant difference in tone (in terms of how encouraging or discouraging and prohibitive) and in the complexity of words being used. It was thus found that the nature of early childhood experience affects a child's academic and other abilities later in life.

This brings to mind the life stories of some local sex workers. These ladies were being ministered to by a few ministries I know, one of which reaches out to and empowers local sex workers to pursue alternative

---

159 Irene Ng, "Singapore's Education System; Growing worry of social immobility", *The Straits Times* (16 February 2011), A25.
160 David Shenk, "The 32-Million Word Gap", *The Atlantic* (9 Mar 2010) based on Shenk's book, *The Genius in All of Us: Insights Into Genetics*, Talent, and IQ (Anchor, 2010); Betty Hart and Todd R Risley, "The Early Catastrophe: The 30 Million Word Gap by Age 3" (2003, Spring) *American Educator*, pp. 4-9.

work options, build their families and improve their lives. One of the ladies was a third-generation sex worker. Her grandmother was a sex worker in Geylang. So was her mother. She now has a number of children of her own. Without intervention, it's quite likely that her children will also become sex workers in Geylang. Why? I was told these ladies grew up, and lived their entire lives in Geylang. They have never had the opportunity to go to school, but have very low levels of basic skills such as language and social skills, and character values such as determination, commitment, patience, the capacity to plan for the future, delayed gratification, etc. In one case, when the ministry workers helped a lady find a job as a waitress, she went AWOL after a few days. She could not cope with the different environment. In another case, one of the ladies was charged for affray (fighting) and my colleagues kindly acted as her defence lawyers *pro bono*. They tried to advocate for probation instead of imprisonment. But the lady did not turn up for the meeting with the probation officer. It happened more than once. The probation officer had no choice but to give a negative report. The lady was eventually sentenced to prison.

A superficial understanding of the issues may lead one to the view that these sex workers are in the sex trade by choice. But a more holistic understanding and sensitivity to the underlying systemic, social, economic and cultural issues suggest otherwise. Social mobility has not been available to some of these ladies. They have few alternatives. Sex work is all that their mothers and themselves have known. But the ministry workers have been investing time and care into the next generation, the children of these sex workers. The ladies are beginning to recognise that their children may have a way out—opportunities to pursue a different, perhaps better life. The ladies themselves then resolve to make decisions which help their children succeed.[161] That is the principle of social mobility encompassed in the Jubilee Law—capacity building and empowerment of the next generation.

Second, the Jubilee Law provided that all Israelites' debts were to be released. And all debt slaves or bondservants, along with their families, should be liberated and returned to their original or ancestral land and hometowns.[162] OT Israelites who fell on hard times and were unable to repay their debts can "sell" themselves along with their families into slavery.[163] An Israelite thief who was convicted and unable to make multiple-fold restitution would also have to be made a debt slave.[164] The law provided that such an Israelite debt slave was not to be treated like a slave but a hired hand.[165]

There are other OT legislation pertaining to Israelite debt slaves.[166] Deuteronomy 15:13-14 even provides that the former master or creditor must "liberally" bless the ex-slave with tools, clothes and food to have an opportunity at rebuilding his life. People were expected to sponsor the empowerment of the poor. Not just the poor, but one's own debtor!

Debt is a very sinister thing. In one *pro bono* case I did, an elderly man who had a sickly father and a dependent son had to borrow money

---

161 See e.g., Esther CL Goh and Shamini Praimkumara, "Understanding The Impact Of The Mother-Child Relationship On Sex Workers' Decision To Enter And Leave The Streets—Lessons For Social Work Practice", *Journal of Social Work Practice* (2015).
162 Leviticus 25:40-41.
163 Leviticus 25:39.
164 Exodus 22:1.
165 Leviticus 25:40.
166 For instance, Exodus 22:2 and Deuteronomy 15:12 provide that Israelite debt slaves would only serve a 6-year bond at the maximum and must be liberated on the 7th year. It is not clear whether these laws in Exodus 22 and Deuteronomy 15 are in conflict with Leviticus 25. Rabbinical scholars and Christian theologians are divided on this: Jonathan Burnside, *God, Justice and Society* (Oxford University Press, 2011) at 231. It appears that Leviticus 25 relates to severe debt, since it relates to debt slavery of entire families (and not just single persons) and the 'sale' of a family's entire plot of land.

from loan sharks to pay the medical bills. He had nowhere else to go to raise funds. He worked at a coffee shop making drinks, earning about $800 every month. He couldn't even borrow money from the licensed moneylenders (which in any event previously charged interest rates as high as 40 per cent) because of his poor credit rating. After he borrowed money from the loan sharks, the latter harassed him to borrow more money or else provide them with ATM cards. The harassment worsened to the point that he succumbed. The provision of ATM cards to loan sharks constitutes an offence under the *Moneylenders Act* (Cap. 188). My colleague and I wrote representations on his behalf to plead for the charges to be dropped. They were not dropped and he was ultimately convicted and sentenced. The Singapore High Court observed that victims of loan shark activities are often the "poor and vulnerable who desperately need loans but cannot get them from legitimate sources",[167] as a result of which some of them are forced to turn to crime. This anecdote profoundly impacted how I understood the poor in Singapore. The poor often end up with serious debt, and their problems become aggravated, because of the dire financial circumstances they find themselves in. Debt begets hardship. Hardship begets greater hardship.

On the other hand, there can be profound impact when God's people actually practise Jubilee principles. I was told that an anonymous donor once contributed a substantial sum of money specifically to pay off the debts incurred by migrant workers who had been injured at work. These debts were in respect of employment agent fees. These workers would have lost their jobs and would have been unable to pay off the debts. It may seem a small thing but it means the world to these workers who would otherwise have had to work for several years up to a decade to pay

---

167   *Ong Chee Eng v Public Prosecutor* [2012] 3 SLR 776 (HC).

off the debts. Also, the Methodist Welfare Services (the charity arm of the Methodist Church) administered a jubilee fund in 2015 (Singapore's golden jubilee) approximately amounting to S$1.7 million to disburse one-time gifts to help about 850 families in its care to pay off debts incurred from arrears for utility, phone, rental bills etc.[168]

Thirdly, interest-based lending to Israelites (sometimes referred to as "usury") is prohibited under Leviticus 25:36-37.[169] This prevents exploitative creditors from charging exorbitant interest. It also prohibits the enforcement of the debt against the debtor unto his bankruptcy, that is, taking away everything from his basic possessions to his liberty. The implication of this was that capital financing was done through interest-free loans, like charitable or joint ventures (e.g., venture capital financing). Risks were thus shared: Creditor and debtor stand or fall together. From an economic perspective, this would also prevent speculative financing of unjustifiably risky or unsustainable ventures and accumulation of toxic debt. This law shows me the importance God places on finance. Why was this necessary? Because the poor are always disadvantaged when it comes to finance. Finance is needed if one is to participate in the economic life of the community. Without finance, it is almost impossible to buy a house, obtain resources to generate income, etc. Yet, the poor have little or no bargaining power when negotiating financial transactions. Often, they have little property to begin with to provide as collateral for credit. The anecdote I mentioned earlier of the elderly man who had to turn to loan sharks to borrow money to pay his father's medical bills is illustrative of this.

---

168   Theresa Tan, "Methodists in Singapore to help the poor clear their debts", *The Straits Times* (7 December 2014).
169   See also Exodus 22:24; Deuteronomy 23:20.

Fourthly, Leviticus 25:35 provides that an Israelite must help to financially maintain a poor fellow Israelite, to the extent of allowing the latter to live with him if he has no shelter. Leviticus 25:37 also prohibits an Israelite from providing a poor Israelite food at a *profit*.

Evident from the above, the Jubilee Law is inextricably bound with principles of social justice. God intended Israel to be a community of social justice set apart from the surrounding nations.[170] In Deuteronomy 15:4, God declared through Moses: "[T]here will be no poor among you; for the LORD will bless you in the land that the LORD your God is giving you for an inheritance to possess". Was it idealism that the Israelites were to expect that there would be no poor persons in their society? Certainly not. Given that a few verses down that passage, in Deuteronomy 15:11, it is declared, "there will never cease to be poor in the land." However God expects that His people are generous to the poor and needy, and "not harden [their] heart or shut [their] hand against" them.[171]

There is no contradiction here, but a tension between God's intent and humanity's reality. God's intent was that given His bountiful material blessings to Israel, there would be more than enough for everyone if the Israelites were to live justly. The reality is that the Israelites would fail. Hence, God expressly commanded in the same verse: "[F]or there will never cease to be poor in the land. Therefore I command you, 'You shall open wide your hand to your brother, to the needy and to the poor, in your land'".[172] It is significant that Jesus quoted from this verse, saying " for you always have the poor with you".[173] Contrary to some misconceived views that this undermined social justice in the New Testament, Jesus was

---

[170] Timothy Keller, *Generous Justice: How God's Grace Makes Us Just* (Hodder & Stoughton, 2010), 25-26; Grant Osborne, *The Hermeneutical Spiral: A Comprehensive Introduction to Biblical Interpretation* (IVP Academic, 2006), 189.
[171] Deuteronomy 15:7-8.
[172] Deuteronomy 15:11.
[173] Matthew 26:11.

affirming the biblical injunction in Deuteronomy 15:11 for God's people to be open-handed to the needy and the poor, albeit that generosity in worshipping Jesus during His Incarnation was a higher priority.

The socioeconomic laws in the Jubilee Law are manifestations of God's commandment in Deuteronomy 15:11. It was by faith in God as a provider of material and spiritual blessings that the Israelites were to live justly. The result would have been that there would be no poor among them. The Jubilee Law is fundamentally interwoven with social justice.[174]

Jubilee Law and the Sabbath

The Jubilee Law also provides that the land shall be set to rest or lie fallow during the Jubilee year.[175] This is an extension of the seven-yearly Sabbath rest of the land provided for in Leviticus 25:1-7, which is in itself an extension of the weekly Sabbath rest of all people from labour.[176] This rest is notably extended to the "servants", "livestock", the "sojourner" or foreigner.[177] These people, and obviously the animals, are unlikely to have any bargaining power to request for rest. The law is therefore deliberately intended to provide for protection from abuse of power.

In this respect, I find it extremely disconcerting that some Christian employers deny their workers proper daily rest or weekly days off. I have come across Christian employers who do not allow their foreign domestic workers (FDWs) to have any off-day at all, at least prior to the legislative amendments on mandatory day-offs for FDWs. Even after the mandatory

---

174 Cf., Kevin DeYoung & Greg Gilbert, *What Is the Mission of the Church? Making Sense of Social Justice, Shalom and the Great Commission* (Crossway, 2011) at 149-151.
175 Leviticus 25:11.
176 Leviticus 25:11.
177 Exodus 20:10.

day-off, compliance has not been widely observed.[178] But this same principle applies to any employer of any type of worker. In a recent *pro bono* legal matter I took up, a foreign manual labourer worked an average of 12 hours a day seven days a week for 14 months until he got injured at the workplace and could not work any further. In some other anecdotes I have heard, poor locals and migrants working as cleaners work excessively long hours on their feet, catching only less than four to five hours of sleep. For that reason, some of the poor locals do not go home to sleep but choose to sleep on the streets near their workplace. On the other end of the spectrum, in many professional industries, the workplace culture and expectations are such that long hours, late nights, work over weekends and other such practices are encouraged or facilitated. In August 2013, a 21-year-old Bank of America Merrill Lynch intern, Moritz Erhardt, was found dead in his shower after working for 72 hours straight, having died of an epileptic seizure.[179] Such practices are in fact common in certain parts of the financial services industry.[180] This is not unheard of in Singapore as well. From anecdotes

> **God intended Israel to be a community of social justice set apart from the surrounding nations.**

---

178 A research survey shows that about 40% of FDW respondents reported not having a weekly day off and also not receiving compensation in lieu (as required by the law); many FDWs reported not having a full 24-hour day off but a significantly trimmed day off, being allowed to leave only after morning chores and having to return by a curfew time to prepare dinner: TWC2, "The Right to Rest: the effectiveness of the 'day off' legislation for Foreign Domestic Workers" (11 June 2015), http://twc2.org.sg/2015/06/11/theright-to-rest-the-effectiveness-of-the-day-off-legislation-for-foreign-domestic-workers/.
179 Maev Kennedy, "Bank intern Moritz Erhardt died from epileptic seizure, inquest told", *The Guardian* (22 November 2013).
180 Paul Gallagher, "Slavery in the City: Death of 21-year-old intern Moritz Erhardt at Merrill Lynch sparks furore over long hours and macho culture at banks", *The Independent* (20 August 2013); Jillian Berman, "A 21-Year-Old Intern Had To Die To Get Wall Street To Change Its Ways" (2 October 2014).

shared by friends, clients would simply drop an email and demand a same-day or same-night turnaround for a work product. In some circumstances, such urgency may be justifiable. But in many others, it is to be doubted. No consideration at all is given to the different stakeholders involved. As a client, would you demand such timelines? As a service-provider, would you take up such work at the expense of yourself, your family, your other commitments, your employees, and so on?

Jesus Himself declared that He is the Lord of the Sabbath.[181] His declaration implicitly affirmed the principle of the Sabbath, while clarifying that it is not about the strict letter of the law but the spirit of the law. That is, the principle of rest. And this principle seeks to benefit people, not burden them. This accords with Jesus' call to enter into His rest.[182] How could a Christian employer expect to enter into Jesus' rest while depriving his worker of physical rest? It is in rest that we sharpen, equip and ready ourselves for productive work. Yet, it is in faith in Jesus that there can be rest. This raises the issue of whether we allow ourselves to constantly practise being at rest? Or, are our pace of life, the impetus for economic growth, for productivity and for meeting targets, our margins and deadlines, so hectic and strenuous that rest is a rarity? Is it because we are wittingly or unwittingly pursuing financial or personal gains?

Another important aspect of the rest which Jesus offers is by way of Him sharing in our burdens, by sharing the oxen yoke with Him. Imagine you and Jesus carrying the yoke on your necks, side by side, working the field. We can have rest even in labour. Because Jesus is working alongside us. As employers or managers, do we unduly burden our subordinates or do we work *alongside* them like Jesus?

Coming back to the Jubilee Law, during the Sabbath rest of the land, there was to be no sowing or reaping from the land. Whatever the land

---
181 Matthew 12:8.
182 Matthew 11:28.

provided would be consumed for food. Because under the Law, both the 49th and 50th years would be rest years, that would be two years without sowing or reaping. This demands faith that God would provide everyone with sufficient food throughout the year from the Sabbath produce of the land. This echoes the narrative of God's provision of manna and quail to the Israelite pilgrims in the Sinai desert.[183] There, God instructed the Israelites to collect for six days, manna which appeared like dew drops every morning. The collection of the sixth day would be sufficient to provide food for the sixth *and* seventh day. It was described that "whoever gathered much had nothing left over, and whoever gathered little had no lack".[184] Those who collected more than was necessary found their excess food rotting. This same theme runs through the Sabbath and Jubilee legislation. Integral to the Sabbath is faith. This faith sets Israel apart from all other nations. The Sabbath was thus holy, i.e., set apart, and sacred.

Yet, the Sabbath rest years did not mean that the Israelites were to be wastrels. Instead, they were free to pursue other endeavours. This would include household activities and capital-building activities, e.g., digging wells and building irrigation systems.

The Sabbath years also allowed for nature to enjoy a cyclical, seasonal pattern of rest and harvest. This has great significance in terms of creation care. It resonates of the stewardship bestowed by God on humanity right after the creation of the world. For Israel, this meant good stewardship of the land because it belonged to God. For us, this means we must conduct our lives properly as regards nature and the environment. It is significant that the people who would especially be adversely affected by environment degradation are the poor, needy and foreign workers. In May 2015, a heat wave in India claimed almost

---

183   Exodus 16.
184   Exodus 16:18.

2,000 lives. Reportedly, "[m]ost of the deaths have been of construction workers, homeless people and the elderly".[185] The poor and needy are especially vulnerable to dangers because they do not have the means to mitigate suffering or injustice, whereas the rich and powerful would have the resources and ability to protect themselves. This is the reason for many other socioeconomic justice laws especially favouring or protecting the weak and marginalised in the society or economy.

Reflections on the Jubilee Law
The Jubilee Law shows us God's intent for the socioeconomically marginalised to be given reasonable opportunities to participate in the social and economic life of the community. Such provisions range from short-term (weekly Sabbath) to long-term (e.g., redistribution of land), social (communal celebration of the Day of Atonement) to economic (e.g., debt cancellation), liberation (e.g., release from debt slavery) to prohibition (e.g., prohibition of usury). These provisions enable the rich and poor alike to unite in a common national identity rooted in God's covenant as regards to their land, to all participating in communal worship, to partaking in economic activities to pursue the good life, and to have moderation and sufficient rest. And these are to be followed by faith in God's faithfulness. This would thus set Israel holy apart from, and as a witness for God to, the other nations.

Gleaning laws

The Mosaic Law provides that landowners are not to reap the maximum possible harvest of their land, but to leave leftovers for the socioeconomically weakest to glean for themselves.[186]

---

185 "India's Killer Heat", *The Straits Times* (30 May 2015).
186 Deuteronomy 24:19-22; Leviticus 19:9-10; 23:22.

The Book of Ruth shows an example of how the gleaning laws were practised. Ruth was a Moabite, a foreigner, a widow. The socioeconomic structure of the agrarian patriarchal society in those days meant that only males had access to socioeconomic opportunities.[187] When Ruth's husband passed away, she made a decision to follow her mother-in-law Naomi, who was an Israelite. In Ruth 2, she went to Boaz's land to glean from it.

A few comments are helpful. First, gleaning was a dangerous activity in those days. Those were the days of the judges, when Israel was a lawless country.[188] Boaz and Naomi alluded to the danger of men potentially assaulting the gleaning poor.[189] The other landowners probably did not observe the gleaning laws. And they probably made sure to keep the gleaning poor off the land by sending their workers to 'assault' them. In contrast, Boaz expressly instructed his workers to allow the gleaning poor to glean.[190]

Secondly, Boaz was regarded by Naomi, who was actually Boaz's relative,[191] as one who had shown "kindness"[192] to her and Ruth. It's important to understand what the "kindness" displayed by Boaz was. To Boaz, observing the Mosaic Law on gleaning was a matter of justice. It cannot be fathomed that I should be lauded as "kind" because I paid my taxes in accordance with the law since it is my lawful duty.[193] The "kindness" that Boaz showed to Naomi was Boaz going beyond his lawful

---

187 For this reason, the Mosaic Law provided for the idea of a male kinsman-redeemer to take over the obligations and also benefits of being the male authority in the family when the male figure has passed away. But we will not study this here.
188 Judges 17:6.
189 Ruth 2:8-9, 22.
190 Ruth 2:9.
191 Ruth 2:1.
192 The Hebrew word for this is "*hesed*" or "*chesed*", which is sometimes also translated as "lovingkindness" or "mercy".
193 Ruth 2:14-16.

duty, that is, Boaz was kind to Ruth by giving her food when he did not have to—so much food that there was leftover for Ruth to bring home to Naomi. He gave her more to glean than was required. Boaz allowed her so much to glean, and Ruth was so diligent, that she gleaned about an ephah, i.e., 22 litres, of barley.[194] That could fill a whole truck today! It was so much that Ruth could go into the city to trade for other things.

The principle from the gleaning laws is that capital owners are not to maximise their profits, but should transfer some profits to empower the socioeconomically weakest. Yet, the gleaning laws do not provide for welfare handouts.[195] The poor and needy must work with their own hands. Nevertheless, they are not to exploit it for greed. Deuteronomy 23:24-25 provides that people gleaning cannot pick food excessively. Implicit in this is that God will provide enough for the landowner and the needy person. It is again resonant of Exodus 16, i.e., God's provision of manna and quail for Israel. It also reflects the view that all land belongs to God anyway. He can decide how the harvest of the land can be distributed. This law is especially important for the poor and needy because gleaning could be a matter of life and death for them.[196] The law reveals God's intent for the socioeconomically marginalised to be participating in the communal economic life of society with dignity and not undue dependence.

Tithing laws

Another Mosaic Law stipulation on socioeconomic justice is the tithing law. It requires that the Israelites set aside in storehouses a tenth of their harvest each year in order to participate in a worship celebration

---

194   Ruth 2:17-18.
195   Kevin DeYoung & Greg Gilbert, *What Is the Mission of the Church? Making Sense of Social Justice, Shalom and the Great Commission* (Crossway, 2011), 143-144.
196   Jonathan Burnside, *God, Justice and Society* (Oxford University Press, 2011), 236.

feast before God.[197] It sounds oxymoronic but the Israelites were required to rejoice and consume whatever food or drink (yes, including alcohol!) that they desired.

Every third year, there would be a special feast for the Levites, the migrants and refugees, the orphans and the widows. These people would otherwise have been unable to celebrate the tithe feast because they had no land and thus no harvest. God is concerned with including the socioeconomically marginalised—even the foreigners or non-Israelites—in community worship.[198] This also includes them in the mainstream social life of the community. These groups of people are then obliged to fulfil their religious obligations to God.[199]

The focus of the tithing laws is not so much on provision of sustenance since it is only once every three years. Instead, the aim is egalitarian participation in the faith and social life of the community. No person should be excluded because he is too poor.

Intended beneficiaries of socioeconomic justice laws

Many passages considered thus far refer to "the sojourner, the fatherless, and the widow" as the intended beneficiaries of socioeconomic justice laws. Other intended beneficiaries referred to in the Bible include daily wage earners, the poor, the disabled or infirmed, prisoners and slaves.[200]

Does this mean only foreigners, orphans and widows are allowed to benefit from this law? No. The Mosaic Law provides for paradigm examples rather than specific ambits.[201] It was given in a narrative and

---

197 See Deuteronomy 14:22-29; Deuteronomy 16:13-15; 28:12-15; Malachi 3:6-10.
198 See also Deuteronomy 29:10-12; 31:12; 2 Chronicles 30:25.
199 Numbers 9:14; Exodus 12:19; 12:48-49; Leviticus 17:12-13, 15, 18; 18:26; 20:2; 24:16.
200 Job 29:12-17; Psalm 146:7-9; Malachi 3:5; Trent C. Butler, ed., *Holman Bible Dictionary* (Holman Bible Publishers, 1991), 828.
201 Gordon Fee and Douglas Stuart, *How To Read the Bible For All Its Worth*, 2nd edn (Zondervan, 1993), 169-171.

also has to be interpreted with a narrative hermeneutic approach.[202] The Israelites were supposed to start from these paradigms and extend their application to situations which fall within the intended purpose of the law.

One example is Leviticus 19:14: "Do not curse the deaf or put a stumbling block in front of the blind, but fear your God. I am the Lord" (NIV). A modern legalistic construction may suggest that this law only applies to the deaf and the blind. What if the hearing or visual impairment is 70 per cent as opposed to 100 per cent? What about the mute? Did this law therefore implicitly permit the Israelites to curse the mute? Proper hermeneutics would suggest that God required the Israelites to treat disabled persons generally with respect.

Indeed, Jesus' teachings magnified the spirit and purpose of the Mosaic Law in contradistinction to the Pharisees' legalistic and pedantic interpretations. This short discursive on interpreting the Mosaic Law brings into focus who the intended beneficiaries of these socioeconomic justice laws are. The common theme is that the intended beneficiaries have specific needs preventing them from fully participating in the life of their community.[203]

Widows and orphans were vulnerable socioeconomically because of the patriarchal society Old Testament Israel was. Entitlements to land, inheritance and so on were familial and clan-based, which were represented by the male family figure.[204] This meant that widows and orphans would be deprived of economic opportunities. Without an opportunity to inherit land, one would have struggled to find an income source. The alternative option in those days would be working as a hired hand earning daily

---

202 Jonathan Burnside, *God, Justice and Society* (Oxford University Press, 2011), 11-14.
203 Trent C Butler, ed., *Holman Bible Dictionary* (Holman Bible Publishers, 1991), 828.
204 E.g., see Numbers 27, 36: See book's website on "Zelophehad's inheritance".

wages. But landowners would have employed male workers, not widows and children. The story of Ruth and Naomi mentioned above illustrates this. Hence the need for the gleaning laws.

However, the broader principle to be drawn from a paradigmatic interpretation of the Law is that it was intended to provide opportunities for the socioeconomically disenfranchised in general. On this, we consider the "sojourner" next.

Treatment of foreigners

The Mosaic Law required Israelites to treat the "sojourners", the non-Israelites, the foreigners, among them justly:

> You shall not wrong a sojourner or oppress him, for you were sojourners in the land of Egypt. (Exodus 22:21)

> When a stranger sojourns with you in your land, you shall not do him wrong. You shall treat the stranger who sojourns with you as the native among you, and you shall love him as yourself, for you were strangers in the land of Egypt: I am the Lord your God. (Leviticus 19:33-34)

> [The LORD] executes justice for the fatherless and the widow, and loves the sojourner, giving him food and clothing. Love the sojourner, therefore, for you were sojourners in the land of Egypt. (Deuteronomy 10:18-19)

> If your brother becomes poor and cannot maintain himself with you, you shall support him as though he were a stranger and a sojourner, and he shall live with you. (Leviticus 25:35)[205]

---

205 See also Exodus 23:9; Jeremiah 7:6; 22:3. Zechariah 7:8-10.

Thus, the Israelites were to support, maintain and provide food, clothing and shelter for the "stranger" and "sojourner". The Hebrew words for "stranger" and "sojourner" are *"ger"* and *"towshab"* respectively, which are used in the Bible to mean "foreigner", "guest", "resident alien", "foreigner" or "inhabiter". *"Towshab"* refers to long-term foreign residents whereas *"ger"* suggests a transient stay. Collectively, this would encompass any foreigner, including refugees, émigrés, transient migrant workers and permanent residents.

Why is this significant? It is the tendency of sinful human nature that the majority and the powerful oppress the minority and the powerless. It is also human nature that the majority would likely express xenophobic, racist, ethno-nationalistic behaviour against the minority. We have seen this throughout human history. Recent examples include the persecution of ethnic minority groups such as the Rohingyas, the Kachins, the Chins, the Karen, the Shan, etc., in Buddhist-Burman-majority Myanmar since the country's independence in the 1940s; ethnic Hoa Chinese in Vietnam which led to the refugee boat people crisis in the 1970s; Christian ethnic minorities in Vietnam including Hmong, Degar and Montagnards; ethnic Vietnamese and indigenous people in Cambodia; hill tribes in Thailand; Dalits or the 'untouchables' in India; and the Christian Indians in Hindu-majority states in India such as Orissa, e.g., Christian Indians were massacred in 2008-2009 for refusing to change their faith. Since 2014 to date, the terrorist group Islamic State in Iraq and Syria (ISIS)[206] has been persecuting anyone who does not submit to their version of Islam, including Christians and Shia Muslims, as well as ethnic groups such as the Assyrians. ISIS has beheaded victims, killed thousands of civilians, and displaced hundreds of thousands of people whom they consider to be

---

206   Also known as the Islamic State in Iraq and the Levant (ISIL).

different from them.[207]

Singapore is not immune to this. During the 2011 General Elections, the public discussion on mainstream media and online media regarding hot button issues included the topic of foreigners. Some of the views and comments made, many of which were anti-foreigner in sentiment, reeked of irrational xenophobia. Foreigners were blamed for infrastructure problems and employment issues. After the Little India Riot in December 2013, there was a heightened mood of suspicion and ill will towards foreigners. Comments were made on online media against foreigners from South Asia. As a result, several civil society groups and activists issued a statement registering their "alarm" of the "recent surge of racism and xenophobia" in Singapore.[208] A 2014 survey by the Institute of Policy Studies (IPS) suggested that more than 30 per cent of citizens and permanent residents felt that nationality-based prejudice had risen over the past five years.[209]

> **Jesus' teachings magnified the spirit and purpose of the Mosaic Law.**

Even within some Singapore churches, we sometimes treat fellow believers of different ethnicities or nationalities differently. This may happen at a person-to-person level or even, in how we conduct church. Believers of every ethnicity and nationality are of the same faith, praising

---

207 See generally UN Declaration on the Rights of Persons Belonging to National or Ethnic, Religious and Linguistic Minorities GA A/RES/47/135 (1992); Minority Rights Group International, World Directory of Minorities and Indigenous Peoples, http://www.minorityrights.org/directory; Peter Grant, ed., "State of the World's Minorities and Indigenous Peoples 2014, Events of 2013", *Minority Rights Group International* (2014). See Roads of Success' video of Christians in Syria recounting the persecution of ISIS: https://www.youtube.com/watch?v=ALf_6FLNg44
208 Civil society statement on racism and xenophobia (28 May 2014).
209 IPS Survey on Race, Religion and Language (2014).

the same God in the same body of Christ.[210] There is neither Jew nor Greek, slave nor free, male nor female.[211] There should be no distinction in terms of ethnicity, socioeconomic status or gender. We will be praising God shoulder-to-shoulder in heaven. CS Lewis' words are poignant:[212]

> There are no ordinary people. You have never talked to a mere mortal... it is immortals whom we joke with, work with, marry, snub and exploit—immortal horrors or everlasting splendors... [We must take] each other seriously—no flippancy, no superiority, no presumption.

We cannot treat another human being with flippancy, superiority or presumption just because he is from a different ethnicity or nationality, speaks a different language, looks different or practises different cultural customs.

No doubt, many racial, ethnic-linguistic, nationality or religious disputes are complex and multi-faceted. They are not *merely* religious disputes. They are not purely about ethnic pride or nationalism. But a common thread underlying these problems is the notion of us-versus-them, the fear of the 'Other', and an insecurity about entrenched power and socioeconomic structures.

This was the Pharaoh's sentiment when he oppressed the Israelites in Egypt.[213] It was in that context that God required the Israelites to love the foreigners in their midst as their own. God was saying, "Look, you were oppressed as a minority people group in Egypt and you knew how terrible it was. I am the God who rescued you from that oppression. You cannot now turn around to oppress other minority groups." God knows

---

210 Ephesians 4:4-6.
211 Galatians 3:28.
212 CS Lewis, *The Weight of Glory* (HarperOne, 2001) at 45-46.
213 Discussed above in "Exodus: Freedom from Oppression into a Worship Community".

the tendency for the majority in power to maintain its domination and hegemony. So God explicitly commanded the Israelites to not only limit themselves, but to positively love the foreigners as themselves. This calls for Christians and the Church to conduct a radical self-reflection in relation to power and differences.

Treatment of workers, orphans, widows and the poor

The Mosaic Law also makes it clear that those who are socioeconomically weakest are to be protected from abuses.

> [The LORD] executes justice for the fatherless and the widow, and loves the sojourner, giving him food and clothing. Love the sojourner, therefore, for you were sojourners in the land of Egypt. (Deuteronomy 10:18-19)[214]

> You shall not wrong a sojourner or oppress him, for you were sojourners in the land of Egypt. You shall not mistreat any widow or fatherless child. If you do mistreat them, and they cry out to me, I will surely hear their cry, and my wrath will burn, and I will kill you with the sword, and your wives shall become widows and your children fatherless. (Exodus 22:21-24)

Harsh words but it reflects the severity with which God views the potential abuse of power against the weak. It has been suggested by critics[215] that such verses do not refer to socioeconomic justice but merely legal justice. It is difficult to understand such a criticism in the light of the various provisions in the Mosaic Law which provide for substantive rights to these beneficiaries. And what would have been the "legal" justice which God executed for these people? If it is procedural fairness in adjudication

---

214 See also Deuteronomy 27:19.
215 E.g., Andrew S Kulikovsky, "Justice and the Bible" (January 2007).

of disputes, that has already been provided for elsewhere in the Law, why would God single out these people? It is clear that the references to "justice" in respect of these vulnerable groups refer to substantive socioeconomic justice rights and protection. On such rights, Nicholas Wolterstorff observes:[216]

> Seeing that rights are claims to guarantees against threats makes clear that rights are God's charter for the weak and defenceless ones in society. A right is the legitimate claim for protection of those too weak to help themselves. It is the legitimate claim of the defenceless against the more devastating and common of life's threats which, at that time and peace, are remediable. It is the claim of the little ones in society to restraint upon economic and political and physical forces that would otherwise be too strong for them to resist.

Justice also required that the poor and needy not be economically oppressed by way of exploitative or unfair employment practices.

> You shall not oppress a hired worker who is poor and needy, whether he is one of your brothers or one of the sojourners who are in your land within your towns. You shall give him his wages on the same day, before the sun sets (for he is poor and counts on it), lest he cry against you to the Lord, and you be guilty of sin. (Deuteronomy 24:14-15)[217]

---

216 Nicholas Wolterstorff, *Until Justice and Peace Embrace* (Wm B Eerdmans Publishing, 1983), 84.
217 See also Leviticus 19:13.

For the wageworker, his daily wages would determine whether he had enough food for the day or shelter for the evening. Paying him the wages due to him is literally a matter of life and death.

Under Deuteronomy 24:12-13,[218] a lender must let a poor borrower have his cloak for the night, which is his security for the loan. It is a moral and legal obligation. Not merely a good thing to do. Can you imagine? I lend you money to buy a house. The world's wisdom says if you can't pay your mortgage payments, I will foreclose, sell the house, repay myself with the proceeds and if the debt is still outstanding, I can continue to sue you until full repayment is made. But God's Law says, hold your hands; if your poor borrower cannot pay you, don't take away his house. Let him stay in it, otherwise he would have no roof over his head. This prevents the poor, who are more vulnerable than other types of borrowers, from being exploited.

The Law also provides that poor persons who desire to make offerings to God but cannot afford it can do so with less expensive options. Thus in Leviticus 5:7, 11-13, regarding sacrifices for forgiveness of sins, an exception is provided for poor persons: If they cannot afford a lamb, then two turtledoves or pigeons; if they can't afford that, then flour would do.

This shows us that God desires sincere, not ostentatious and lavish displays, of worship. It shows us that God's forgiveness is grace on His part, and not a matter of how much we can give to him. All are invited to worship God, whether rich or poor.

This calls us to reflect on how we conduct our church activities and relationships. Are they universally accessible or do they tend to repel the less well-off? Apart from providing subsidies for poorer members, do our church activities ensure anyone of any means can participate? For

---

218 See also Exodus 22:25-27.

example, holding a year-end watch night service until midnight would mean poorer members would have to take a taxi home. This might already repel some members from even attending the service. In my church, we have a lady who would quietly arrange carpooling for the poorer members. Do informal outings with church members involve going to expensive eateries? These same issues would apply to any social context and not just within the church. Sensitivity to these issues is important to ensure that social participation is egalitarian and not divided by financial means or status.

Finally, as mentioned above, God demands that people respect the handicapped, see Leviticus 19:13-14. The Hebrew word for "oppress" in that verse is "*ashaq*" which is used in the Bible to mean defraud, violate or do violence. Surely this doesn't mean that it's alright to oppress non-handicapped people. So why did God expressly highlight the handicapped for protection? The significance to me is that, as with the other passages examined in this chapter, God is especially protective of the weak and marginalised.

Mercy in the Mosaic Law

In the Mosaic Covenant, mercy as *racham* and *chesed* are found in the narrative rather than in the Law. For example, when Moses asked for the Lord to reveal His glory to him,[219] the Lord's reply was: "I will be gracious to whom I will be gracious, and will show mercy [*racham*] on whom I will show mercy [*racham*]".[220] In Deuteronomy 30:3, God declared under the Covenant that if the Israelites obeyed Him, He would restore their fortunes and "have mercy [*racham*]" on them. *Racham* appears therefore to be relating to forbearance from wrath and judgment.[221]

---

219   Exodus 33:12-23.
220   Exodus 33:19.
221   See Deuteronomy 7:2; 13:7; 28:50; Joshua 11:20.

Racham is juxtaposed with *chesed*, which surfaces in the biblical narratives concerning the conduct of interpersonal relationships, including God's covenantal relationship with Israel, which is often translated as "steadfast love" or "faithfulness" within the Mosaic Covenant.[222] We have seen earlier in the book of Ruth that *chesed* is the central motif in the narrative. It is significant that this narrative is meant to parallel our relationship with God as the one who shows us *chesed*.

D. Justice, Mercy and Righteousness Beyond the Mosaic Law

Having considered the conception of God's justice, mercy and righteousness in the Mosaic Law, we turn to the biblical passages on justice in the rest of the Old Testament which also reveal the same themes. These are predominantly the words of the prophets during the exilic and post-exilic periods. These were often of God rebuking His people for, among other things, their failure to do justice and live righteously.

Injustice and Unrighteousness are a Sin Issue

From many of these passages, I have come to the view, unsettling as it may be, that *the failure to do justice is sin*. Perpetrating injustice by acts or omissions is to sin against God. My participation in injustice is sin. Consider the following passages:

> Ah, sinful nation, a people laden with iniquity, offspring of evildoers, children who deal corruptly! They have forsaken the

---

222 Exodus 15:13; 20:6; 34:6,7; Leviticus 20:17; Number 14:18,19; Deuteronomy 5:10; 7:9,12.

LORD, they have despised the Holy One of Israel, they are utterly estranged... Wash yourselves; make yourselves clean; remove the evil of your deeds from before my eyes; cease to do evil, learn to do good; seek justice, correct oppression; bring justice to the fatherless, plead the widow's cause. (Isaiah 1: 4, 16-17)

And the word of the LORD came to me: "Son of man, say to her, You are a land that is not cleansed or rained upon in the day of indignation... Her princes in her midst are like wolves tearing the prey, shedding blood, destroying lives to get dishonest gain... The people of the land have practiced extortion and committed robbery. They have oppressed the poor and needy, and have extorted from the sojourner without justice. And I sought for a man among them who should build up the wall and stand in the breach before me for the land, that I should not destroy it, but I found none. Therefore I have poured out my indignation upon them. I have consumed them with the fire of my wrath. I have returned their way upon their heads, declares the Lord GOD'... " (Ezekiel 22:23, 24, 27, 29-31)

He who oppresses the poor shows contempt for their Maker, but whoever is kind to the needy honors God. (Proverbs 14:31)

The above passages reveal to me that God considers injustice as sin. In Isaiah 1, God declared His people as "sinful", "laden with iniquity", "evildoers", having "despised" God. Why? Because they did not "do good; seek justice, correct oppression [or] bring justice to the fatherless [and] plead the widow's cause". In Ezekiel 22, God declared that He had judged and punished His people for "oppress[ing] the poor and needy, and hav[ing] extorted from the sojourner without justice".

We learn that both acts and omissions are sinful. Actively causing injustice by way of oppression and exploitation,[223] and the failure to seek justice and correct oppression[224] are sinful.[225] And oppression includes the forces which deprive people of what is basic for community life,[226] and the exploitation of power and privileges to deprive others of rights in the community.[227]

Job, who was deemed by God to be "blameless and upright, who fears God",[228] considered it a sin against God if he failed to do justice.[229] In Job 29 and 31, Job articulated how he had done justice and pursued righteousness:

> ... because I delivered the poor who cried for help, and the fatherless who had none to help him. The blessing of him who was about to perish came upon me, and I caused the widow's heart to sing for joy. I put on righteousness, and it clothed me; my justice was like a robe and a turban. I was eyes to the blind and feet to the lame. I was a father to the needy, and I searched out the cause of him whom I did not know. I broke the fangs of the unrighteous and made him drop his prey from his teeth. (Job 29:12-17, NIV)

---

223 Ezekiel 22:28, 29; Proverbs 14:31; Malachi 3:5.
224 Isaiah 1:17; Jeremiah 5:28.
225 Trent C Butler, ed., *Holman Bible Dictionary* (Holman Bible Publishers, 1991), 828.
226 Micah 2:2; Ecclesiastes 4:1.
227 Mark 12:40; Trent C Butler, ed., *Holman Bible Dictionary* (Holman Bible Publishers, 1991), 828.
228 Job 2:3.
229 Job 31:23, 28.

> If I have denied justice to any of my servants, whether male or female, when they had a grievance against me... If I have denied the desires of the poor or let the eyes of the widow grow weary, if I have kept my bread to myself, not sharing it with the fatherless—but from my youth I reared them as a father would, and from my birth I guided the widow—if I have seen anyone perishing for lack of clothing, or the needy without garments, and their hearts did not bless me for warming them with the fleece from my sheep, if I have raised my hand against the fatherless, knowing that I had influence in court, then let my arm fall from the shoulder, let it be broken off at the joint. For I dreaded destruction from God, and for fear of his splendor I could not do such things... then these also would be sins to be judged, for I would have been unfaithful to God on high. (Job 31:13-28, NIV).

Justice, Mercy and Righteousness is True Worship

God considers seeking justice and showing mercy as true worship. Isaiah 58:6-10 states:[230]

> Is not this the fast that I choose:
>> to loose the bonds of wickedness,
>> to undo the straps of the yoke,
>
> to let the oppressed go free,
>> and to break every yoke?
>
> Is it not to share your bread with the hungry

---

[230] See Kevin DeYoung and Greg Gilbert, *What Is the Mission of the Church? Making Sense of Social Justice, Shalom and the Great Commission* (Crossway, 2011), 155-156; John Calvin, *Calvin's Commentaries*, vol. 8, Isaiah 33-66 (Baker, 1998), 233.

>   and bring the homeless poor into your house;
> when you see the naked, to cover him,
>   and not to hide yourself from your own flesh?
> Then shall your light break forth like the dawn,
>   and your healing shall spring up speedily;
> your righteousness shall go before you;
>   the glory of the Lord shall be your rear guard.
> Then you shall call, and the Lord will answer;
>   you shall cry, and he will say, 'Here I am.'
> If you take away the yoke from your midst,
>   the pointing of the finger, and speaking wickedness,
> if you pour yourself out for the hungry
>   and satisfy the desire of the afflicted,
> then shall your light rise in the darkness
>   and your gloom be as the noonday.

Jeremiah 9:23-24 states: "Let him who boasts boast in this, that he understands and knows me, that I am the Lord who practises steadfast love, justice, and righteousness in the earth. For in these things I delight, declares the Lord." In Amos 5:22-24, God rejected the offerings and the "noise" of His people's worship songs and demanded that "justice roll down like waters, and righteousness like an ever-flowing stream". This vivid and forceful image emphasises that justice must be constant, abundant and dynamic in the lives of God's people. Without these in their lives, they do not truly know God and are not truly worshipping Him.

In Micah 6:6-8, God said that He did not desire from His people great sacrifices or ostentatious material offerings. Instead, if they could only do three simple things, they would be acceptable to God. What were these three things? Micah 6:8 (also known as the Micah Mandate) declares:

> He has told you, O man, what is good; and what does the Lord require of you but to do justice [*mishpat*], and to love kindness [or mercy: *chesed*], and to walk humbly with your God?

> • • •
> **Perpetrating injustice by acts or omissions is to sin against God.**

The tone of frustration in the Micah 6 passage should not be missed. Here, the prophet effectively pleaded with his people: Look, it's really not that hard, the entirety of the Mosaic Law which God gave can be summed up in this; just do justice, love mercy and walk humbly with God! It's especially significant that the Micah Mandate was implicitly referred to when Jesus rebuked the Pharisees in Matthew 23:23. Jesus said: "Woe to you, scribes and Pharisees, hypocrites! For you tithe mint and dill and cumin, and have neglected the weightier matters of the law: *justice and mercy and faithfulness*. These you ought to have done, without neglecting the others. You blind guides, straining out a gnat and swallowing a camel!" (Emphasis added). Justice, mercy, faithfulness and walking humbly with God are thus foundational in our covenantal relationship with God. I will elaborate on the Micah Mandate and its universal application to us later.

God's Judgment on Sins of Injustice and Unrighteousness

Because God's people failed to do justice and pursue righteousness, He judged and punished them.[231] Jeremiah 22:3-5 states:

---

231 Amos 2:6-7; 4:1; 5:11.

Thus says the Lord: Do justice and righteousness, and deliver from the hand of the oppressor him who has been robbed. And do no wrong or violence to the resident alien, the fatherless, and the widow, nor shed innocent blood in this place. For if you will indeed obey this word, then there shall enter the gates of this house kings who sit on the throne of David, riding in chariots and on horses, they and their servants and their people. But if you will not obey these words, I swear by myself, declares the Lord, *that this house shall become a desolation.* (Emphasis added)

In Jeremiah 34, God declared that He handed Judah over to Babylon because Judah failed to observe the Jubilee Law. Zechariah 7:9-10 also declares: "And the word of the Lord came to Zechariah, saying, "Thus says the Lord of hosts, Render true judgments, show kindness and mercy to one another, do not oppress the widow, the fatherless, the sojourner, or the poor, and let none of you devise evil against another in your heart." And what happened when God's people failed to do this? God declares in verses 11-14:

But they refused to pay attention and turned a stubborn shoulder and stopped their ears that they might not hear. They made their hearts diamond-hard lest they should hear the law and the words that the Lord of hosts had sent by his Spirit through the former prophets. Therefore great anger came from the Lord of hosts. "As I called, and they would not hear, so they called, and I would not hear," says the Lord of hosts, "and I scattered them with a whirlwind among all the nations that they had not known. Thus the land they left was desolate, so that no one went to and fro, and the pleasant land was made desolate."

Justice and Righteousness Expected Universally in Governance

Finally, the wisdom of King Lemuel's mother in Proverbs 31 to the king is poignant. What kind of wisdom might we expect the King's mother to talk about? Perhaps, the wisdom to govern subordinates and armies; how to relate to foreign nations in times of peace and war; how to ensure the economic prosperity of his nation. In the oracle, the king's mother tells him three main things. The first is about avoiding hedonism and lust.[232] The second is about finding an excellent spouse.[233] And the third is this: Proverbs 31:8-9:

> Open your mouth for the mute, for the rights of all who are destitute. Open your mouth, judge righteously, defend the rights of the poor and needy. (Proverbs 31:8-9)

Proverbs 29:14 declares that "[i]f a king faithfully judges the poor, his throne will be established forever".[234] In Nehemiah 5, Nehemiah was filled with righteous anger against the nobles and officials in power for oppressing the poor. In Daniel 4:27, the prophet Daniel counselled King Nebuchadnezzar of Babylon to "break off [his] sins by practicing righteousness, and [his] iniquities by showing mercy to the oppressed, that there may perhaps be a lengthening of [his] prosperity". The King took no heed of Daniel's advice and God turned him into a beast-like wild man eating grass for seven years. Indeed, if the character of the universal God who is sovereign over the universe is just and righteous, it

---

232 Proverbs 31:2-7.
233 Proverbs 31:10-31.
234 See also Psalm 72:2-4, 12-14.

is no surprise then that human kings established under His sovereignty are expected to reflect that character.[235] This applies even to pagan kings.[236] It should therefore also be no surprise that the various legal codes of other ancient Near/Middle East nations, the most famous of which being the Code of Hammurabi, also contained legal provisions on social justice.[237] This is because the God of the whole universe is a God of justice and righteousness.

God's Favour on the Poor

Throughout the Old Testament, God reveals a special closeness to, and favour on, the poor. Various passages declare that God will exalt and lift up the poor. Hannah, the prophet Samuel's mother, prayed and declared that "[t]he Lord makes poor and makes rich; he brings low and he exalts. He raises up the poor from the dust; he lifts the needy from the ash heap to make them sit with princes and inherit a seat of honor. For the pillars of the earth are the Lord's, and on them he has set the world".[238] The psalmists similarly declare God's special favour to give hope and personally take action to lift up and rescue the poor.[239] God also declares his favour on those who care for, and identify with the poor,[240] and conversely, those who do not are far from God.[241] The poor are especially inclined to know and worship God.[242]

---

235 Ezekiel 34:4; Jeremiah 22:15-16; Psalm 72:1-4; Trent C Butler, ed., *Holman Bible Dictionary* (Holman Bible Publishers, 1991), 828.
236 Daniel 4:27; Romans 13:1-4.
237 See Victor P Hamilton, *Handbook on the Pentateuch*, 2nd edn (Baker Academic, 2005), 201; Jonathan Burnside, *God, Justice and Society* (Oxford University Press, 2011), 2-10; see footnote 137.
238 1 Samuel 2:7-8.
239 Psalm 9:18; 12:5; 113:7-8; 132:15; Isaiah 25:4.
240 Psalm 41:1-2; Proverbs 16:19-20; 22:9; 28:27; 29:7.
241 Proverbs 21:13; 28:27.
242 Isaiah 29:19.

Chesed as Covenantal Faithfulness

The Old Testament beyond the Mosaic Law continues to use the word *chesed* to largely mean covenantal faithfulness, often translated as "steadfast love" or "loyalty".[243] In most cases, the word refers to God's steadfast love and faithfulness within His covenant. Sometimes, *chesed* is used to refer to "good deeds" but even so, it likely refers to deeds in respect of covenantal faithfulness to God.[244] There are also instances where *chesed* refers to acts of kindness and favour.[245]

E. Reflections on Justice, Mercy and Righteousness in the Old Testament

This survey of Old Testament passages on justice, mercy and righteousness shows us a few things. God's justice and righteousness are concerned with right living, right relationships and right conduct. This includes personal holiness and *social* holiness, sexual ethics and *social* ethics, legal-adjudicative justice *and socioeconomic* justice.

God has expressed an especial concern for the socioeconomically weak and marginalised persons in the community. God sees injustice as a sin problem for individuals and the nation of Israel. Conversely, just and righteous living is true worship of God.

We see that God intends His justice and righteousness to be the way

---

243 See e.g., 1 Samuel 15:6; 20:8,14,15; 2 Samuel 2:5,6; 3:8; 7:15; 9:1, 3, 7; 10:2; 15:20; 16:17; 22:51; 1 Kings 2:7; 3:6; 8:23; 20:31; 1 Chronicles 16:34, 41; 17:13; 19:2; 2 Chronicles 1:8; 5:13; 6:14,42; 7:3,6; 20:21; 24:22; Ezra 3:11; 7:28; 9:9; Nehemiah 1:5; 9:17, 32; 13:14, 22; Isaiah 16:5; 40:6; 54:8, 10; 55:3; 57:1; 63:7; Jeremiah 2:2; 9:24; 16:5; 31:3; 32:18; 33:11; Daniel 1:9; 9:4; Hosea 2:19; 4:1; 6:4,6; 10:12; 12:6; Joel 2:13; Jonah 2:8; 4:2; Micah 6:8; 7:18,20; Zechariah 7:9.
244 2 Chronicles 32:32; 35:26.
245 Ruth 1:8; 2:20; 3:10; Esther 2:9, 17; Job 6:14; Proverbs 11:17; 21:21; 31:26.

of life for citizens of the Kingdom of God. This way of life was also to be a vision for all of humanity. God's intended vocation for Israel was to be a witness of His glory and His righteousness to the surrounding nations that they may inquire of, and worship, Him. In summary, we see that *God intends for His people to manifest His Kingdom by living justly and righteously, by including the marginalised into His Kingdom community.*

Israel failed in this given task. For that reason, God judged Israel and punished them, exiling them from the land He gave to them, just as He promised He would do if they failed to obey Him.[246]

Yet, God did not leave His people without hope. Many of the prophets during the time around the exilic period prophesied of a Messiah who would restore the Kingdom of Israel. Isaiah foresaw that this Messiah would be one who would "bring forth justice to the nations" and "establish justice in the earth".[247] He would bring about the Jubilee Year of the Lord and restore the ruins of the Kingdom; He would bring "good news to the poor", "bind up the broken hearted", "proclaim liberty to the captives" and free from "prison... those who are bound".[248] This Messiah would possess, rule over, and draw all "the nations" from the "ends of the earth".[249] He would bring about everlasting peace, justice and righteousness to the world.[250] The Messiah would establish an eternal kingdom, removing all

> **God's justice and righteousness are concerned with right living, right relationships and right conduct.**

---

246 Deuteronomy 28.
247 Isaiah 42:1-4; see also Psalm 45; Isaiah 11:1-5.
248 Isaiah 61:1-4.
249 Psalm 2:8-9; Isaiah 11:10-14; 56:3-8; Zechariah 14:16.
250 Isaiah 9:6-7; 11:6-9; Ezekiel 34:23-32.

previous earthly kingdoms.[251] In other words, the Messiah would be the perfect epitome of God's Kingdom and the King who would establish God's Kingdom eternally in the entire world. That person is Jesus. That is the message which all the gospel narratives sought to tell: The Messiah or the Christ has come and Jesus is He! On that note, we turn now to the New Testament.

Chapter Summary

- The Old Testament reveals God's intent for His Kingdom people to live lives of justice, mercy and righteousness.
- God's justice is about His desire for egalitarian inclusion of all persons to freely and fully participate within His community and their enjoyment of His gracious provision.
- The failure to do justice is sin.
- A life of seeking justice and showing mercy is true worship of God.
- Because God is just and righteous, justice and righteousness are expected to be practised universally in governance, including by pagan rulers.

---

251 2 Samuel 7:16; Isaiah 9:6-7; Daniel 2:44-45.

Discussion Questions

1. Which Bible passages caught your attention? What did you learn from those passages? What implications would those biblical truths have on your life?
2. What did you learn about God's justice, mercy and righteousness respectively? How does this impact your relationship with God, with others and with the world?
3. How are the above biblical truths being expressed in your life and your faith community? Which of them are missing in your life or faith community?
4. What is your response to God in the light of what you have gleaned from these truths?

INTERVIEW: Dr Goh Wei-Leong

• • •

Dr Goh Wei-Leong, a family physician and Adjunct Assistant Professor in the Department of Family Medicine (NUS), worships at Katong Presbyterian Church. He co-founded and chairs HealthServe, an NGO and charity that reaches out to the under-served communities of foreign workers in Singapore.

He is Co-founder and Director of Linking Hands, a medical networking agency. He also chairs the Christian Medical & Dental Fellowship (CMDF) of Singapore where medical missions, student work, ethics and marketplace engagement are growing ministries. He is the Southeast Asian regional general secretary of the International Christian Medical and Dental Association (ICMDA).

Wei-Leong serves with Operation Mobilisation (Singapore) as an OM Associate (Local Ministries) and in OM East Asia Pacific (Relief and Development). He is currently the chairman of the board of OM MTI (Mercy Teams International).

1. Do you think that social justice is a key expression of Christian discipleship and witness? Why or why not?

Discipleship is following our Lord Jesus who was almost always partial to the poor. The entire Bible has social justice themes throughout. God's centre is our 'margin'. Throughout his ministry, Jesus was always concerned with social justice even in his daily interactions with people. At the start of His ministry in Luke 4, he emphasises social justice.

2. How do you pursue social justice as an expression of Christian faithfulness?

As a doctor, I'm confronted with issues of justice, poverty, life threatening situations, and even death. Many of these issues are connected with people at the margins. My own practice is in a very poor neighbourhood. Through my vocation, I try to frame the way I practise medicine with a biblical lens—in the way I treat my patients and how I help them beyond giving medicine.

In addition, I've started new initiatives and platforms, HealthServe being one of them. I did it because the institutional Church finds these expressions a lot more difficult. I also often network and read to expand my vocabulary, discover fresh ideas and to be more creative in my expression.

3. Tell me more about HealthServe, Linking Hands, and these other organisations you founded.

HealthServe was started eight years ago and the primary reason for starting it was because I sensed an undercurrent of change in our social space—more migrants in Singapore. These migrants are fellow image bearers who do not have much access to medical care and are pushed to the margins.

HealthServe provides that safe space for the flourishing and wellbeing of people made in His image even when they have not yet acknowledged Him as Creator. This space bridges communities, brings healing and keeps hope alive for a common humanity. It is through this space that Christianity confronts everyday matters which we often rather not see, like injustice, poverty and ill health in the migrant community. In a world where we rob each other of the liberties God gives us, social justice is breached and HealthServe attempts to address that through the various expressions of her ministry.

The individual, community and society at large are intersecting daily in the social, emotional and spiritual realms besides the more tangible physical needs. Social justice is brought to the fore as these issues synapse with each other. HealthServe often reconnects the various realms when there are gaps. This reconnection is realised in HealthServe through active service and advocacy.

Linking Hands is a web-based portal which links global partnerships in medical missions. We started about 15 years ago to connect doctors to the needs around the world. One of the hospitals Linking Hands sends students for medical electives at is a missions hospital called Christian Fellowship Hospital in Oddanchatram, India. Until today, they model a missions hospital where social justice is framed in biblical and robust social justice functioning. For example, the hospital director's pay and the janitor's pay has a mere 40 per cent differential.

Linking Hands, while promoting collaboration and partnership in medical missions, opens the world to those who plug into God's mission and world. For young students and medical professionals, signing up for a Linking Hands programme means that the issues of the world are experienced in a diverse cultural setting and their worldviews are challenged.

4. Why do you do this work? What got you started on it?

I just saw the need and I went in. I never went in knowing the fully developed framework. I sort of learnt on the job. The people around me, inspiration, reading, exposure, stories. People I've met all over the world. My time in Mongolia and India got me started doing this work.

Mongolia was where I rediscovered Jesus and my first introduction to missions was the JCS (Joint Christian Service) model. I witnessed self-sacrificing service by missionaries from different agencies and denominations serving in collaboration and partnership with each other. This was the norm in missions which I was introduced to and it left an indelible mark in the future endeavours of HealthServe and Linking Hands.

Early in the course of my journey in Christian missions in the late 1990s I was introduced to the Dalit Freedom Movement which had just been birthed in India. Social justice and advocacy, which were new to me then, were discussed and acted upon. I learnt from my Indian friends, who were at the forefront of the Dalit Freedom Network as they campaigned for the freedom of the low caste Indians, the untouchables. That formed the framework for me for the subsequent work in HealthServe and Linking Hands.

My exposure to the international Christian community, where I saw people working among the poor and my constant exposure to people doing this work led me to reflect on my own faith and the gospel. The Bible became more alive and challenging at the same time.

5. How do you ground or relate your work with these organisations in your faith?

I think constant reflection on the Bible on one hand and the issues on the other, and talking with people are key. While I serve the poor, I also talk to the theologians and check the Bible out. The Lausanne Movement which is about "The whole church taking the whole gospel to the whole world, framed in the language of love" has been instrumental in moving me to question my faith in action where it matters.

6. Do you evangelise to the people you work with?
I have become less anxious in needing to fulfil my set goals of "sharing" the Gospel. Sharing my faith is more integral in my life now, ministry and work intertwined, proclamation and social action woven together. Evangelism as a result is now more active in my work, ministry and everyday life.

In HealthServe, we don't overtly "share" the Gospel. Yet there have been countless opportunities to share our stories. We serve the marginalised because we are disciples of Jesus and people we serve are image bearers; not as a means to "bring them to church".

7. These organisations are not tied to any local church. Why not?
Just as the body has different parts, organisations like HealthServe and Linking Hands are part of the Church. However the institutional church is suspicious of unfamiliar forms of church. It's like the ear saying to the toe: "You're so different, we can't be from the same body."

The problems of liberation and liberal theology in the middle of the last century caused a pendulum swing away from social action and vilified it. Proclamation [of the Gospel] and saving of individual souls became paramount. With this backdrop, any attempt to associate the Gospel with social action, advocacy and activism is largely viewed with much caution and suspicion. Meanwhile, a generation that came to faith as teenagers with Billy Graham rallies and Campus Crusade programmes are now in leadership in our local churches. Unfortunately the same yardsticks of faith and spirituality are stuck in the form of programmes these leaders are familiar with.

Against this backdrop, fresh expressions of the Gospel in action can be a challenge and that is why the Church is seldom the early adopters of organisations like HealthServe, Linking Hands or TeamZero, let alone pioneering them.

However, once a critical mass, credible voice and transformational presence is acknowledged by society and the Christian community, the Church is then quick to embrace the ministry that she overlooked simply because of her worldview and practice.

HealthServe was largely unnoticed by the Church in her early years. However when her own members began to serve and engage faith in a ripe but risky environment, robust discipleship is realised. This was quietly but powerfully brought back to the Church.

8. What do you think should be the role of the local church in relation to your organisation?

To embrace us. To be part of us. To encourage us. Not to have the parachurch/church divide. We are all part of the Church.

Churches can help by revisiting and reflecting on the Bible with us. Being the Church together with us can mean being involved in the global scene like Lausanne Movement, WEA and Micah Global as much of the theologising is being done there for our benefit.

9. How does your local church view or support you in this ministry?

It has taken them a long time to accept that my work at HealthServe, Linking Hands, TeamZero, etc., is part of a regular church ministry because it is so new. So my local church, only in recent years, has become more open. They were not too enthusiastic about it initially. They were still more interested in the convenient annual Vacation Bible School (VBS) and Christmas Rally. Be that as it may, they are beginning to understand

and are increasingly curious and excited about societal issues. The young people in my home church, especially the Millennials, are asking questions that many of us church leaders have not asked. Today's church leaders (baby boomers) grew up doing big rallies and stuff. I feel the world has moved and changed. They still bring back this old teenage stuff. I bring to church the things I grew up with. I run church the way I saw church 30 years ago. But today, church is different. I think the way for us to move on is to allow much more discussion and conversation about these topics. Lastly, allow the Millennials and the people from Generation Y to lead the discussion and be a part of it.

10. Any other thoughts or comments on the topic?
More conversations on this are needed. The other thing is that we have to approach this with much humility and patience because we have to realise that people are at different stages of their life journey. I cannot expect you to suddenly come on board when I have not taken the time to educate you and help you to see how this is important.

The Church must plug into international resources like the Lausanne Movement. There is so much thinking going on regarding this topic around the world. Sadly our churches are only concentrating on the type of music that they play in their church worship service. We need to go beyond that.

People join HealthServe because they are attracted to the cause. And so we have that advantage of a very clear cause, in this case, with migrant workers. Whereas churches have this whole wide range of causes and they have the whole community to look after. And so when the church is not talking about social justice issues, then the people who think, who feel that God is leading them to this will naturally come and look for a place where they can grow and it happens to be in this para-church.

Social media seems to be driving the surge in interest in social justice. We must respond accordingly.

My home church allowed me to explore the world outside the gates of Joo Chiat Lane and left the gates open for me to walk in and out; often I bring many with me. The Church began to realise the richness of this and many are serving in agencies like Prison Fellowship, local community centres and nursing homes. We acknowledge them as we do overseas missionaries. This is transforming the landscape of my local church. Even our values and DNA have evolved as a result. Most Katong Presbyterian Church members can tell you that "KPC is a missional community framed by the Word, led by the Spirit and undergirded with prayer" and that our five values are, "We are disciples making disciples; bridge builders across generations; lovers of all people; caretakers of the earth; upholders of justice and mercy". I think it's exciting and there is hope!

4

How did Social Justice Evolve Through the Bible? Justice, Mercy and Righteousness in the New Testament

Both of His hands
Are equally skilled
At showing me mercy
Equally skilled
At loving the loveless
Equally skilled
Administering justice
Both of His hands

—Jon Foreman, "Equally Skilled" (2007)

Jesus set aside His divine glory and entered the world as a human being to show us the Kingdom of God. He did so by living in a way that fulfilled the will of His Father, living out God's justice and righteousness perfectly, thereby manifesting—proclaiming and demonstrating—the Kingdom for people to see, hear, touch, smell and taste. God's justice and righteousness, which we have studied in the Old Testament, was more lived out and exhibited than didactically preached about in the New Testament. We therefore consider first the life of Jesus the Messiah and King of God's Kingdom.

A. The Model of Jesus

Jesus and the Jubilee
When an organisation officially opens for business, the first thing it would do is to explain its mission and vision. What is its purpose? What does it stand for? Who does it want to serve? Similarly, Jesus' opening declaration

of his public ministry is especially revealing. He began his public ministry in Luke 4:18-19 by declaring in a synagogue the opening words of the prophecy in Isaiah 61:1-2:

> The Spirit of the Lord God is upon me,
>   because the Lord has anointed me
> to bring good news to the poor;
>   he has sent me to bind up the brokenhearted,
> to proclaim liberty to the captives,
>   and the opening of the prison to those who are bound;
> to proclaim the year of the Lord's favour.

Isaiah 61 is a prophecy of the Year of the Lord's favour, i.e., the Jubilee Year. It was prophesied to be a year when the Lord would bring liberation, comfort, reconciliation, justice and righteousness. Jesus declared that He would bring good news to the poor, liberty to the captives, healing to the afflicted and freedom to the oppressed. He proclaimed the year of the Lord's favour, the Jubilee, at the commencement of His public ministry.

Indeed, the Jubilee Law is, for the Christian, a precursor to and a shadow of a Jubilee which would be of a different character from that of the Old Testament. Jesus declared Himself to be the fulfilment of the Law and the Prophets.[252] Jesus is the fulfilment of the Jubilee Law. Jesus is the Jubilee.

Recall that the Jubilee Year in Leviticus 25 climaxes on the Day of Atonement.[253] Before Jesus declared the opening words of Isaiah 61, He went into the wilderness and was tempted by Satan to sin. Jesus is the

---

252 Matthew 5:17; Luke 24:44.
253 Leviticus 25:9.

scapegoat on which the sins of the world were imputed—the scapegoat that was let loose to go into the wilderness to face Azazel as part of the Atonement rituals.[254] Jesus would also be the goat that was to be killed, whose blood would be used for the atonement of the sins of the people. The New Testament explains that Jesus was the sacrifice of a fundamentally different character,[255] the high priest who would live forever and was perfect, unlike the high priests of old.[256] It is through this atoning sacrifice of Jesus on the Cross that believers in Him can be reconciled with God.[257] It is no coincidence that the Jubilee year is intended to climax on the Day of Atonement. Reconciliation with God is the premise for reconciliation between people and between humanity and creation.[258] For the Christian, reconciliation with God in Jesus by His atoning sacrifice transforms Him to live a life of justice and righteousness.

Leviticus 25:1-6 also makes clear that the Jubilee year is a super Sabbath year. In Matthew 12, Jesus declared himself to be the Lord of the Sabbath. As Christians, we understand Jesus to be our Sabbath rest.[259] Also, we understand that as people who truly follow Jesus, our spiritual debts to God have been released insofar as we release our own debts vis-à-vis others.[260] Not only have our spiritual debts of sins been released, we understand that our spiritual bondages to sin have also been broken.[261] Indeed, it is telling that Jesus' public ministry

> **Jesus is the fulfilment of the Jubilee Law. Jesus is the Jubilee.**

---

254 See Leviticus 16.
255 Hebrews 9-10.
256 Hebrews 7-8.
257 2 Corinthians 5:18.
258 Victor P Hamilton, *Handbook on the Pentateuch*, 2nd edn (Baker Academic, 2005), 292.
259 Hebrews 4, Matthew 11.
260 Matthew 6:12.
261 Romans 6.

often involved healing people afflicted with physical, psycho-emotional and spiritual infirmities. The release of debts and bondages in the Jubilee Law is fulfilled in Jesus' release of our spiritual debts and bondages. The receipt of land as inheritance provided in the Jubilee Law is fulfilled metaphysically as the receipt of salvation as inheritance.[262] At the same time, it is also significant that Jesus did not declare the whole of Isaiah 61 to be fulfilled in His ministry during His first incarnation, as we know it. There remain aspects of the prophesied events unfulfilled. Nevertheless, it is paramount to understand that, for Christians, Jesus is our Jubilee.

What does the fact that Jesus is our Jubilee have to do with social justice? Everything. It is no coincidence that the Jubilee Law was primarily legislation of socioeconomic justice. It reflects God's especial concern for the socioeconomically weakest. At the same time, it should be realised that the "poor", "captives", "blind" and "oppressed" referred to by Jesus in Luke 4:18-19 were not *only* the socioeconomically poor or infirmed or physically enslaved or oppressed. Jesus was *also* referring to the socially, emotionally and spiritually poor and oppressed.[263] Jesus magnified the Mosaic Law and, applying the spirit rather than the letter of the law, extended its application in radically different ways.[264]

Mary's Magnificat

Mary's Magnificat in Luke 1:46-55 deserves special attention because it is part of Luke's narrative to establish and confirm Jesus as the fulfilment of God's promises about His Kingdom. Its subversive nature brings out certain key themes regarding justice, righteousness and power. The hymn is as follows:

---

[262] Ephesians 1:11, Romans 8:17, Hebrews 9.
[263] Kevin DeYoung and Greg Gilbert, *What Is the Mission of the Church? Making Sense of Social Justice, Shalom and the Great Commission* (Crossway, 2011) at 36-40.
[264] Matthew 23:23.

And Mary said,

"My soul magnifies the Lord,
> and my spirit rejoices in God my Savior,

for he has looked on the humble estate of his servant.

For behold, from now on all generations will call me blessed;

for he who is mighty has done great things for me,
> and holy is his name.

And his mercy is for those who fear him
> from generation to generation.

He has shown strength with his arm;
> he has scattered the proud in the thoughts of their hearts;

he has brought down the mighty from their thrones
> and exalted those of humble estate;

he has filled the hungry with good things,
> and the rich he has sent away empty.

He has helped his servant Israel,
> in remembrance of his mercy,

as he spoke to our fathers,
> to Abraham and to his offspring forever."

The rich theology in the hymn reveals three key aspects about the Gospel of Jesus: Worship, power in God's Kingdom, and God's faithfulness in fulfilling His promise of establishing His Kingdom.

First, Mary worshipped God in faith as a response to what God was doing through her. She had earlier been informed by an angel of the Lord in Luke 1:26-38, corroborated by her cousin Elizabeth's prophecy,[265] that

---

265   Luke 1:39-45.

she—a virgin, no less—would bear a son who is the Son of God, and who would be the eternal King on the throne of David.[266] Mary understood this meant that her child would become the Messiah who would re-establish the Kingdom of Israel, the Kingdom of God, foretold long ago by her ancestors, prophesied about in the Scriptures. For too long, Israel, which had once been a nation, was subjugated as an oppressed people. Her child was to be the liberator of Israel. But even she did not realise how this Messiah would go about fulfilling that role. Mary, however, knew in faith that, to be the mother of the Messiah was surely a miracle and an act of favour from God. Her response was simply to worship God.[267] She was grateful that God would do such a "great thing" for her and through her.[268]

Second, Mary's hymn is subversive in its context. God chose a simple, poor young girl to be the mother of the Messiah. It's not only about Mary's social status. The corollary is that the Messiah would grow up in such socioeconomic circumstances. Mary contrasts the humble with the proud and mighty, the poor with the rich, congruous with the prophets of old in the Scriptures.[269] This is also in line with the theme of the Gospel of the Kingdom of God as reflected in other passages in the New Testament: Jesus the King of Kings contrasted with Caesar, Herod and Pilate (among others); they represent earthly kings who exercise power to oppress people, not bring welfare to the people. Jesus, on the other hand, exercises His divine power by choosing to be a lowly human being, born into poverty, who would later be subject to marginalisation, oppression, and injustice.[270]

---

266 Luke 1:32-33.
267 Luke 1:46-47.
268 Luke 1:49.
269 Luke 1:51-53.
270 See generally Scot McKnight and Joseph B. Modica, eds., *Jesus is Lord Caesar is Not: Evaluating Empire in New Testament Studies* (InterVarsity Press, 2013).

The most powerful person in existence, God Himself, establishes Himself as King by choosing to defer power, by identifying with, and serving, the lowest, the oppressed, the marginalised, the victims of injustice.

At the time in Luke 1, Mary would not have known that her son would do these things. What she knew was that her son, the promised Messiah and King, would have to live in lowliness until the time came for him to take his throne. For that reason, she sang of God exalting the humble but bringing down the proud. Power is inverted in God's Kingdom: Those who wield power and abuse it will be brought low, while those who are humble in heart will be exalted. This theme of the Gospel of God's Kingdom would be seen in Jesus' life, in the Apostles' life, in the early Christians' lives, and in Mary's life. This is the inversion of power in God's Kingdom: The meek are strong, the humble elevated and the last shall be first.

Third, Mary believed that the birth of the Messiah, her son, was the fulfilment of God's gracious covenant with Abraham.[271] Mary knew her history and theology: The promised eternal Kingdom of God was consequential to the covenant that God had made with Abraham. If Mary's son was really the Messiah, the King of God's established Kingdom, that promise and covenant was fulfilled. This was the mercy, steadfast love and faithfulness of God.

The song of Mary is beautiful also because it is the Gospel for the whole world. It is the Gospel of a righteous good King who would be established as an eternal King in an eternal Kingdom. It is the Gospel that this powerful King identifies with those of us who live in brokenness, in suffering, in injustice, in oppression. It is the Gospel that God's Kingdom will surely be established. We have hope that on that day, all brokenness and suffering will cease. It is the Gospel that while we believe and wait for

---

271   Luke 1:54-55.

that day, we live in the spirit of the Kingdom, deferring power, rectifying injustice, healing brokenness and alleviating suffering.

The Cross: Cosmic Justice, Social Justice

In Chapter 3, we examined the Exodus narrative and its significance to our understanding of God's justice. The Exodus narrative is a key theme by which we can understand Jesus' work on the Cross. We had considered in Chapter 2 how Jesus' work on the Cross inaugurates the new form of God's Kingdom. The intersection between the Exodus narrative and God's Kingdom is this:

By Jesus' work on the Cross, the New Covenant is established through which every person who believes would be redeemed from sin.[272] And every person who was once a slave of sin could be freed to become a slave of righteousness.[273] This is of fundamental importance. God's Word reveals that the root problem underlying all suffering, brokenness, injustice and oppression in the world is sin. By the Cross, the bondage, power and effects of sin are neutered. Whereas we all had previously been destined to share the same fate as the firstborns in Egypt, God had passed over us because of Jesus, our Passover lamb. And the ultimate purpose of our deliverance, redemption and liberation is to be included into God's community, God's family,[274] God's household,[275] God's Kingdom. Once, we were all strangers and foreigners to one another and to God, but because of the Cross, we are now fellow citizens with other saints.[276] Once we were not a people, but now we are God's people.[277]

---

[272] Ephesians 1:7.
[273] Romans 6:16-17.
[274] Ephesians 1:5.
[275] 1 Peter 2:5.
[276] Ephesians 2:19.
[277] 1 Peter 2:10.

Because of the Cross, where there had been violence, resentment, discord, segregation or discrimination, there can now be peace, harmony and reconciliation.[278] There may be *shalom* for the whole person, for the whole community. *God meting out cosmic justice on the Cross is the means of availing social justice on earth.*

Jesus' Life and Ministry

Jesus' entire life was an embodiment of God's especial closeness to the poor. "For you know the grace of our Lord Jesus Christ, that though he was rich, yet for your sake he became poor, so that you by his poverty might become rich".[279] He was born into, and lived a life of, poverty. Throughout His public ministry, Jesus fed the hungry, healed the sick, stood against racism and sexism,[280] and associated with the socially marginalised including women,[281] the infirmed and the poor,[282] 'sinners' and tax collectors.[283] In Luke 7:11-16, Jesus had "compassion" on a poor widow who had just lost her son and brought her son back to life. In telling the Parable of the Good Samaritan to a crowd of Jews, Jesus made a non-Jew, i.e., the Samaritan, the hero of His story.[284] At the synagogue, Jesus singled out the poor widow for praise.[285] He would often make physical contact with lepers, who would have been shunned by everyone else.[286]

Jesus instructed His disciples to "[s]ell [their] possessions, and give to the needy"[287] because God would provide for their needs, and that their

---

278 Ephesians 2:11-22; 2 Corinthians 5:18-19; Colossians 1:19-22.
279 2 Corinthians 8:9.
280 John 4:27.
281 Luke 8:2-3; Luke 7:44-47.
282 Luke 7:22.
283 Luke 5:27-32.
284 Luke 10:25-37.
285 Mark 12:42-43; Luke 21:3-4.
286 Mark 1:40-42; Luke 5:12-13.
287 Luke 12:33.

> **God meting out cosmic justice on the Cross is the means of availing social justice on earth.**

true wealth should be in heaven rather than on earth. Indeed, Jesus said that by giving to the poor, one will have treasures in heaven.[288]

In Luke 14:12-13, Jesus exhorted his followers not to invite to their dinners or banquets people who could repay them with such reciprocal invitations and hospitality. Instead, He told them to invite the poor, the crippled, the lame and the blind. The context to this has to be understood. The patronage system was a well-entrenched feature during the time of the Roman Empire. The rich and powerful would trade favours, opportunities and influence with those who were slightly less rich and powerful for rewards such as banquets, dinners, etc. This is not foreign to us in Singapore and Asia as well. The notion of harnessing one's social connections or *guanxi* is well-known and often practised here as well. But Jesus told His followers to do something radical. Don't throw banquets for people so that they can give you something in return. Instead, throw banquets for the poor and needy, people who cannot give you something in return. Why? Because this is how the Kingdom of God works.

Another key teaching of Jesus which has become an oft-quoted basis for Christian witness is Jesus' call for His disciples to be salt and light of the earth. Jesus said "[i]n the same way, let your light shine before others, so that they may see your good works and give glory to your Father who is in heaven".[289] When we consider the examples of "good works" in the New Testament, we find that the New Testament frames acts of justice and righteousness as "good works". "Good works" are acts

---

288   Mark 10:21.
289   Matthew 5:13-16.

which benefit others in love and in a morally good way, for example, bringing up children, showing hospitality, washing the feet of saints, and caring for the afflicted.[290] It is to be generous and ready to share our wealth.[291] Tabitha or Dorcas was said to have been "full of good works and acts of charity".[292] Other translations simply translate the latter phrase as "alms-deeds" (KJV, Darby). In this regard, the NIV and NLT translate the verse as "always doing good and helping the poor". The Greek word for "alms" or "alms-deeds" is "*eleemosune*", which means beneficence to the poor. In Matthew 6:2, Jesus said "... when you give to the needy, sound no trumpet before you, as the hypocrites do in the synagogues and in the streets, that they may be praised by others". It should be observed that Jesus said "when" not "if". In Luke 11:40-42, Jesus criticised the Pharisees for failing to give as "alms" what was "inside" of them. He went on to equate their failure to sincerely and truly give "alms" as "neglect[ing] justice and the love of God". In Acts 10:1-5, the Gentile Roman Centurion, Cornelius, was visited by an angel of God who declared to him that his "prayers and... alms have ascended as a memorial before God".

In Matthew 23:23, Jesus rebuked the religious teachers of the day for neglecting the "weightier matters of the law", which are "justice [*krisis*], mercy [*eleos*] and faithfulness". In Matthew 9:13 and 12:7, Jesus quoted Hosea 6:6 and reaffirmed the paramount priority of covenantal faithfulness. The two verses are set out here for comparison:

> Go and learn what this means, 'I desire mercy [*eleos*], and not sacrifice.' For I came not to call the righteous, but sinners. (Matthew 9:13)

---

290   1 Timothy 5:10.
291   1 Timothy 6:18.
292   Acts 9:36.

> For I desire steadfast love [*chesed*] and not sacrifice, the knowledge of God rather than burnt offerings. (Hosea 6:6)

It should also be mentioned that in Luke 3:11-14, when the crowds asked John the Baptist what sort of fruits they should have in keeping with repentance, his reply was for those who had food and clothes to share with those who had none, for the tax collectors to collect no more than what they were authorised to do, and for the soldiers to not extort money by threats or false accusations and to be content with their wages.[293] This is illustrative of living justly and righteously. Conversely, perpetuating those acts was evidently sin.

Parable of the Good Samaritan
One of the most well-known parables of Jesus is the Parable of the Good Samaritan. The Luke 10:25-37 version of it is perhaps most useful for our study. The narrative begins with a lawyer asking Jesus what the requirements to inherit eternal life were. Jesus asked the lawyer what he thought the requirements were. The lawyer gave the two Greatest Commandments. Jesus said, yes, that's correct. Do that and you will live. Do that and you will have eternal life. Do that and you will know God.[294] Do that and you will enter into the Kingdom of God.[295]

The lawyer probably wanted to nail Jesus to a position, and 'justify' himself. What was the lawyer justifying? It's likely that he wanted to limit the scope of who falls within the term "neighbour". He probably thought, well, I can't be loving the whole wide world, can I? And as any lawyer worth his salt would do, he asked Jesus: What does "neighbour" mean?

---

293 Luke 3:8, 10.
294 John 17:3.
295 Mark 10:17-23; Luke 18:18, 24-25.

Jesus' answer to him expounded on more than the question of what "neighbour" means, but also what it means to "love" one's neighbour.

First, we are not told about the identity of the victim in the story. Was he Jew, Samaritan, or Gentile? It did not matter. The lawyer ultimately recognised the point when he accepted that the "one who showed him mercy" was being a neighbour to the victim. Loving your neighbour means loving whomever you encounter who is in need.[296] This is regardless of the person's ethnicity or nationality or socioeconomic status.

Second, Jesus deliberately chose a Samaritan as the hero of the story. Why? Some background is needed. The Samaritans were the mixed-ethnicity descendants of former Israelites of the Northern Kingdom and the foreigners whom the Assyrians brought into the land. The pure Jews, as it were, were from the Southern Kingdom of Judah. The Jews considered the Samaritans to have messed up their religion. So the Samaritans were deemed to no longer truly worship Yahweh. Historically, when the Jews were rebuilding Jerusalem, the Samaritans also caused trouble for them.[297] This historical animosity continued until the time of Jesus. In Luke 9, Jesus' disciples went ahead of Him to make arrangements for His arrival at a Samaritan village. However, they were rejected by the village. The disciples asked Jesus for permission to call down fire from heaven to consume the village, but Jesus rebuked them for the suggestion.[298] What then was the significance of Jesus' choice of the Samaritan in the Parable? Jesus was suggesting that Samaritans can also inherit eternal life and enter the Kingdom of God. In John 4, Jesus deliberately passed

---

296 Nicholas Wolterstorff, *Justice in Love* (William B Eerdman, 2011), 131-133; Timothy Keller, *Generous Justice: How God's Grace Makes Us Just* (Hodder & Stoughton, 2010), 76.
297 Ezra 4:10, 17; Nehemiah 4:2.
298 Luke 9:51-55.

through Samaria and stopped to proclaim the Gospel of the Kingdom to the Samaritan woman at the well. The woman was convicted of the Gospel and told of Jesus to her town. Thereafter, Jesus proclaimed the Gospel to the other Samaritans in the town and they believed.[299] More importantly, however, we must return to the starting point of this Parable, which was about the purported requirements for eternal life—love God and love neighbour. Jesus was highlighting that the Samaritan in the story had loved a neighbour by showing mercy to the victim *in contrast* to the Jewish priest and Levite. This is significant because Jesus showed that on the Cross, He was tearing down all prior hostilities and reconciling all divided factions, ethno-national groups and indeed doing away with all distinctions to draw the whole world to Him.[300] In Christ, there can be no room for racism or xenophobia.

Third, Jesus went into great detail to describe how the Samaritan hero had compassion on, and loved, the victim. As Charles Spurgeon observed, the Samaritan loved the victim: (1) Without asking questions; (2) without attempting to shift the labour from himself on to others; (3) without any selfish fear; (4) with self-denial; and (5) with great tenderness and care.[301] Spurgeon went on to point out that Jesus is even greater than the Good Samaritan in relation to the believer: We were not only half but altogether dead in our trespasses and sins.[302] Jesus was even more generous than the Good Samaritan: Instead of only wine and oil, Jesus gave His blood to heal our wounds; instead of only paying for the innkeeper's care of the victim, Jesus paid for all our sins not with money but with his own life. In this light, the moral bar is raised unimaginably high. Jesus called

---

299 John 4:40-42.
300 Ephesians 2:14-18.
301 Charles Spurgeon, "The Good Samaritan" (delivered on 17 June 1877 at the Metropolitan Tabernacle Pulpit), *Spurgeon Gems Vol. 23*, Sermon No. 1360.
302 Ephesians 2:5.

His disciples to love one another as He loved them.[303] Even if one were to take the view that such Christ-like love is only reserved for fellow believers (which already is humanly impossible in my opinion), then the love expected of us for our neighbours has to be at least as the Good Samaritan's. And the imperative for this is that Christ has already loved us with an even greater love than that. There was therefore to be no prescribed limit on how much we are to love our neighbour. The love to be granted is to restore the neighbour to a state of *shalom* or wellbeing.

At the same time, the acts of the Good Samaritan were portrayed as nothing out of the ordinary to him. It was a simple matter. He encountered a person in dire need. He met those needs. It was not like he went out of his way to seek out some grand and noble thing to achieve. It is as Mother Theresa has said, "Not all of us can do great things. But we can do small things with great love". The Good Samaritan's conduct belies a lifestyle, a way of life, of just and righteous living. I say it is a lifestyle because it is only when it is a way of life, a well-established norm, that such a loving response could be a matter of course. The Good Samaritan did not worry about disruptions to his schedule when he cared for the victim; or if he did worry, he did not let it stop him.[304] The Good Samaritan did not let fear of danger stop him from venturing out to help the victim. Instead, he was sensitive to the needs of the victim.[305] Justice is a lifestyle, and just and righteous conduct should be an ordinary way of life for God's Kingdom people.

Matthew 25: Two Parables and the Final Judgment

It is appropriate then to consider next, Jesus' discourse in Matthew 25. The Matthew 25 teachings are set in a broader sermon on "the end of the

---

303 John 13:34; 15:12.
304 Robert Solomon, *Following Jesus in a Fallen World* (Armour Publishing, 2009) at 265.
305 Martin Luther King, Jr's sermon "I've Been to the Mountaintop" delivered at Bishop Charles Mason Temple on 3 April 1968.

age".[306] Jesus emphasises that no one but the Father knows the day or the hour of the end.[307] However, Jesus went on to discuss in Matthew 25 how this eschatology should impact the way His followers ought to live.

Parable of the Ten Virgins and Parable of the Talents

Jesus began by telling the Parable of the Ten Virgins.[308] Five of the virgins had flasks of oil with their lamps, while the remaining five did not. When the bridegroom came to bring the virgins for the marriage feast, those who did not have the oil had to go out to buy oil. But by the time they returned, it was too late and the door to the marriage feast had shut. Jesus concludes this Parable by warning His disciples to "watch" since they did not know the day or the hour.[309] In other words, the Parable of the Ten Virgins teaches us that Jesus' followers cannot afford to delay in following Him and living in accordance with His teachings.

Then in Matthew 25:14-30, Jesus tells the Parable of the Talents. First, it should be pointed out that in the Parable, there were three servants, each given money (talents) "according to his ability".[310] In relation to the Master, they were of equal status, i.e., servants. The only difference among them is their ability and hence the amount of talents given. Presumably, these were all believers who knew their Master.

Second, two of the servants invested the money entrusted to them. They each doubled their investments. But the absolute amounts were different. The servant with greater ability and thus with a greater sum of money entrusted to him had a greater absolute sum in returns. But

---

306 Matthew 24:3.
307 Matthew 24:36.
308 Matthew 25:1:13.
309 Matthew 25:13.
310 Matthew 25:15.

the Master gave the two servants the same commendation and reward.[311] The third servant however did not invest the money entrusted to him. This is despite the sum being the least of all. The Master condemned the servant for being "wicked and slothful".[312]

Applying the above two observations to Christians today, the point then is that each individual believer is given, by the grace of God, a unique set of "talents". These "talents" could be money, time, resources, skills and abilities, relationships, and so on. Different individuals receive different types and amounts of "talents".[313] All that we are expected to do is to be faithful to steward those "talents" given to us "according to our ability". This means that we are not expected to produce the same results as someone else. We only need to be sensitive to how God desires of us to steward what He has given to us.

Third, the Master even ordered the third servant to be cast into "the outer darkness" where there will be "weeping and gnashing of teeth".[314] This parable was told by Jesus to describe the Kingdom of God. This is of profound importance for us who are professed believers. A person may be a professed Christian, may call on Jesus' name, and may even do great things in Jesus' name, but it may turn out that Jesus does not know him.[315] Only those who do the will of the Father will be recognised by

> **Justice is a lifestyle, and just and righteous conduct should be an ordinary way of life for God's Kingdom people.**

---

311 Matthew 25:21, 23.
312 Matthew 25:26.
313 1 Corinthians 12:4-11.
314 Matthew 25:30.
315 Luke 13:25-28; Matthew 7:21-23.

Jesus.[316] Am I saying that I think believers can lose their salvation? I think that is the wrong question and wrong premise. The real question is this: Do I really believe in, and follow, Jesus? If I do, I would properly invest the talents entrusted to me; I would seek to do the will of the Father, that I may have fruit.[317] It should follow also that I would seek the justice and righteousness of God. I think there is a necessary connection between the stewardship of talents in this passage and the next passage. This connection hints to us what the stewardship of our talents is supposed to achieve. It is revealing then that the next passage, Jesus' final word in this discourse on the end of the age about the Final Judgment, is about the fruit of the righteous believer. And as we shall see, the fruit is of a certain nature, which reflects again, just and righteous living.

The Final Judgment: Of Sheep and Goats

In Matthew 25:31-46, Jesus reveals that there will be a Final Judgment of every person. He will separate people like a shepherd separating sheep and goats. I think the metaphors of sheep and goats are to suggest to us that the sheep and goats will graze and live alongside one another in the same pasture. Only when the shepherd comes will there be a separation.[318]

The separation is for the purpose of directing them to their ultimate destiny: The unrighteous will go away into eternal punishment, but the righteous into eternal life, i.e., the Kingdom prepared before the foundation of the world for them.[319]

Who are the righteous and the unrighteous? Jesus refers to two categories of persons. The first category is for people who are deemed "righteous" and who have cared for the "least of these [Jesus'] brothers" in

---

316 Matthew 7:21.
317 Matthew 7:17-18.
318 See also Matthew 13:24-30.
319 Matthew 25:46.

material, tangible ways: Giving food, drink and clothes, showing hospitality, and visiting the sick and imprisoned. The "least of these" appears to refer to the lowest, the oppressed, the marginalised and the weak. It is also noteworthy that the word "stranger" in the passage is translated from the Greek word *"xenos"* which means foreigner or alien and also sometimes refers to guests. No prizes for guessing that this word is the root word for "xenophobia". Jesus' reference to "brothers" appears to suggest that He is referring to those within the Church. In other passages, He referred to "brothers" as those who do the will of the Father.[320] He also referred to His disciples as His brothers. In other words, the "least of these" referred to in Matthew 25 refers to fellow Christians in need.[321] As we will see later, the New Testament Church understood that they were to live as one community similar to how Old Testament Israel lived as a community of justice and righteousness under the Mosaic Law, albeit no longer under the legal demands of the Law but under the grace of the New Covenant.

In contrast, the second category is for people whom Jesus did not call "righteous". These people were described as having encountered others who were in need but refused, neglected or failed to do anything to meet those needs. It is also interesting that in verse 45, the word "brothers" is absent. So this category of people had failed to care for the "least of these". It is also telling that this second category of people expressed no surprise at the fact that Jesus was judging them. In fact, they called Jesus "Lord". Their surprise however was at the fact that Jesus had criticised them for failing to care for Him, whom He equated with the "least of these".

This passage is congruous with other portions of the New Testament which makes clear that the true believer of Jesus will love Him and obey

---

320 Matthew 12:50.
321 Kevin DeYoung and Greg Gilbert, *What Is the Mission of the Church? Making Sense of Social Justice, Shalom and the Great Commission* (Crossway, 2011), 162-165; cf., Thio Li-ann, *Jubilee and the Destiny of Nations* (Armour Publishing, 2014), 26.

His commandments, abide in Him, and will thus bear fruit.[322] It is faith expressing itself through love.[323] It is faith expressing itself through works.[324] Indeed, the illustration in James 2:15-16 is resonant of the Matthew 25 passage: "If a brother or sister is poorly clothed and lacking in daily food, and one of you says to them, 'Go in peace, be warmed and filled,' without giving them the things needed for the body, what good is that?" And similarly in 1 John 3:17: "But if anyone has the world's goods and sees his brother in need, yet closes his heart against him, how does God's love abide in him?" True faith necessarily results in good works and love, not merely as an emotion, and perhaps sometimes in spite of any emotion, but as action. This includes acts of love to the oppressed and the marginalised. Indeed, this was how the New Testament Church understood the teachings of Jesus.

B. The Model of the Church

Against the backdrop of the biblical narrative of the Kingdom, with the prior understanding of Israel as a community of God's people, the New Testament Church who believed in and followed Jesus understood their community to be the new community of God's people which was modelled after the nation of Israel, albeit no longer under the Law but under the grace of the New Covenant.

In Acts 2:42-47, we see that they shared their lives intimately with one another, devoting their time to worshipping God, fellowshipping, the apostles' teaching, the breaking of bread and praying. In terms of how they conducted their economic affairs, Acts 2:44-45 is telling: "And all who

---

322   John 15:1-17.
323   Galatians 5:6.
324   James 2.

believed were together and had all things in common. And they were selling their possessions and belongings and distributing the proceeds to all, as any had need". They were following what Jesus had told them to do: To "[s]ell [their] possessions, and give to the needy".[325] They were loving one another by sharing all that they had. Hence in Acts 4:34-37, the early Church was described as such:

> There was not a needy person among them, for as many as were owners of lands or houses sold them and brought the proceeds of what was sold and laid it at the apostles' feet, and it was distributed to each as any had need. Thus Joseph, who was also called by the apostles Barnabas (which means son of encouragement), a Levite, a native of Cyprus, sold a field that belonged to him and brought the money and laid it at the apostles' feet.

This was a fulfilment of Deuteronomy 15:4: "But there will be no poor among you". It has been suggested that it is not mere coincidence that Luke's description of the early Church's state of affairs was in the same vein as that of Deuteronomy 15:4.[326]

Later on, the early church had to appoint a special group of helpers known as "deacons" to assist in administering a daily food distribution programme.[327] The church also set up a support system for widows among them.[328] (I had previously thought that it was not feasible or possible for any human community to exist like this in *today's world*. I was wrong. I

---

325 Luke 12:33.
326 Timothy Keller, *Generous Justice: How God's Grace Makes Us Just* (Hodder & Stoughton, 2010), 59.
327 Acts 6:1-7.
328 1 Timothy 5:1-10.

discovered The Simple Way, co-founded by Shane Claiborne. I cannot properly describe this amazing faith community comprising of the poor, among the poor, so I shall simply commend to you Claiborne's book, *The Irresistible Revolution: Living as an Ordinary Radical*.[329])

The mutual contribution of material provisions for one another was not confined to local churches in the nearby vicinity. In the epistles, we see that churches in other cities contributed to churches with less.[330] It is significant that the sharing of material goods within the Church was expressed by Apostle Paul to be a matter of "fairness" and not mere charity.[331] Simply put, it is only fair that Christians who have more share with those who have less and are in need.[332] Even so, this was not a mandatory obligation—it was a privilege or grace to be able to share.[333]

The New Testament Church also continued to help the poor and needy. Tabitha, also known as Dorcas, was lauded for "always doing good and helping the poor".[334] Paul exemplified this and exhorted the Ephesian church to follow likewise in Acts 20:35: "In all things I have shown you that by working hard in this way we must help the weak and remember the words of the Lord Jesus, how he himself said, 'It is more blessed to give than to receive'". In Romans 12:8, Paul urged the Christians in Rome to do acts of

> **True faith necessarily results in good works and love as action.**

---

329 Shane Claiborne, *The Irresistible Revolution: Living as an Ordinary Radical* (Zondervan, 2006).
330 2 Corinthians 8-9; Acts 11:27-30.
331 2 Corinthians 8:13-14. See also Romans 12:13.
332 Kevin DeYoung and Greg Gilbert, *What Is the Mission of the Church? Making Sense of Social Justice, Shalom and the Great Commission* (Crossway, 2011), 168.
333 2 Corinthians 8:4, 6.
334 Acts 9:36.

mercy with cheerfulness. The Jerusalem Council specifically requested Apostle Paul to "remember the poor" in his ministry.[335] And if there is any doubt that the early church's care for the poor and needy was only for believers among them, Galatians 6:10 clearly suggests otherwise: "So then, as we have opportunity, let us do good to everyone, and especially to those who are of the household of faith". It is heartening to note that the early Church's expression and practice of justice, mercy and righteousness continued into the first few centuries. Collections were made within the churches to disburse to the widows, orphans, poor, sick, sojourners, imprisoned, slaves grown old, shipwrecked mariners, those working in the mines or islands, and not just for Christians but also non-Christians.[336]

It is also important to appreciate the New Testament Church's practices and convictions in contrast to the socioeconomic and cultural context of the Roman Empire.[337] Roman society at the time was hierarchical and highly stratified by wealth, class, ancestry, location, sex, among others: The powerful elite would take intentional steps to reinforce social stratification and express their disdain for lower social classes.[338] The wealthy elite, who controlled and held most of the power, property and positions, constituted 2-3 per cent of the population. Such positions were hereditary and thus highly protected. The elites, being

---

335 Galatians 2:10.
336 Paul Barnett, "Jesus, Paul and Peter and the Roman State" in Michael Nai-Chiu Poon, ed., *Pilgrims and Citizens: Christian Social Engagement in East Asia Today* (ATF Press, 2006) at 74-75.
337 See generally Scot McKnight and Joseph B Modica, eds., *Jesus is Lord Caesar is Not: Evaluating Empire in New Testament Studies* (InterVarsity Press, 2013).
338 David Nystrom, "We Have No King But Caesar: Roman Imperial Ideology and the Imperial Cult" in Scot McKnight and Joseph B. Modica, eds., *Jesus is Lord Caesar is Not: Evaluating Empire in New Testament Studies* (InterVarsity Press, 2013), 25-26; Judith A Diehl, "Anti-Imperial Rhetoric in the New Testament" in Scot McKnight and Joseph B Modica, eds., *Jesus is Lord Caesar is Not: Evaluating Empire in New Testament Studies* (InterVarsity Press, 2013) at 25-26, 44, 61.

landowners, were thus able to exploit hired labourers and indeed any other persons of lesser socioeconomic status.

A key feature of Roman society was patronage. People of lesser socioeconomic status could receive material goods, security and protection from the elite landlords, who fulfilled the role of "patrons". Social stratification and inequality were reinforced through various acts and means. Against the backdrop of this context, Jesus's Gospel was shockingly counter-cultural. For instance, His exhortation to the rich young man to "love your neighbour as yourself" would have meant that the rich young man was supposed to not only ignore the socioeconomic distinctions between himself and his neighbours but to surrender any privileges as a member of the elite.[339] Jesus's proclamation of an upside-down kingdom where the first will be last and the last will be first[340] strikes at the heart of the prevalent socioeconomic cultural norms of the day.

This Roman socioeconomic context also helps us understand the tensions and problems addressed in the New Testament epistles. For instance, the social division addressed in the Pauline letters to the Corinthian church can be understood as a division between the "wise", educated and elite believers on one hand and the uneducated and members of the lower classes on the other hand.[341] And Paul's rebuke to the Church regarding the Lord's Supper—"[o]ne goes hungry, another gets drunk"—can be understood in this context as referring to the division between the wealthy believers who could afford to have a substantial meal at the Lord's Supper whereas others could

---

339 Matthew 19:19.
340 Matthew 19:30.
341 1 Corinthians 1.

not.[342] Another example is the rebuke in James' epistle regarding the distinction between the rich believers and the poor believers and the display of partiality and favouritism for the former.[343] The believers there were merely (perhaps unwittingly) practising the social cultural norms of the day.

What this suggests to us is that the apostles and disciples were keenly aware of how Jesus's Gospel of God's Kingdom demanded wholly different attitudes, lifestyles, paradigms, behaviours and relationships from those of the prevailing socioeconomic cultural norms in their social milieu. Much has been written or spoken about Christianity being 'counter-cultural'. But Jesus's Gospel and Kingdom are not counter-cultural for the sake of being counter to everything or anything. Instead, it is important to recognise the nub of the culture which the Gospel of God's Kingdom was counter to. And it appears that one key aspect of this culture was the unequal socioeconomic cultural practices and relationships. The apostles and disciples understood that the demands of the Gospel on the New Testament Church inevitably meant that the believers in the Church who were also wealthy and elite members in society had to surrender their privileges and thus deprive themselves of the power and positions which they enjoyed in the secular society outside of the Church.

The pertinent question this raises for us is: *What are the socioeconomic cultural norms and practices which we have (wittingly or unwittingly) adopted in our faith communities today?* Are there any such practices which Paul or James, if they were alive today, would severely reprimand us for?

---

342   1 Corinthians 11:17-34; Judith A Diehl, "Anti-Imperial Rhetoric in the New Testament" in Scot McKnight and Joseph B Modica, eds., *Jesus is Lord Caesar is Not: Evaluating Empire in New Testament Studies* (InterVarsity Press, 2013), 62-63.
343   James 2.

C. Reflections on New Testament Survey

It is important to reiterate that the New Testament has to be understood in light of the larger biblical narrative of the Kingdom of God. God's justice, mercy and righteousness which we have studied in the Old Testament is lived out and exhibited in the life of Jesus the Messiah or the Christ, who is also the perfect expression of God's Kingdom.[344] He is the perfect fulfilment of the God-given vocation of Israel, which Israel failed to be. The early Church did not miss this. They lived their lives as a community which was modelled after what was supposed to have been Old Testament Israel in accordance with the Mosaic Law. And God's justice and righteousness are in the core DNA of Kingdom life and Kingdom community.

The Church as a Community of Justice and Righteousness

In Chapter 2, I mentioned that the Church is the community of God's Kingdom. It follows from the preceding discussion that as the community of God's Kingdom people, the Church is to be a community manifesting God's character of justice and righteousness.

The Church's community life

In this respect, an important reality of God's Kingdom has to manifest in the Church's counter-cultural[345] conduct of its communal life. The reality is that in Christ, there are no distinctions as to race, ethnicity or language,

---

[344] C René Padilla, *Mission Between the Times* (Langham Monographs, 2010), 202.
[345] Joel Willitts, "Matthew" in Scot McKnight and Joseph B Modica, eds., *Jesus is Lord Caesar is Not: Evaluating Empire in New Testament Studies* (InterVarsity Press, 2013), 92.

social, political or economic status, or sex.³⁴⁶ All are equally welcome into the Kingdom of God. This means that within the Church community, two things must happen. First, the community must embrace one and all. Second, the community must practise justice and righteousness as between its own members. In practice, however, the Church historically has had difficulty with both. Even in the New Testament Church, James rebuked some Church members for showing bias and favour towards the rich,³⁴⁷ for neglecting to provide for the poor,³⁴⁸ for failing to do right by the low-paid wage worker.³⁴⁹ The rebuke which James had for the early Church could easily be applied to us today.

In Singapore, the Church is rightly or wrongly often perceived as predominantly English-speaking middle-class.³⁵⁰ Nothing wrong with that, of course. Anecdotally, local church congregations are more often than not separated by ethnicity or language, and perhaps as an effect rather than a cause, by socioeconomic background. In this respect, we must be constantly self-reflective. Is it a concession that given the circumstances and with the aim of fulfilling Christ's mission of discipleship, we are segregating congregations on the basis of language and culture, or is it the fear of diversity and the chauvinistic desire to ignore, barely tolerate, subordinate or eliminate pluralism?³⁵¹ Importantly, we must also constantly examine whether the way we do church intentionally or

---

346 Galatians 3:28; Colossians 3:11.
347 James 2:1-9.
348 James 2:15-16.
349 James 5:1-5.
350 Terence Chong and Hui Yew-Foong, *Different Under God: A Survey of Church-going Protestants in Singapore* (Institute of Southeast Asian Studies, 2013); Leonard Lim, "Who are Singapore's Megachurch Members? Many from working class: Study", *The Straits Times* (14 January 2013); Terence Chong, "Christian Evangelicals and Public Morality in Singapore", *ISEAS Perspective* (20 March 2014).
351 C René Padilla, *Mission Between the Times* (Langham Monographs, 2010), 182, citing Lesslie Newbigin, "What Is 'A Local Church Truly United'", *The Ecumenical Review 29* (April 1977), 124 and Peter Wagner, *Our Kind of People: The Ethical Dimensions of Church Growth in America* (Atlanta: John Knox Press, 1979), 147.

> **The Church is to be a community manifesting God's character of justice and righteousness.**

unwittingly alienates or marginalises people from different social and economic backgrounds.

Some years back, two youths started attending my church's youth service. They were adorned with tattoos, piercings and such, and certainly looked very different from the rest of the youths. They came from a different socioeconomic background as compared to most of our church youths, and spoke mainly in Hokkien and Mandarin whereas the rest of the youths spoke in English. The couple joined our youth gatherings for awhile but left eventually. I suspect one significant reason was that they simply felt uncomfortable in our church. One might take the view that perhaps it was inevitable and there was nothing which could have been done about it. But if the youth group's composition was sufficiently diverse to begin with, perhaps there would have been less discomfort.

Another consideration is that in many of our local churches, we have employers and foreign domestic workers (FDWs) attending the same church. It is heartening to know of FDWs coming to know Jesus through the efforts of the employers. If the Church is to be a community in which master and servant are to live together under the rule of God's Kingdom (consider Paul's letter to Philemon regarding Onesimus), how would that look like in our churches today?

Justice only within the Church?

You may then be wondering: If the call to express justice, mercy and righteousness is meant to be expressed within the community of God's people, does it mean that as Christians, justice is to be practised *only* in relation to fellow Christians within the Church? I have been struggling with this question for some time. A literal reading of the Final Judgment passage in Matthew 25 suggests this, given Jesus' reference to "brothers".[352] So also the passages concerning how the early Church conducted their faith community. On the other hand, Jesus taught in the Sermon on the Mount to love *even* our enemies.[353] He did not qualify or limit such love for enemies. More significantly, the Parable of the Good Samaritan makes it clear that loving one's neighbour is not limited by the identity of the neighbour. Rather, the neighbour is the person in need whom you encounter. The fact that the early Church through to the first few centuries practised generous care among primarily, but *not only*, Christians, is also telling.

I will be honest to say that I have not yet come to a firm view on this, but it appears to me for now that the call to love our neighbour is a call to love *anyone* who crosses paths with us. It follows from this that the people who are more likely to receive our love, and the amount of resources we expend on seeking justice for, and extending mercy to, them, is necessarily connected with the closeness of our neighbourly relationship.

It follows also that when we are rooted in our local church, the needs of our church members are a priority. This is supported by Paul's remark in Galatians 6:10: "Let us do good to everyone, and especially to those who are of the household of faith". Why? Because our fellow believers are our direct and immediate neighbours. It would be strange for someone to spend much time and resources on loving neighbours who are strangers halfway across the globe but refuse to do the same for a needy neighbour who is sitting right next to him in church on a Sunday morning. Indeed,

---

352 Kevin DeYoung and Greg Gilbert, *What Is the Mission of the Church? Making Sense of Social Justice, Shalom and the Great Commission* (Crossway, 2011) at 162-165.
353 Matthew 5:43-48.

Jesus' explicit call for His disciples was to "love one another" so that the world may know that they are His disciples.[354] And by "one another", He meant fellow disciples.

This view of the Church as the primary locus of justice is perhaps surprising. Because the world has taught us that social justice is about causes, whether global and national, about societal structures and power dynamics, and so on. But here we have God's Word telling us that biblical social justice is about manifesting justice and love in the local community you are a part of, and in the wider community of the universal Church.

Biblical social justice is the caring aunties in my local church preparing food for, doing laundry for and checking in on, our oldest church member. Recently by God's grace, they went to visit her just in time. They were there to do the elderly member's laundry. But the door was locked. Something was amiss. So they broke the lock, and found the elderly lady on the floor, smelling of dried urine, hip fractured. They rushed her to hospital for surgery. Thank God she is now alright and has been transferred to a hospice. Her children do not care for her. So our church members come together to help her. Financially. Emotionally. Drafting her will. And so on.

Biblical social justice is the young adults in my local church contributing money to purchase a fridge and a washing machine for a needy neighbour of one of our church members.

Biblical social justice is the congregation in a local church comprising of members of different ethnicities and languages, coming from countries including China, India, Myanmar, Indonesia, Malaysia and Singapore worshipping together without distinction.

Biblical social justice is James 2—being impartial in treatment and service between the rich and the poor in my local church. Biblical social justice is 1 John 2—the brother-in-Christ who has must share with the

---

354   John 13:35.

brother who has not. Biblical social justice is 1 John 4—the person who does not love his brother or sister in Christ does not love God. It is about ensuring that anyone, whether rich or poor, can participate fully in our local church's community activities. It is as simple as carpooling and giving rides to members (who cannot afford to drive or take a cab) for late nights after small group meetings. So it appears to me that while biblical social justice is to be expressed *vis-à-vis* everyone, the *primary* locus of the believer's expression of justice, mercy and righteousness is his local faith community as a matter of course and not of principle or restriction.

The Church's witness to the world

It is also significant that this call to love one another is intrinsically tied to the Church's vocation, which was Israel's vocation, to witness to the world. In John 17:20-21, Jesus' prayer to the Father was as such: "I do not ask for these only, but also for those who will believe in me through their word, that they may all be one, just as you, Father, are in me, and I in you, that they also may be in us, so that the world may believe that you have sent me". By loving one another and thereby being in unity—"all be one"—the world may believe that Jesus is sent from the Father. Francis Schaeffer in his book, *The Mark of the Christian*, argues that John 13:35 informs us that the world has a right to judge that an individual is not a true Christian if he does not love other Christians. He further argues that John 17:21 is "the final apologetic"—we cannot expect the world to believe that the Father sent the Son, that Jesus' claims are true, and that Christianity is true, unless the world sees some reality of the oneness of true Christians. Even the famous atheist philosopher Bertrand Russell thought that the most important reason for the growth of the Christian Church before Constantine was the unity of the Christian republic in a hostile environment.[355] He also noted that soon after the Church came into political power, it became divided and turned against one another. The unity of fellow Christians and the love for one another are the Church's unique identifying mark and its Final Apologetic. I discuss the issue of the Church's witness to the world and its relation to social justice further in Chapter 6.

Justice and Righteousness and the Ethics of Love and Good Works
The passages surveyed in this chapter also suggest that although the New Testament does not appear to expressly refer to this core DNA of justice and righteousness of God's Kingdom, it was remoulded into a new paradigm: The ethic of love and good works as the fruit of true faith and righteousness. Yet, there is no disconnect between the Old Testament and the New Testament.

The New Testament is replete with references to "righteousness". These references are mostly related to the relationship between the individual and God, with only a few references relating to the relationship between the individual and other people. However, we see in the New Testament that righteousness, being an individual right before God, comes through faith. And Galatians 5:6 declares that the only thing that counts is faith expressing itself through love.

There is no disconnect between the Old and New Testaments when it comes to this ethic of love. The Greatest Commandment declared by Jesus[356] is also the highest calling on Israel in the *shema* confession: "Hear, O Israel: The Lord our God, the Lord is one. You shall love the Lord your God with all your heart and with all your soul and with all your might".[357]

---

355 Bertrand Russell, *History of Western Philosophy* (Routledge, 2006), 310-312.
356 Mark 12:28-30; Matthew 22:34-40.
357 Deuteronomy 6:4-5.

Further, Jesus was saying that the very essence and marrow of the Law and the Prophets is love: Love God, love neighbour. This relationship between the Old and New Testament is like this—the Old Covenant is like children who are given a Lego set with an instructions manual but who simply cannot build the end product properly because they don't know what it looks like; the New Covenant is like children shown the end product (that is Jesus Christ) and given the freedom to explore and build the product with the guidance of a helper (the Holy Spirit). Justice and love are interwoven across the Old and New Testaments. They are part of the same Lego set but with different modes of instruction.

Justice is necessary for love; justice is a partial expression of love.[358] Former Archbishop of Canterbury, William Temple, said: "Love, in fact, finds its primary expression through Justice… love should be the predominant Christian impulse, and that the primary form of love in social organisation is justice".[359] And the imperative for this ethic of justice and love has always remained the same for God's people whether during the Old Testament or New Testament. It is the imperative of covenantal faithfulness between God and His people.

As a round up on this chapter, we considered that *the Church is to be God's Kingdom community manifesting the Kingdom to the world through her life of justice and righteousness*. We turn to the next chapter in which we will consider how this is undergirded by covenantal faithfulness.

---

358 Daniel Koh, "Justice: A Christian Social Ethical Perspective" in Daniel Koh and Kiem-Kiok Kwa, *Issues of Law and Justice in Singapore* (Armour Publishing, 2009), 30; Nicholas Wolterstorff, *Justice in Love* (William B Eerdman's Publishing Company, 2011).

359 William Temple, *Christianity and Social Order* (Penguin, 1942), 55, cited in "The Influence of Religion" in Sir Alfred Denning, *The Changing Law* (Stevens & Sons Limited, 1953), 107, cited in Andrew Phang, "A Passion For Justice—The Natural Law Foundations Of Lord Denning's Thought And Work", GJCT 05:2 (Jan 2006); Harold J Berman, *The Interaction of Law and Religion* (Abingdon Press, 1974) at 81-91.

Chapter Summary

- Jesus' life and work on the Cross, and the practice of the New Testament Church, embody God's justice, mercy and righteousness.
- While justice is to be expressed *vis-à-vis* everyone, the primary locus of the believer's expression of justice, mercy and righteousness is his local faith community as a matter of course and not of principle or restriction.
- Justice and mercy in the Old Testament were remoulded in the New Testament into a new paradigm of love and good works as the fruit of true faith.
- The Church is to be God's Kingdom community manifesting the Kingdom to the world through her life of justice and righteousness.

Discussion Questions

1. Which Bible passages caught your attention? What did you learn from those passages? What implications would those biblical truths have on your life?
2. What did you learn about God's justice, mercy and righteousness respectively? How does this impact your relationship with God, with others and with the world?
3. How are the above biblical truths being expressed in your life and your faith community? Which of them are missing in your life or faith community?
4. How does your knowledge of Jesus Christ as your King, the King of God's Kingdom, impact your life? In particular, how does this impact your life in terms of justice, mercy and righteousness?
5. What is your response to God in the light of what you have gleaned from these truths?

INTERVIEW:
Joshua Tan Kuan

• • •

> Joshua Tan is a final year medical student at the National University of Singapore. He is keen on serving migrant workers by meeting their health needs and building bridges to share the gospel. He desires to serve in medical missions in the future and in doing so, extend the glory of God's kingdom.

1. Do you think that social justice is a key expression of Christian discipleship and witness? Why or why not?

Yes! In order to truly answer this question we need to see how the character of our God fits in with social justice. From the Old Testament, we see how our God desires for his people to live in harmony with creation in obedience to their God. We see God's heart for the poor and oppressed in Israel. In the New Testament, we see Jesus' heart for the sick, poor, and the oppressed as well. He healed the sick and encouraged the marginalised (e.g., the Samaritan woman). In doing all this, he intended not to bring about social change *per se*, but to point people to Christ through witnessing and discipleship. True discipleship leads to a change of heart, which leads to a change of societal attitudes which advances social justice.

2. How have you pursued social justice as a matter of Christian discipleship?

I feel that the migrant construction worker population in Singapore is marginalised. So much can be done for our brothers from a distant shore. We can look into fair wages, appropriate working hours with adequate rest, adequate nutrition, the list goes on. Above and beyond these matters of social justice, they, too, are in desperate need of the Gospel of grace. They may not have gotten to hear of the Gospel in their homeland due to religious oppression or the lack of local churches. Little of that exists on our shores. We can definitely do something about this.

3. What do you think is the local church's role in relation to justice and mercy? Any personal experience in this regard?

Churches need to appreciate that social action is a manifestation of God's love in us. Often times, churches struggle with marrying the ministry of Gospel proclamation with justice and mercy. From my understanding of the Word, Gospel proclamation should be central and paramount in all that we do. But justice and mercy ministry should follow closely behind.

This does not mean that churches should preach the Gospel then act justly and show mercy. Rather it means that in all that the church does, Gospel proclamation should be the goal. Justice and mercy are very important and should complement Gospel proclamation.

However, from my personal experience, some churches struggle with this concept. They are unwilling to embrace justice and mercy ministry as an in-road to Gospel proclamation.

4. What is the relationship between the local church and the individual Christian in relation to justice and mercy?

Going back to the definition of a Church, it is a body of believers in which

Christ is their master, their head. Christ calls us to preach the Gospel to all nations. Christ also calls us to love one another, to act in His likeness, which embodies justice and mercy. Therefore every individual of the Church should seek to preach the Gospel, love others by upholding justice and showing mercy.

Often times, members of the Church are inactive in Gospel proclamation or acting in love for justice and mercy. This cannot be the case. Every individual must make it a point to follow in Christ's likeness, no matter what! They must seek God's heart and lead radically sold out lives for Christ.

5. What do you think is the relationship between social justice and evangelism?

Evangelism is paramount in all that we do. That is, we always need to be ready to evangelise but there may be many occasions where evangelism occurs after acting for social justice.

Social justice alone will not be sufficient to save people from sin. Social justice can demonstrate the power of Christ in our life. But if we don't speak forth words of life (i.e., the Gospel), others may just perceive us as very good and pious Christians.

6. What do you observe about the Singapore Church in relation to justice and mercy?

The Singapore Church is often perceived to be at extremes with regards to this issue. Some will say that this Church does a lot of mercy ministry but is weak in their preaching. Another will say, this church preaches a lot but doesn't have any mercy ministry.

This is sorely discouraging. Over time I have come to see that Christians and churches should not condemn each other. Rather, they should encourage each other. This can be done through communication, conviction and collaboration.

Communication: Churches should be keen to find out what other churches are doing. I speak for my church. We are located in Lavender but we probably do not know who the other churches within 1 km radius of our vicinity are. Churches should not be afraid to come to the table to talk. Churches should not be afraid to be open about their ministry and plans. After all, we all work as one body of Christ. We must communicate to advance the body of Christ.

Conviction: Different churches have been apportioned different yokes. Churches must appreciate these differences yet move to share their convictions with each other, so that all may be built up in every part.

Collaboration: With effective communication and a shared conviction, churches should then work together in collaboration so that they can effectively share resources, manpower, and expertise.

7. Do you think more young people today are concerned about social justice? Do you find that they struggle with their local church's attitudes towards social justice?

It is hard to say. Personally, I come from a church where a few young people are concerned but the majority of young people are too absorbed by the worries of daily life that they choose not to be involved in social justice. Some will say that it is not their portion. Others will claim that they do not have time.

There are a few passionate youths who are very concerned about social justice. Although they may feel a burden to get their church involved, they may consider that the local church's lack of interest discouraging but not hindering their work. Thus they carry on with their passions in their service.

5

What does Social Justice Mean to Me? Social Justice, the Micah Mandate and Covenantal Faithfulness

Few will have the greatness to bend history itself, but each of us can work to change a small portion of events. It is from numberless diverse acts of courage and belief that human history is shaped. Each time a man stands up for an ideal, or acts to improve the lot of others, or strikes out against injustice, he sends forth a tiny ripple of hope, and crossing each other from a million different centers of energy and daring those ripples build a current which can sweep down the mightiest walls of oppression and resistance.

—Robert F Kennedy

The arc of the moral universe is long, but it bends towards justice.

—Martin Luther King, Jr

A. Social Justice: In Search of Meaning

Where does all this discussion about justice, mercy and righteousness leave us? After surveying the biblical narrative, I saw more clearly how our just God is extremely concerned with the socioeconomically marginalised. Every passage I read which involves this group of people, I sense God's desire: Include them in My community; give them the means to have dignity and to participate in worshipping Me. It became clear to me that *the biblical view of social justice is to enable every person to freely and fully participate in community—at the highest, a community which worships God.*

Biblical social justice is like family members of vastly different heights at a dinner table: Some are so short they cannot reach the table; some are so tall they have to bend very low to reach the table. Justice is to build a table and chairs of varying heights suited to each person so that the whole family can share a meal and have meaningful conversations round the table.

> **Biblical social justice is to enable every person to freely and freely participate in community.**

The problem with the term "social justice" is that there is no fixed definition and people have used it for a whole variety of things.[360] Nevertheless, I adopt the term "social justice" as a convenient expression to distinguish justice as it pertains to social aspects of people and communities, as opposed to legal-adjudicative justice. The former may encompass the latter, but not the reverse. This is because the law cannot perfectly obtain holistic justice for a person. We turn now to consider the place of social justice in the biblical worldview.

B. Imperative of the Micah Mandate: Covenantal Faithfulness

I have encountered Christians who, or Christian writings which, are extremely critical towards any suggestion about social justice. Some reject the notion of social justice or at least socioeconomic justice having a place in New Testament Christianity. Micah 6:8 is an Old Covenant expression of God's mandate to His people, some would argue. Yet, if we view the

---

360 See book's website on "Social Justice as Term of Art"; Kevin DeYoung & Greg Gilbert, *What Is the Mission of the Church? Making Sense of Social Justice, Shalom and the Great Commission* (Crossway, 2011), 180-183.

Micah Mandate to seek justice, love mercy and walk humbly with God based on a purely semiotic reading of verses in the New Testament, then I think we would tend to have a myopic understanding of this Mandate.

Instead, the Micah Mandate is borne out of a narrative of grace and covenantal faithfulness, both in the Old Testament and the New Testament. In the Old Testament, the Israelites were constantly reminded regarding social justice laws and exhortations that the impetus for doing justice is the heritage story of their redemption from slavery in Egypt and God's abundant provision for them, first in the desert, then in the Promised Land. Hence, for example, in Deuteronomy 24:17-18, in a section on various social justice laws, God reminded the Israelites: "You shall not pervert the justice due to the sojourner or to the fatherless, or take a widow's garment in pledge, but you shall remember that you were a slave in Egypt and the Lord your God redeemed you from there; therefore I command you to do this". That same narrative is paralleled in the New Testament. Christ has redeemed us from bondage to sin and remains our provider.

The Micah Mandate in Micah 6:8 declares:

> [The LORD] has told you, O man, what is good; and what does the LORD require of you but to do justice [*mishpat*], and to love kindness [mercy; *chesed*], and to walk humbly with your God?

For all that the Lord has done, what does the Lord require of His people? "Require" is too tame a word. It is not, after all, a request by God. It is a command, a decree, a *demand*. In other words, *God demands His people to do justice, love mercy and walk humbly with Him. This is God's justice demand.*

It is significant that Micah 6:8 is contextualised in a prophetic declaration pointing to Christ. It is a reminder of God's grace and a call for His people to return to mercy or *chesed*, that is, both covenantal faithfulness and lovingkindness. Consider the context of Micah 6:8. Micah 6 is an indictment by God against His people.[361] The charge is this: God had been faithful to His people, having redeemed them from bondage and delivered them to the Promised Land.[362] Yet, what had they done in response? He then asked a series of rhetorical questions in verses 6-7 about the unacceptability of their ostentatious worship offerings. God says these offerings were not what He desired. Instead, what is it that God expected—demanded—of His people in response to His covenantal faithfulness? Micah 6:8. It was to express covenantal faithfulness (*chesed*) to God by living rightly in accordance with the requirements of justice and righteousness expressed in the Mosaic Law under the Old Covenant.[363]

Consider further textual context to Micah 6. Micah 4 speaks of the "Mountain of the Lord" where the "Lord's temple" will be established; it speaks of everlasting peace among nations and the Lord's ultimate plan of restoration. Micah 5 speaks of a ruler that will rise from Bethlehem who will rule in the name of God and with everlasting peace. Micah 6:8 is preceded by Micah 4 and 5, which is the prophecy of Jesus Christ as the everlasting King.

For us Christians living on this side of history, we are grafted into the covenant through Jesus Christ.[364] As Christ's followers, we are God's covenantal people. And the establishment of His Kingdom and reign had already begun. Because we have received God's *chesed*, His covenantal

---

361 Micah 6:1-2.
362 Micah 6:3-5.
363 Carson, et. al., *New Bible Commentary* (IVP, 1994), 830.
364 Romans 11:17, 24

faithfulness, His mercy, His grace, His love, His redemption, His salvation, His provision, His abundance… then what does God require—what does God demand—of us? Our covenantal obligation based on our Kingdom citizenship, *our response to God's covenantal faithfulness must be to live justly, love mercy (loving-kindness and faithfulness), and walk humbly with God.*

Micah 6:8 is therefore the precursor and variation of the imperatives in the two Greatest Commandments that Jesus would later teach, i.e., love God, love neighbour; or *love God by loving our neighbour.*[365] In other words, Jesus exhorted us to express our covenantal faithfulness to God. And *to live justly, love mercy and walk humbly with God is to love God and to love our neighbour.*

C. The Micah Mandate for the Christian

The Micah Mandate to seek justice, love mercy and walk humbly with God is such a tall order. As a follower of Christ, I struggle with expressing covenantal faithfulness to God. I struggle because I often fall short. My walk with God is often hampered by distractions I allow into my life. And ever since I came to better understand God's character of, and desire for, justice and righteousness, I am made aware of my sin of neglecting to do justice and show mercy. I have too much apathy. Too little resolve to do right. I am too selfish to love my neighbours. At times, I feel overwhelmed by the fact there's too much to be done for the needy. Too many issues. Too many persons in need. I become filled with guilt. I look away from the

---

365   1 John 4:7-21.

problem altogether. The Micah Mandate is too difficult for me.

Yet, that is where the Gospel of grace comes in. I have to keep reminding myself of Ephesians 2:1-10. I had fallen short of God's justice and righteousness that I was dead in my transgressions. But it is purely by God's grace and mercy alone that even though I was in sin, I have been saved into the Kingdom of God *only* because of Jesus. It has nothing to do with my prior good works. Or my future good works. It is by God's grace alone! And the amazing thing is that by grace, because I am secure in my salvation, I can then go about doing the good works which God had prepared for me to do long before I was born. That I should "walk" in these good works.[366]

How does one walk in good works? The Bible seems to use "walk" in three different ways. First, the Bible often uses the term "walk" in God's "ways" or "path" or "love"[367] to mean to live one's life in accordance with God's ways.[368] To walk in "good works" is thus to live a life of "good works". Second, the Bible refers to walking in God's "truth" or God's "light" to mean living according to His revealed truth.[369] Conversely, walking according to the ways of the world results in sin and thus death.[370] Third, the Bible refers to walking "with" God. That is the usage in Micah 6:8. The same usage is applied with reference to Noah who walked with God and who was deemed by God to be righteous.[371] Likewise, Enoch walked faithfully with God.[372] Hebrews 11:5 observes that Enoch did not see death because he "pleased God". Malachi 2:6 also uses the phrase

---

366 Ephesians 2:10.
367 Genesis 17:1; Deuteronomy 5:33; 8:6; 10:12; 1 Kings 2:3-4; Isaiah 2:3; Jeremiah 7:23; Micah 4:5; Zechariah 3:7; 1 John 2:6.
368 Ephesians 4:1; 5:2; Colossians 1:10.
369 Psalm 26:2-3; 56:13; 86:11; 89:15; Isaiah 2:5; 2 Corinthians 5:7; 1 John 1:7; Revelation 21:24.
370 Ephesians 2:1.
371 Genesis 6:9.
372 Genesis 5:22-24.

"walk with" in relation to Levi the priest who walked with God "in peace and uprightness". A Bible commentator observes that this type of "walk" suggests an intimate communion with God, for in the word "*hithhallekh 'eth ha-'elohim*", "*eth*" denotes intimacy and fellowship.[373] Such a walk necessarily involves walking in God's ways and in His truth. The Bible also exhorts Christian disciples to walk by the Holy Spirit, to be led by the Spirit.[374] And walking by the Holy Spirit necessarily involves walking in all three senses discussed above.

Herein lies the power of the Gospel. God's grace in Christ enables me to be deemed just and righteous before God even though I am not actually just and righteous. This is because I am hidden in Christ, and God sees Christ and not me. It is in the safe sanctuary of Christ that I have the space to slowly become just and righteous in fact, i.e., my sanctification process. This is a profound mystery. God's act of pouring His wrath on a sinless Christ for our sins of injustice and unrighteousness becomes a satisfaction of cosmic divine justice. In other words, *God took injustice upon Himself as the cost of our injustice in order to fulfil cosmic justice and make us just.* This is truly amazing grace!

God's grace also *empowers* me to become just and righteous by way of the Holy Spirit. The Holy Spirit empowers me to be a witness of Christ[375] because the Spirit Himself is a witness of Christ[376] and guides me into the truth of Christ.[377] The Spirit produces in me fruit.[378] And the Spirit enables me to walk in "good works", to "walk humbly with God", to "do justice". In other words, *I am justified to live justly.* The

---

373 HC Leupold, *Exposition of Genesis* (Baker Book House, 1942), 241-242.
374 Galatians 5:16, 18, 25.
375 Acts 1:8.
376 John 15:26-27.
377 John 16:13.
378 Galatians 5:22.

justice demand has been fulfilled to become *our grace-fuelled response of justice.*

This grace-fuelled response of justice is not mere rhetoric, semantics or highfalutin theory. A grace-fuelled response of justice is a *fundamental heart* attitude. The heart is deceitful; God searches the heart and examines the mind to give to each person according to his ways, according to the fruit of his deeds.[379] When our motivation for pursuing justice is anything other than a grace-fuelled response of worship to God, it is necessarily problematic. It would be self-seeking (e.g., to feed one's pride or to elicit praise from others), ideological, worldly and/or human-centric. None of these are practically or philosophically sustainable. This is because the self-serving person would do well to find other better ways to serve himself than to pursue justice, which entails much sacrifice when taken to its conclusion. An ideological motivation dictates that only limited forms of justice may be dispensed to only limited groups of people. A worldly motivation is nihilistic since on that worldview, there is no ultimate reality and all justice would end in futility and meaninglessness. A human-centric motivation leads to frustration because people are imperfect and bound to disappoint. I've met social justice activists who are full of anger, disappointment and bitterness. And understandably so. Henri Nouwen wrote that much of what many of us do, even the best of good causes and most well-intended, are done to tend to our own wounds and needs.[380]

For many of us, fighting poverty and oppression in the world or caring for the needy and sick is entangled with our need for recognition and praise, our desire for sensationalism and our own curiosity, and so on. We may discover that the wounds and needs which belie the oppression

---

379 Jeremiah 17:10.
380 Henri Nouwen, *Peacework: Prayer, Resistance, Community* (Asian Trading Corporation, 2009), 27-34.

we fight against are the same wounds and needs underlying our own actions. "We too are part of the evil we protest against," Nouwen declared.

Only the grace-fuelled response of justice as worship to God is coherent and sustainable because it leaves the practical and philosophical knots to a sovereign, all-powerful God. This may seem like an intellectual cop-out, but it's not. It provides an eternal impetus for our faithful devotion to justice because it is founded on an eternal relationship with a gracious God. It provides a holistic robust framework for justice which is extended to all peoples. It is not nihilistic because it is focussed on the ultimate everlasting reality. It may be difficult but not frustrating because it is ultimately empowered by, and directed towards, a good and loving God. Its source is not in our wounds and needs but the goodness of God.

This grace-fuelled response of justice also answers the problem I often struggle with: There are so many people to love, communities to serve, problems to solve—which do I focus on? Wouldn't we burn out from helping everybody? In a sense, that is the burden of the Christian—everyone and anyone is a neighbour whom we could love. It is often the case that many civil society groups and activists organise themselves around specific causes and interests. As a Christian, fortunately and unfortunately, I cannot be confined to specific causes or communities. Instead, I have to take heed from my executive director, Jesus Christ, through the Holy Spirit, who leads me through the seasons in my journey. *The only way to follow Jesus in pursuing justice is to walk humbly with God, guided by the Holy Spirit.* That is to be constantly in intimate communion with God.

That was how Jesus went about His ministry on earth. Jesus said that everything He did was according to His Father's direction and revelation.[381] He would withdraw to quiet places to pray.[382] Mark 1:32-39 illustrates this clearly. One night, the entire city gathered around Jesus to seek His healing and deliverance for the infirm and spiritually oppressed. This must have gone on all through the night. Early the next morning before sunrise, Jesus went to a quiet secluded place to pray. His disciples came looking for him, saying that everyone was looking for him. Most likely, they were still seeking Jesus' supernatural healing and deliverance. What was Jesus' response? His response was "no". They would go to the next town so that He could preach the Gospel there. That was His purpose. This can be understood to mean a few things. But one important reason, I think, for why He refused to keep at His healing and deliverance work is because His Father had directed Him to move on to the other towns.

> **The only way to follow Jesus in pursuing justice is to walk humbly with God, guided by the Holy Spirit.**

Realising this, as well as understanding the Parable of the Talents,[383] has given me great comfort. In this light, I do not have to be overwhelmed by the immensity of the world's problems and needs. I only need to be concerned with the person, the community, the cause that God directs me to. I only need to rely on the Spirit's guidance in taking me to where Jesus already is, ministering to the people in need. For where Jesus is, I, His servant, also must be.[384] Yet, I do not have to do

---

381 John 5:19.
382 Luke 5:16.
383 Matthew 25:14-30.
384 John 12:26.

everything to solve every aspect of a problem, or meet every need of a person. I only need to properly invest the 'talents' which God has given me. Those matters which are beyond me and my 'talents', I can seek help from other members of the Church who have been given the 'talents' appropriate for the task. Such a diversity of 'talents' is the architecture of the Church intended by God for the common good.[385] An understanding of calling and vocation also puts into perspective the relationship between one's work and one's expression of faith in pursuing social justice. One may be called vocationally as a professional social worker and within that capacity seek social justice daily for his clients. The fact that he is doing it professionally does not in any way undermine it as an expression of his faith. Indeed, I know many social workers who tirelessly serve clients with great love, aiding them whose needs are deep and plenty. In sum, *pursuing justice is stewardship of our God-given talents.*

Understanding justice and righteousness through the paradigm of Kingdom citizenship, I also begin to understand it is about having a daily *lifestyle* of justice and righteousness. It's not about *doing* things. It's not about merely loving the *idea* of social justice,[386] or being simply an armchair advocate and "slacktivist".[387]

Hence, *all we need to do as Jesus' disciples is to humbly walk closely with God to live justly and love mercy as an expression of covenantal faithfulness.* But what about the Great Commission? Where is the place for evangelism in all this? We turn to consider this in the next chapter.

---

385 1 Corinthians 12.
386 Eugene Cho, *Overrated: Are We More in Love with the Idea of Changing the World Than Actually Changing the World?* (David C Cook, 2014) reprint edition.
387 Charlotte Robertson, "Slacktivism: The Downfall of Millennials", *The Huffington Post* (14 October 2014); Laura Seay, "Does slacktivism work?", *The Washington Post* (12 March 2014).

Chapter Summary

- The biblical view of social justice is to enable every person to freely and fully participate in community—at the highest, a community which worships God.
- God demands His people to do justice, love mercy and walk humbly with Him.
- Our response to God's covenantal faithfulness must be to live justly, love mercy (loving-kindness and faithfulness), and walk humbly with God.
- To live justly, love mercy and walk humbly with God is to love God and to love neighbour.
- God took injustice upon Himself as the cost of our injustice in order to fulfil cosmic justice and make us just.
- We are justified to live justly. The justice demand has been fulfilled to become our grace-fuelled response of justice.
- A grace-fuelled response of justice is a fundamental heart attitude.
- Only the grace-fuelled response of justice as worship to God is coherent and sustainable because it leaves the practical and philosophical knots to a sovereign, all-powerful God.
- The only way to follow Jesus in pursuing justice is to walk humbly with God guided by the Holy Spirit.
- Pursuing justice is stewardship of our God-given talents.
- In sum, all we need to do as Jesus' disciples is to humbly walk closely with God to live justly and love mercy as an expression of covenantal faithfulness.

Discussion Questions

1. Do you agree with the above conception of biblical social justice? How would you explain the essence of biblical social justice?
2. Do you agree that the Micah Mandate is a call upon your life to respond to God's covenantal faithfulness to you and your faith community? How is the Micah Mandate being manifested in your life and your faith community?
3. How does your understanding of God's grace affect your life and your faith community? In particular, how does it affect the manifestation of the Micah Mandate in your life and your faith community?
4. What do you struggle with when it comes to living justly, loving mercy and walking humbly with God?
5. What is your response to God in the light of what you have gleaned from these thoughts?

INTERVIEW: Michael Chiam

• • •

Having spent more than 14 years serving in the international humanitarian sector, Michael is no stranger to global poverty issues and social evils that are prevalent in impoverished and oppressed communities in the developing countries. Beyond his senior management experience, his last stint as Head of Operations with World Vision Singapore saw him providing direct oversight of some 30 global development projects in about 25 countries worldwide. Outside of work, Michael also volunteers with The Navigators as a mentor in the 20-30s ministry. Michael has an MBA in NGO Leadership and is happily married to his wife, Lynette—a passionate social activist and now, a key volunteer with Hagar Singapore.

1. Do you think that social justice is a key expression of Christian discipleship and witness? Why or why not?
Yes, social justice is a key expression of Christian discipleship and witness. Social justice is not the ultimate message but it is a key expression of our love for the world. As Christians, we are compelled by God's love and

the biblical command to seek justice, rescue the oppressed, defend the orphan and plead for the widow (Isaiah 1:17).

Justice is an integral part of the Gospel. God is the God of justice. Righteousness and justice are the foundation of God's throne. If we know or see of any injustice and do not do anything about it, how can we call ourselves a disciple of Jesus? The second greatest commandment is: Love your neighbour as yourself (Matthew 22:39). For me, the equation is simple:

The Gospel = Love + Social Justice = Authentic expression of our faith.

NO SOCIAL JUSTICE = NO LOVE = NO GOSPEL.

2. How do you pursue social justice as an expression of Christian faithfulness?

During his years of ministry, Jesus went about feeding the poor, healing the sick, and aligning himself with the marginalised, and outcast communities.

Personally, I'm convicted of this—to be a follower of Christ, we need to act justly, love mercy and walk humbly with God (Micah 6:8), and that in itself, is social justice. We cannot proclaim to love Jesus yet not do all these things.

3. Tell me more about your work with Hagar.

Hagar is a Christian international non-government organisation (INGO) dedicated to the recovery and economic empowerment of women and children who are survivors of extreme human rights abuse, particularly human trafficking, gender-based violence, and sexual exploitation, regardless of religion and background.

Our purpose is singular; we restore broken lives. We welcome the toughest of human conditions. We focus on the individual. We do whatever it takes for as long as it takes to restore a broken life.

Each year, Hagar works to restore the lives of over 1,000 women and children who have been trafficked, abused and sexually exploited. Human trafficking and gender-based violence are prevalent in the countries we work in. For women and girls, the threat of sexual exploitation and abuse is grave; 10 per cent of these clients have intellectual disabilities. Hagar receives into our care those who have suffered the worst of human conditions and many are referred to Hagar by local governments and non-governmental organisations in the country. We walk the whole journey with each individual, ensuring holistic healing, legal and physical protection, social rehabilitation, education and economic empowerment for her eventual reintegration into society.

The ultimate goal is to help each of these survivor victims get over her painful past, realise her innate potential and put her on the path of self-sustainability where she will be able to help herself in the long run.

4. Why do you do this work? What got you started on it?
God's grace got me started. The opportunity came at the point when I left another Christian international NGO after 14 years, and I was praying for my next season in serving God. I still very much wished to serve in another humanitarian-based agency and it was at that same time that Hagar Singapore was on the lookout for a new Executive Director. By God's divine appointment, one day I bumped into one of Hagar's board members (and a former colleague!). God had placed my name in her mind and she approached me and told me about Hagar. I believe it was God's timing and grace. It's definitely a journey of faith, trusting Him every day to bring the right people and resources in to do His work.

5. Do you evangelise to the people you work with?
I was brought up with The Navigators. In the early years of my walk with the Lord, my understanding of evangelism was very narrow. Present the gospel, and do Bible study with the individual. I am still with The Navigators but after joining a Christian INGO, my understanding of evangelism has broadened. Many of our beneficiaries have come to know Jesus because of our persistent love in reaching out to them and our walking the whole journey with each of them when many had given up on them. As staff, we share our personal faith with these survivors to encourage them to look to Jesus as their ultimate source of hope, strength and renewal. Complete restoration can only happen with Jesus living in our lives. We are the expression of God's love. And this is evangelism: "For I was hungry and you gave me something to eat, I was thirsty and you gave me something to drink, I was a stranger and you invited me in, I needed clothes and you clothed me, I was sick and you looked after me, I was in prison and you came to visit me" (Matthew 25:35-36, NIV).

6. Is Hagar tied to any local church. Why or why not?
No, Hagar is not tied to any local church. This allows us to work in certain environments and countries. We collaborate with the local churches in our work among the afflicted communities. And there are quite a number of local churches that are partnering and supporting us in our work.

7. What do you think should be the role of the local church in relation to para-church organisations like yours?
Both parties should focus on their respective roles, functions and strengths. The church should focus on preaching the Gospel, outright evangelism and equipping the people with knowledge and skills to grow in their walk with God and to be a blessing to the communities. As for para-church

organisations like Hagar, we should focus on meeting the physical and felt needs of people in a tangible way, point them to Christ in everything we do, and connect them with churches for continuous support and follow-up.

8. How does your local church view or support you in this ministry?
There are quite a number of local churches that are partnering and supporting us in our work. For my own church, while they are supportive of Hagar's work, they are not able to partner us in tangible ways as they have already pre-committed to supporting other missions organisations and internal ministries.

INTERVIEW:
Timothy Weerasekera

● ● ●

Timothy has always been keenly aware of the difference between right and wrong and has been irked by issues of injustice since an early age. In young adulthood he wrote a well-received undergraduate thesis on human trafficking in Singapore and began his involvement in the anti-human trafficking space. He now co-facilitates the Scarlet Web, a faith-based coalition of anti-trafficking organisations and individuals. His professional experience is in both the public and private sectors where he was involved in national policy review and leadership development, respectively. Timothy is a graduate of the Bible College of Wales and feels a strong call to improve the lives of children and the oppressed in Africa. He tries his best to live according to the requirements set out in Deuteronomy 10:12 and Micah 6:8, "... to fear the LORD your God, to walk in obedience to him, to love him, to serve the LORD your God with all your heart and with all your soul," (NIV) and "... to act justly and to love mercy and to walk humbly" with his God.

1. What does the Scarlet Web do?
The Scarlet Web is a coalition of faith-based anti-human trafficking (AHT) organisations that come together for the primary purpose of intercessory prayer over the issue. Secondarily, it is an attempt to connect the different organisations and ministries with each other as well as with believers who are passionate about service in this area.

2. What made you start the Scarlet Web?
I didn't really start the Scarlet Web. I just happened to be in the right place at the right time when God decided to reveal a vision for a web of organisations to collectively provide a better support structure to the work done in the industry. I was made aware of a need for such a grouping from my Honours studies, where I discovered that while there were several brilliant organisations doing good work, their leaders didn't really seem to know each other on a personal level. I did feel it important that cohesion existed so that groups that were largely working in silos could come together to form a unified whole.

3. How do you ground or relate your work with the Scarlet Web in or with your faith?
As the Scarlet Web is first and foremost a prayer network, it is by default rooted in one of the fundamental tenets of Christianity. Although there are several organisations in Singapore that work against human trafficking, the Scarlet Web consists only of Christian organisations because of fundamental beliefs about human value and morality, and that, too, grounds the Scarlet Web in our faith.

4. Do you consider your work with the Scarlet Web an expression of Christian social justice and mercy?

In a way. The Scarlet Web is not a frontline ministry. We assist the NGOs on the ground with the work that they do, for example, connecting them with legal aid for cases they are facing. Apart from that, we often pray as an expression of our faith and to intercede for the women and girls on the streets—which is equally a cry for social justice and mercy.

5. The Scarlet Web is not tied to a local church. Why not?

The Scarlet Web was birthed independent of a local church when God assembled a team of people who could catalyse the formation of a network for NGOs and church ministries involved in anti-human trafficking and red-light district ministries. It has no financial outlay nor input and is not doctrinally aligned with any particular denomination. Although the Scarlet Web is not tied to a church body, it is closely affiliated with one which operates in the vicinity of Geylang.

6. What do you think should be the role of the local church in relation to movements like the Scarlet Web?

The local church must ideally realise that just as the hand cannot say to the foot, "I have no need of thee", so too a church cannot say no to a faith-based NGO or a para-church organisation. The trouble with human trafficking and prostitution is that it is far too large to be solved by one organisation alone. As such, different members of this community should come together to contribute to the larger pool of information, strategy and most importantly, corporate prayer. The battering ram of the Kingdom must be held by more than just a few soldiers if the gates of hell are to fall.

6

Discovering Justice and Mercy Ministers in Singapore: Social Justice and Evangelism

Christianity, whatever else it is, is an explosion.
Unless it is sensational there is simply no sense in it.
Unless the Gospel sounds like a gun going off it has not been uttered at all.

—Gilbert Keith Chesterton

A friend told me that once, while talking to his Christian colleague about biblical justice, his colleague said that social justice is a distraction from the Christians' primary mission of evangelism. I've heard statements like this before. Other statements or questions I've heard are: Wouldn't social justice be pointless without evangelism? Isn't it like feeding a man a meal today only to leave him to perish forever? And yet some others think that social action is only a means to evangelism.

A. My Journey in Discovering Justice and Mercy Ministers in Singapore

Before I attempt to address this issue, I want to continue where I left off in Chapter 1. My friend invited me to volunteer with a ministry called Geylang Bless God (GBG) started by a church located in Geylang, Oikos Fellowship. So I did. I went with my then girlfriend, now wife.

Every Wednesday, GBG would prepare cookies and head out to the streets of Geylang—male and female volunteers alike—and offer the sex workers or prostitutes cookies along with prayers. My first excursion was a culture shock. I had never seen so many sex workers before. They were lining the streets. In some small lanes, they were huddled together in tight packs. The ladies and their pimps were situated at different streets, according to their nationalities. In one back alley, it was so dark that at first, I couldn't tell how many people there were. From a distance away, I saw shadows shifting like smoke dancing from a pyre. When I stepped closer, I was shocked to find hundreds of South Indian male workers loitering around, moving about, watching a line of ladies that stretched along the alley. The ladies had their backs against the walls (perhaps both literally and figuratively). The volunteers would boldly step up to the ladies and offer cookies and prayers. Some ladies would decline. Some were doubtful of our agenda. Some were afraid of their pimps and would not dare to talk to strangers. But many would accept our gifts. In some cases, the ministry had become so familiar that the pimps would welcome the group into their brothel to pray for the ladies. (My first time stepping into a brothel! Who ever said Christian life was dull?) Even when there was a language barrier, the ladies being prayed for would respond visibly, some nodding and praying along, some declaring an "amen", some emotional and teary-eyed from the experience. The women volunteers would end off with hugs for the ladies. Sometimes, the male volunteers would hold the ladies' hands in prayer as well. Often the ladies would be hesitant at first. After the prayer, some would break down. I think it is because they have for too long only known the violence of men. For a man to touch them with sincere and tender love was an inexpressibly emotional encounter. It was a profound experience. I saw for myself how the Kingdom of God could be expressed by way of cookies, prayers and hugs.

On one such Wednesday evening, I encountered a lady from the People's Republic of China (PRC) who chatted with my group after we prayed for her (in Mandarin). We asked her how she came to Singapore. Her story was shocking. It exposed a blind spot in my mental horizon. She explained that back in PRC, a recruiter had offered her a job in Singapore to work as a shop assistant. Certain salary terms were promised. She took on the job and had to pay a significant amount of employment agency fees. When she arrived in Singapore, there was no such job waiting for her. In fact, there was no job at all. Whoever it was whom she met in Singapore told her to raise funds for her own flight home. Well, quite apart from the illegality of it, how was someone like her to find work in a country so foreign? Through a series of events, she ended up doing sex work in Geylang. She found it was the easiest way to earn money quickly.

She shared that some of the other PRC ladies she met wanted to keep doing sex work because they could earn a lot—the younger ones especially, she said. According to her, the police had once arrested her and after finding out that she was working illegally in breach of her work pass, required her to be repatriated back to PRC, albeit using her own means. She was issued a 'white paper' which permitted her to remain in Singapore until her matter was resolved and she could be repatriated home. I had no way of verifying the facts, but that was what she recounted to us. (Her story is congruous with similar stories I would later come across in my volunteer work with migrants.) This was astounding—in front of me was a real person who would be considered a victim of human trafficking. The GBG volunteers gave her their contact details and told her to reach out to them if she ever wanted to. She thanked us and we left her to the streets of Geylang.

The issue of human trafficking surfaced in the public consciousness when the US State Department downgraded Singapore's status as a Tier 2A country in its Trafficking-In-Persons Report. At the time, I was an immature and perhaps presumptuous young law school student. I wanted action and solutions. I wanted them fast. And I wanted the Singapore Church to lead the way. Why not? The Church is called to bear witness to the glory of God. And part of that is to do good works to the praise of God.[388] I wanted the Church to do something about human trafficking. Evidently, I didn't see a point in having a chain of command. I wrote a lengthy email to the then Chairperson of the National Council of Churches Singapore (NCCS) about (among some other issues) human trafficking. He was none other than Bishop Robert Solomon. It was a demanding email. I set out the problem, the proposed solution and requested that he did something about it. Honestly, I expected no reply. That's what happens when people write to busy leaders who have too many things to care about and manage than answer demanding cold call emails. It's like emailing the Prime Minister to ask him to fix your HDB block's garbage chute. (No, I have not done that.)

> **The Church is called to bear witness to the glory of God by doing good works.**

To my pleasant surprise, I got an email reply from Bishop Solomon's personal assistant who said that he wanted to meet me. I thought perhaps he was going to meet me to size me up, or rebuff every point in my email. You know how some people do that when they just want to shut you up and never hear from you again—they give you a thorough explanation without actually listening to you. Then they conclude the matter. When I showed up at his office, I was expecting something like that. I received none of that. He sought to listen to me to understand where I was coming from. He raised a few anecdotes based on his own experience and knowledge to respond to some points. And I just went on. At the end, he said, "Okay, if you want NCCS to address human trafficking, that's really not how NCCS works; but you come up with a proposal and I'll see what

---

388 Matthew 5:16.

the Methodist Church and the Methodist Welfare Services (MWS) can do, bearing in mind the resources we have."

I was surprised. Motivated. Empowered. Much later, I also found out that Bishop Solomon made sure to find a mature Christian to journey with me. This person was Dr Goh Wei-Leong, the co-founder of HealthServe. The journey after the meeting with Bishop was a long one. I did a lot of research on the issue. I roped in some friends and classmates to help. I talked to NGOs in Singapore and overseas.

Then a friend introduced me to someone he knew at HealthServe, a community development NGO based in Geylang. I attended Healthserve's orientation on an unassuming Tuesday morning, during which a staff explained what HealthServe does—it runs an almost-free medical clinic in Geylang and a partner clinic in Little India, a *pro bono* legal clinic, a migrant drop-in centre and skills classes (e.g., English lessons). It also has case workers assisting workers who have employment problems and work injuries, a food programme for migrant workers who suffered work injuries and thus have no income, and it organises social outreach and counselling to low-income needy locals, etc. They then brought us to a workers dormitory in an industrial area. There, I was introduced to yet another side of Singapore I had previously not known. The rooms which the workers stayed in were small and packed. About 12 workers inhabited one room. The bunk beds were three-levels high, so the space for each worker on the beds, which was the only 'personal space' they had, was the height of a coffin. The mood at the dormitory was solemn and tense. The HealthServe staff asked about it. We were told that one of the workers from South Asia had hanged himself. This was the Singapore which the HealthServe staff and volunteers had to grapple with. And I saw a glimpse of it that evening. I will just present here the reflection I penned right after that evening:

Reflection on Visit to HealthServe and Kaki Bukit Dormitory:

Gathering the scraps of heavy thoughts, I followed the rest of the group as we headed off by car to the Kaki Bukit Dormitory, as part of the HealthServe orientation.

It was a ghetto hidden beneath Singapore. Located in an unassuming industrial area, the dormitory stood tall and alive, breathing with discreet movement from the members of the resident community. It was effectively a flatted factory, with many rooms containing three-level bunk beds. I was told, Jackie said, that by law, only two-level bunk beds were allowed, but of course the authorities 'close an eye'. I wonder how many eyes they have to spare for such laws as these which law students like me would never study about, and most of whom would never bother to in their entire career. Laundry fluttered like the flags of many nations outside each room. It was majestic in its own right. United nations, underground.

A friend of HealthServe came out to greet us. Skin shiny as ebony, and a handshake light as a child. He was one of those kinds of guys. You know from the moment you meet that you could share more than just a few laughs with him; you could count on him to carry the tears back home.

We followed him to his room. I removed my slippers and stepped carefully. It was sacred space. Home, no matter how temporary, is still a home. But they welcomed us with wide grins and extended arms. So I took liberties to delve deeper into the room.

The floor was fresh and smooth. All laundry and whatever that was unclean were outside. Inside, a sanctuary.

In the centre was a small television set which everyone shared. A proud asset, fruit of rough labour. A small fruit. A labour of years.

Most of their income, I found out, was sent home. They flowed north, crossing the Bay of Bengal; some by land along the straits of Malacca, through Yangon and then west through the tributaries familiar only to them.

That is the journey of love mailed home. The journey here is heartache. It costs SGD$8,000. Agents back home need not even spend a cent on marketing. These workers, eager for the 'spotless streets paved with gold', hungry to satisfy the hunger of their families, would sell off their land, equipment and livestock, and take further usury-tainted loans, to come here. They come to a country that exchanges their labour for $18 a day, that enjoys high-rise prosperity and year-round parties built on narrow, 50 cm high bunk beds and two-dollar meals of self-denial, and that pays no attention when any one of them should so despair as to find a false freedom by hanging himself on an unfashionable sarong tied to a fire-alarm sprinkler on the ceiling.

So a 19-year-old man hung himself just a few days before our visit. We were told his body was left dangling for three hours that evening, swaying in the quiet occasional breeze that probably accidentally found its way into this part of the country.

He had paid $10,000 to his agents. Fresh with eagerness, fired up with diligence, and probably fuelled by hunger—of his family—he took up a part-time job; only it was a fraud, and the fraudster ran away with this young man's work permit. His employer told him that without a work permit, he could no longer work for the employer; he could no longer work in Singapore. Those were the rules. That is the law.

This law knew no grace.

So he killed himself. And so it goes.

It blows their minds to have Singaporeans, lawyers, housewives, students, etc., share a meal with them at the same table, so Dr Goh said.

Bridging communities. That was one of HealthServe's mission goals.

I could see Jesus in this. Jesus at a corner of the table: Fishermen on his left, tax collectors on his right. The Levite and the Samaritan. The Jew and the Greek. As Christ reconciled us to himself, we are tasked with the ministry of reconciliation (2 Corinthians 5:18).

Bringing healing. Inspiring hope. Those were the other two aspects of HealthServe's mission. Again, that resonated.

Jesus had compassion for people. Jesus healed. Jesus shared the Gospel of the Kingdom of Heaven.

He said blessed are the poor in spirit, for they shall enter heaven. The mourners and the meek, they shall be comforted and they shall inherit the earth.

As a Christian songwriter penned in his song, "losers, all the lovely losers… never thought you'd hear your name… they shall see the kingdom come to the broken ones… it's for the poor, the broken, the meek" (Jason Gray, "Blessed Be" (2006)).

But to paraphrase Paul, how would these poor, broken, meek know hope without someone sharing it with them

(Romans 10:14, 15)? And how is anyone to share unless he is sent?

As I sat at the HealthServe premises, listening to co-founder and Chairman Dr Goh's sharing, I could not help but notice a decorative wall decal which resembled those gaudy red traditional Chinese papers containing idioms of blessings that are put up everywhere during the Lunar New Year. This one said, in Chinese, "God loves you." Creative.

God's love is not cross-cultural; it is beyond culture. Jesus loves the Chinese and he loves the Sindhis, the Tamils, the Gurkhas, the Punjabs, and all the other people groups. For God so loved the *whole world*, that he gave his only Son, not that they may be condemned, but be saved (John 3:16, 17).

Dr Goh talked about justice and exploitation, among the many issues that are intertwined with the problem of migration; real problems in real lives of real human beings who work as migrants on foreign shores.

Justice. Christians often forget that God's justice (*mishpat*) is covenantal justice, justice that restores peoples and communities to *shalom*, i.e., to live in harmonious and right relationships (*tzedeqah*).

In God's eyes, justice is secondarily about right and wrong. Justice is primarily about the rights that the 'quartet of the vulnerable'—the poor, the widow, the fatherless, the immigrant—are bestowed with by God. "This is what the LORD Almighty says: 'Administer true justice; show mercy and compassion to one another. Do not oppress the widow or the fatherless, the alien or the poor'" (Zechariah 7:9-10, NIV).

In God's eyes, it is not optional. *We owe it to them.*

Justice is a response to a broken world. It is the surrogate of *shalom* when *shalom* has been shattered by sinful nature.

Then grace. Grace is good beyond rights and wrongs. Grace is justice plus.

For those who have received grace, God says: Freely you have received, freely give.

What resonated with me was that HealthServe forgot about justice while yet seeking justice. Under this law, grace increases as justice abounds.

And that is the purpose of humanity. God spoke thus. Seek justice, love mercy, walk humbly with God (Micah 6:8).

***

For some reason, I felt drawn to the staff and volunteers at HealthServe. They seemed humble, unpretentious, sincere, caring. I told them about the human trafficking project I was working on. We explored the issue together. Over time, we became friends and I got to know them and their origins better.

HealthServe was founded by two Christians who sought to serve the "last, lost and least" by providing almost-free medical care. It was established as a secular community organisation to serve anyone and everyone, regardless of race, language, religion, nationality or indeed, any distinction. The clinic is situated in Geylang, in a small sanctuary located at the heart of the red light district. The sanctuary also houses Youth With A Mission (YWAM), High Point Halfway House and other organisations.

Over time, HealthServe evolved organically on a community-centric and needs-focused basis. In other words, when it turned out that many of the clients were foreign workers, sex workers and poor locals, staff and volunteers adapted to tailor solutions and programmes to meet the needs of the clients. Some, but not all, of the staff and volunteers were Christians. They served the clients with sincere care and humility. A majority of long-term clients were migrant workers who suffered workplace injuries and had to wait for many months for their injury claim to be determined. In most, if not all, cases, their employers would have terminated their employment already, so they were jobless and had no income. Some did not even have a roof over their heads. HealthServe found ways to meet these needs, including food coupon programmes and skills classes. There was even one instance when a doctor sponsored a hearing aid for a worker who had lost much of his hearing due to his work. Staff also chipped in and provided money to support him. Most days, the workers and the staff and volunteers just hung out.

Something else happened along the way. Many of the migrant worker clients started attending church services. Some accepted Christ as their Lord. Some got baptised before they returned to their home country. How did it happen? In many cases, it's because the staff and volunteers spent so much time with the workers that as personal friendships developed, the workers were impressed and impacted by the love of the staff and volunteers, and the reason for their love. In a sense, there is nothing peculiar about this. They were simply being a witness in their workplace or place of community service. It's no different from a Christian sharing his faith during lunchtime conversations with his colleagues at work. Yet, in another sense, there is something peculiar about this. The number of people receiving Christ is significant. I need not go into specifics but the percentage I've been told is about 50 per cent of the casework clients.

B. The Relationship Between Social Justice and Evangelism

I shared my journey of discovering Christians who were seeking justice and mercy in Singapore because these real stories shaped my thinking on the relationship between social justice and evangelism. They also serve as case studies to help ground our discussion on this issue.

Social Justice and Evangelism are Both Expressions of Christian Faith
Expressing justice and righteousness is a command[389] as much as the Great Commission itself.[390] It is self-referential in a sense: The Great Commission to make disciples necessarily requires making disciples who express God's justice and righteousness. And disciplers must necessarily already express God's justice and righteousness to disciple others in this. Disciples who do not desire to express justice and righteousness are not true disciples because they do not abide in God's Word.

At the International Congress on World Evangelization at Lausanne in 1974, evangelical church leaders from 150 nations, including prominent Christian leaders like John Stott, Billy Graham and Chris Wright, came together to reflect on the Global Church's mission in the world. One issue which came up was the issue of social justice and evangelism. At the conclusion of the Congress, the leaders made the Lausanne Covenant. Paragraph 5 of the Lausanne Covenant 1974 eloquently explains this view:

> ... Although reconciliation with other people is not reconciliation with God, nor is social action evangelism, nor is political liberation salvation, nevertheless we affirm that

---

389 See Chapter 5 on "Imperative of the Micah Mandate: Covenantal Faithfulness".
390 Matthew 28:19-20.

evangelism and socio-political involvement are both part of our Christian duty. For both are necessary expressions of our doctrines of God and man, our love for our neighbour and our obedience to Jesus Christ. ... When people receive Christ they are born again into his kingdom and must seek not only to exhibit but also to spread its righteousness in the midst of an unrighteous world. The salvation we claim should be transforming us in the totality of our personal and social responsibilities. Faith without works is dead.

Social Justice and Evangelism Need Not Always Go Together
If there were no opportunity to share the Gospel to a hungry homeless person given the circumstances, I would still be obliged to provide food for him. And if a colleague were having a lunchtime conversation with me on my faith, I would seize the opportunity to explain my faith to him (although perhaps I may feel obliged to buy him a drink to continue listening to me).

Following the Lausanne Congress in 1974, some evangelical leaders put forward a follow-up report stating:[391]

> ... There are still occasions when it is legitimate to concentrate on one or the other of these two Christian duties. It is not wrong to hold an evangelistic crusade without an accompanying programme of social service. Nor is it wrong to feed the hungry in a time of famine without first preaching to them, for, to quote an African proverb, 'an empty belly has no ears'...

---

391 "International Consultation on the Relationship between Evangelism and Social Responsibility", *Evangelism and Social Responsibility: An Evangelical Commitment.* (Grand Rapids, Michigan, June 19-25 1982), Section 4.B.

In the case of the Geylang Bless God (GBG) ministry, the fact that the volunteers could not actually explain the Gospel in a language comprehensible to the transient sex workers did not stop them from going out every week to the streets of Geylang to offer them hugs, cookies and prayers. They persisted in their ministry because of love for these ladies, transient as they are, and their calling from the Lord.

Social Justice and Evangelism May be Expressed in Different Ways and to Different Extents for Each Individual

Recall the Parable of the Talents: God gives us different types and amounts of 'talents' to steward. Thus, social justice or evangelism may be expressed in different ways and to different extents in each individual's life. A materially poor Christian may not be able to give money to help needy persons but may be able to help them in kind, e.g., by offering to fix their home electrical appliances. Further, as Kingdom citizens who are obliged to follow the marching orders of the King, the King's calling on us and His spiritual gifts to us must be the central paradigm for how we express our faith.[392]

The case-in-point for me is that of Bishop Emeritus Robert Solomon. When I first naively raised the issue of human trafficking to him via email, he did not ignore my email or give a cursory reply. He was genuinely interested in what I had to say. He was well aware of biblical justice and the Christian's rightful response to human trafficking. But he was not going to roll up his sleeves to start constructing a trafficking shelter. Why not? His calling was to be the Bishop of the Methodist Church in Singapore, to be an overseer, preacher and mentor. Those were also his spiritual gifts. Yet, he did participate in the pursuit of social justice. He did it by opening a

---

392 See *Evangelism and Social Responsibility: An Evangelical Commitment*, Section 4.B. See e.g., Acts 6:8-15; 8:5-13.

vista of opportunities for a young Christian wanting to pursue this cause. He did it by encouraging the young Christian in tangible ways. He did it by orchestrating a mentor to journey with the young Christian. He was faithful to God's calling upon him.

Evangelism and Discipleship are Paramount in Priority

Although evangelism and social justice are seldom in conflict or mutually exclusive, if there is a situation where a choice has to be made, I think evangelism and discipleship are paramount in priority.[393] Why?

First, Jesus considered preaching the Gospel and discipleship to be His priority over acts of meeting physical needs.[394]

Second, as Christians, we believe in both a temporal and eternal perspective of wellbeing.[395] But the temporal is a miniscule fraction of eternity. At the point of our first death, neither wealth nor poverty matters.[396] The only thing which matters is one's eternal destiny.

Third, without evangelism and discipleship, there will be no Christian disciples to sustain Christian social action. Social justice is the consequence of evangelism and discipleship.

Fourth, Christian discipleship has the power to transform hearts for significant social change, which would otherwise be implausible. For instance, scholars studied two Dalit communities in India, the Nadars and Paraiyas in Tirunelveli District in Tamil Nadu, and found that the Dalits' coming to faith in Christ gave them a new identity, dignity and

---

[393] See *Evangelism and Social Responsibility: An Evangelical Commitment*, Section 4.D.
[394] Luke 4:42-44.
[395] Christian Buckley and Ryan Dobson, *Humanitarian Jesus: Social Justice and the Cross* (Moody Publishers, 2010), 63: "[W]e can hurt for the dying, minister to the starving, battle for the afflicted and strive for the forgotten just as Christ did. But we can do nothing for them after their last breath of equality. It is appointed once for a man to die and then to face his Creator".
[396] Hebrews 9:27; Luke 16:19-31.

consciousness which fuelled their character transformation, paving the way for their upward social mobility against centuries of oppression.[397]

Social Justice is the Result and Purpose of Evangelism and Discipleship

Social justice is the result and purpose of evangelism and discipleship. Social justice is the "works" of love which evidence faith.[398] We are saved and made a new creation, a beautiful masterpiece, of God in Christ *so that* we can do good works.[399]

It does not follow that we are automatically transformed into people who are zealous to do good works and seek social justice.[400] That is the reason why Jesus specifically taught His disciples to teach other disciples to observe all that He commanded.[401] It is therefore critical that our discipleship must include biblical social justice.

Speaking for myself, I embarked on a journey of discovering biblical social justice because I wanted to seek God's intent for justice and righteousness. It was then that I discovered the "hole in my Gospel".[402] It is the Gospel which motivates me to pursue social justice.

Social Justice is the Bridge to Evangelism and Discipleship

Social justice paves the way for evangelism and discipleship.[403] It builds authority and credibility for the messenger of the Gospel. Jesus preached the Sermon on the Mount *after* the crowds gathered around Him.[404] These

---

[397] Hwa Yung, "The Integrity of Mission in the Light of the Gospel—Some Reflections from Asian Christianity", *Swedish Missiological Themes 93.3* (2005), 331-332.
[398] Galatians 5:6; James 2:18; 1 John 3:16-18.
[399] Ephesians 2:10.
[400] Titus 2:14.
[401] Matthew 28:19-20.
[402] Richard Stearns, *The Hole in Our Gospel* (Thomas Nelson, 2009).
[403] See *Evangelism and Social Responsibility: An Evangelical Commitment*, Section 4.C.
[404] Matthew 5:1.

crowds had followed Him from Galilee, the Decapolis, Jerusalem, Judea and from beyond the Jordan.[405] Why did these crowds follow Jesus? Because Jesus went about "teaching in their synagogues and proclaiming the gospel of the kingdom and healing every disease and every affliction among the people. So his fame spread throughout all Syria, and they brought him all the sick, those afflicted with various diseases and pains, those oppressed by demons, epileptics, and paralytics, and he healed them".[406] No doubt, there would have been people who followed Jesus because they wanted to witness more of the signs and wonders, the healing and deliverance. And yet some must have been so impressed by Jesus' authority and credibility.[407]

Apart from His authority and credibility, Jesus' works of mercy were what made his "fame spread throughout" the region. His works of mercy were His attraction. They were the bridges which transported people to the message He had for them.

I raised the example earlier of how many of the migrant workers whom HealthServe served came to believe in Christ. It was the justice work that HealthServe was doing which brought the workers to HealthServe in the first place. And it was the great love and care the HealthServe staff and volunteers showed the workers which established their credibility and authority as Christian disciples. In many cases, the workers were puzzled by the goodness of these people. So puzzled that they asked, "Why?" It was at these opportune moments that the HealthServe staff could share their faith.

> **Social justice is the "works" of love which evidence faith.**

---

405 Matthew 4:25.
406 Matthew 4:23-24.
407 Luke 4:32; Matthew 7:29.

In the same vein, in his evaluation of the early missionaries' work in providing public education, Bobby Sng notes the dilemma which the missionaries felt as to how much time the educational work was taking up, as opposed to setting up or building up churches. However, Sng notes that from a long-term point of view, mission schools made an important contribution in undermining the strong psychological prejudice the local community had against Christianity. After years of such hard work, a new generation was made ready to receive the Gospel.[408]

Social Justice and Evangelism are Partners: They are the Demonstration and Proclamation of the Gospel of the Kingdom of God

Jesus both demonstrated and proclaimed the Kingdom of God.[409] He demonstrated by the tangible acts of justice and mercy, of healing the sick and disabled, of delivering the spiritually oppressed, and of friendship with the socially marginalised. He proclaimed by verbal didactic teaching. He was fulfilling His Father's integral mission for Him.[410]

Jesus also sent His disciples out on such an integral mission. In Luke 9:1-2, He commissioned them to do two things: Proclaim the Kingdom of God and heal, i.e., cure diseases and liberate people from spiritual oppression.[411] Preach the Gospel and meet felt needs. They go hand in hand. If Jesus is the Word of God made flesh, our words also must be made flesh.[412]

In September 2001, a coalition of evangelical churches and organisations from around the world that were committed to integral

---

[408] Bobby Sng, *In His Good Time: The Story of the Church in Singapore, 1819-2002*, 3rd edn (Bible Society of Singapore/Graduates' Christian Fellowship, 2003), 156-158.
[409] John Stott, *The Contemporary Christian* (IVP, 1992), 345-348.
[410] E.g., Matthew 9:35.
[411] See also Matthew 10:1-8.
[412] John Stott, *The Contemporary Christian* (IVP, 1992), 349.

mission came together as The Micah Network. They declared in the Micah Network Declaration on Integral Mission:[413]

> Integral mission or holistic transformation is the proclamation and demonstration of the Gospel. It is not simply that evangelism and social involvement are to be done alongside each other. Rather, in integral mission our proclamation has social consequences as we call people to love and repentance in all areas of life. And our social involvement has evangelistic consequences as we bear witness to the transforming grace of Jesus Christ.
>
> ... Justice and justification by faith, worship and political action, the spiritual and the material, personal change and structural change belong together. As in the life of Jesus, being, doing and saying are at the heart of our integral task.

C. Is this the Social Gospel or Liberation Theology?

Some readers might, by this juncture, take issue with all that I've been saying about social justice on the basis that I'm advocating for a "social gospel" in the vein of theological liberalism or a Marxist, unbiblical "liberation theology".

In the West, this issue became hotly contested in the 20th Century because of the association of Walter Rauschenbusch's *Social Gospel* with

---

413 Micah Network, "Micah Network Declaration on Integral Mission" (2001). See also *Evangelism and Social Responsibility: An Evangelical Commitment*, Section 4.C.

theological liberalism. This was followed by the emergence of liberation theology in the mid-20th Century, which were deemed by others as Marxist. Not forgetting the historical context of the Cold War and the ideological war between capitalist democracy and socialist authoritarianism, to put it simplistically. The issue of social justice and evangelism therefore became a divisive one between the Western evangelical Christians and the liberal Christians. This polarization and dialectic resulted in a tendency in the Western Church for the evangelicals to focus exclusively on the spiritual aspects of Christianity at the expense of serving the needy, and for the liberals to neglect the spiritual and focus solely on social and political action.[414]

The Singapore Church was not spared this polarization during the mid-20th Century. Liberal theology crept into various Singapore churches in the 1950s-1960s.[415] This was after all the time of anti-Colonial nationalism, and social and political restlessness was evident in the local population. Under the influence of Dr John Sung, the Bible-Presbyterian Church in Singapore split from the Presbyterian Church and was formed to stand for biblical fundamentalism.[416] Campus Christian groups such as the Varsity Christian Fellowship were formed to stand against liberal theology. This then was the historical-cultural context for the tension between social justice and evangelism. Years have passed since the imminent and real threat of liberal and liberation theology loomed over the Singapore Church. It would therefore be helpful for us to distance ourselves

---

414   John Stott, *The Contemporary Christian* (IVP, 1992), 337-338.
415   Bobby Sng, *In His Good Time: The Story of the Church in Singapore, 1819-2002* (Bible Society of Singapore, 2003), 228.
416   Timothy Tow, *The Singapore B-P Church Story* (Life Book Centre, 1995). Besides liberal Christianity, the Bible-Presbyterian Church also opposed the ecumenical movement which the Church saw to be embracing all religions without regard to doctrine.

from such dialectics, both abroad and in Singapore's history,[417] and consider the relationship between social justice and evangelism biblically and practically.

For a fuller discussion on the "social gospel" and my attempt to address concerns about whether the biblical social justice I've espoused thus far is some form of liberal social gospel, please visit the book's website.[418]

In the final analysis, one must look at the substance beyond the form. It is easy to throw labels and terms like "social gospel" and "liberation theology", but every thought, idea or theology must ultimately be parsed through Spirit-led biblical hermeneutics. It is important for each of us to be clear about the essential truth of the Gospel as expressed in the Bible, which is the authoritative, revealed Word of God. (And if there be any concern that social justice is antithetical to the Reformed mind, check out a video of one of the chief proponents of Reformed theology, John Piper, talking about social justice on *The Gospel Coalition*![419])

D. Social Justice Through Church Ministry or Church Members?

Thus far, I have referred to the Church's need to live a communal life of justice; the Church's duty to love its neighbours; and the Church's vocation to witness to the world through love and unity. I have referred to "the

---

417 I think wisdom is to be gained from S Dhanabalan's speech, "The Church in Singapore-Time to Distance from the West?", Message at the GCF Annual Thanksgiving Dinner (5 September 2003).
418 See resource on book's website on "Social Gospel, Liberal Theology, Liberation Theology".
419 "Social Justice and Young Evangelicals: Encouragement and Concern", *The Gospel Coalition* (28 August 2013), http://www.thegospelcoalition.org/article/social-justice-and-young-evangelicals-encouragement-and-concern.

Church" (with a capital "C") as either a community or the global community of Christ followers rather than the institutional church. In cases where I refer to churches as specific organisations, I have generally referred to them as the "local church". The question which arises now is whether a *local church* should start and run social justice ministries, or leave it to the individual church members and informal communities of disciples to do so independently of the local church.

This would depend on your view of what the mission of the Church is. Kevin DeYoung and Greg Gilbert argue that the unique mission of the Church is to "witness to Jesus by proclaiming the Gospel and making disciples of all nations".[420] They argue that a local church should "tend towards doing those activities and spending its resources on those projects that *more directly*, rather than *less directly*, further its central mission".[421] They appear to imply that local churches running justice and mercy ministries are only less directly furthering their purpose of discipleship. To be honest, I have difficulty with their reasoning.

First, DeYoung and Gilbert draw a distinction between the organic church (that is, the community of individual believers) and the institutional local church. However, the distinction made in the Bible between these two concepts of 'church' does not appear to distinguish the outworking of faith in the individual believer and the institutional church, save that the institutional church, being a collective of individuals, is not required to do things or be something which only individual believers can. So for example, while an individual believer can be a good husband, the church cannot. The church can, however, be a community that loves one another. Also, there are only a few things mentioned in the Bible which only apply

---

[420] Kevin DeYoung and Greg Gilbert, *What Is the Mission of the Church? Making Sense of Social Justice, Shalom and the Great Commission* (Crossway, 2011), 26.

[421] Kevin DeYoung and Greg Gilbert, *What Is the Mission of the Church? Making Sense of Social Justice, Shalom and the Great Commission* (Crossway, 2011), 235.

to the church as a corporate body. Paul clarified that within the church, individuals should be responsible for widows in their extended families. Only when there are widows in the church community who have no family members should the church as a collective step in to help the widow.[422] Another example would be church discipline, in that only in the context of the church as a collective body would it make sense to have discipline in the form of the expulsion of an individual from the community.[423] The Bible does not seem to say that only individual believers should do good works and love neighbours, whereas the church as a collective of individuals should do less good works and not love neighbours as much.

Second, if the central mission of the Church and the believer is discipleship then it follows that the Church as a community of believers must first be disciples living out all that Jesus has taught, which necessarily includes living a life of justice and righteousness.

Third, running justice and mercy ministries and encouraging church members to actively participate in them is a good means of discipleship. I cannot fathom discipleship as *merely* sermons and Bible studies. Discipleship must be hands-on. It is telling that even before Jesus' disciples fully grasped the significance of Jesus' work on earth, He already sent them out to preach the Gospel, heal the sick and liberate the oppressed.[424] Discipleship is on-the-job training and not didactic.

I do not have a conclusive view on this issue (I discuss this further in Chapter 10). The views of some interviewees featured in this book provide additional perspective. I am inclined to think that this is a matter of wisdom and discernment of God's leading rather than of principle, and certainly not of doctrine. Nevertheless, it is important to recognise

---

422 1 Timothy 5:3-16.
423 Matthew 18:15-17.
424 Matthew 10; Mark 6:7-13; Luke 9:1-6; Luke 10:1-22.

that if biblical justice is an integral aspect of Christian discipleship and witness in every individual, then it should follow that it should be an aspiration of a local church to provide platforms for their members to be discipled to grasp and express biblical justice, whether or not it is through a formal church ministry, a para-church organisation ministry, an informal ministry, or otherwise. I say aspire because I understand that different churches may be at different stages of development. Accordingly, it is understandable that there will be churches who are unable to devote resources to disciple members in respect of biblical justice. Godly wisdom and prayer are paramount in this regard.

E. How to Pursue Social Justice and Evangelism in Church Ministry

Many local churches have community outreach ministries and activities which *primarily* seek to evangelise. Based on anecdotal observations, it appears that the modus operandi in these ministries is to organise events or activities which cast a wide net to reach as many people as possible in hope that relationships might be forged between the church members and the beneficiaries. It is then hoped that in those relationships, church members will have the opportunity to share their faith.

I think there is nothing wrong with this approach. It has worked for many churches before and still does. This approach and paradigm shapes the types of activities and programmes organised. Although not always the case, the tendency then would be to conduct programmes which reach large numbers. Many activities tend to be ad hoc and one-off, leaving it to the church members to figure out for themselves if and how they can follow up with any beneficiaries. I have organised several such ad hoc and one-off activities in the past myself. The problem is that they are touch-and-go and superficial. They do not meet real or deep needs, or allow for meaningful relationships to be forged. In many cases, the target beneficiaries are not really interested in what we had to offer in the first place. People who first come into contact with such superficial programmes will probably not come back for more than that initial contact.

An example is how a few years back, when thick haze from forest fires in Indonesia blanketed Singapore, I mobilised a group of Christians to distribute masks and dry food to low-income residents at the Jalan Kukoh area. Armed with masks, we went one night, door to door, and felt good about ourselves after that.

I found out a few things later. First, the residents were already over-served. One resident had four packets of Milo and she gave away the packets to other volunteers who visited her. The residents later also received masks from the Government. Second, the residents were annoyed by the great number of groups visiting them. Third, while we tried to leave a note alluding to our faith in the stuff we distributed to the residents, the truth is it was most likely unfruitful because no meaningful connections were made. Such are the shortcomings of ad hoc and one-off activities.

The Goal of Church Community Ministries
This raises the question: What is the goal of the community outreach platforms we organise? Is it about: (1) Bringing people to church to preach the Gospel to them, or (2) going to people to meet their needs? I think this is the fundamental tension between social justice and evangelism. They are not at odds nor are they mutually exclusive for certain, but having

clarity on the priority and focus helps shape the activities, expectations and intended outcomes. In some cases, there is a sweet spot where both can be achieved.

In my view, subject to specific context, we will generally find goal (1) challenging and disappointing in terms of outcomes. And we will find goal (2) more obtainable. The latter helps achieve the former goal. Why? Because in the process of meeting deep needs, it is often inevitable that the process will be lengthy and difficult, and therefore require great love. Deep relationships can be forged. Think about a person who was brought to your church by his friend and then stayed on. How close was that relationship? Likely the relationship was forged over years. Of course, there are many cases of people walking into church and then staying on. Even so, they also had some form of deep need. And the reason they stayed is often because someone invested much time and effort to meet those needs.

The Christian disciple is called to meet *material* needs and *eternal spiritual* needs. He can and should do the latter regardless of whether he is able to do the former.[425] Yet, it is often the case that by doing the former that there will be opportunity for the latter. Not only opportunity, but credibility. That was how Jesus went about preaching the Gospel. We should seriously consider following His example. In short, *when we meet the deep needs of people, deep relationships can be formed in which a deep Gospel can be sown.*

Which Communities to Serve?
On the premise that meeting deep needs is the better way, the question then is: Whose needs? Many local church outreach ministries confine themselves to the immediate geographical neighbourhood. While

---

425   Mark 2:1-12; Luke 5:17-26.

there may be legitimate reasons for this apart from convenience and expediency, distance really cannot be a significant obstacle to expanding one's territorial scope or focusing on communities which are not within one's immediate vicinity. After all, many churches go to great lengths to organise short-term mission trips in other countries. A little distance in the same country could hardly matter much.

Which communities then should you or your church ministry serve? I think this would depend on three factors:

1. Which communities have significant needs?
2. What are you or your church members passionate about?
3. What resources (skills and talents of members, money, time, physical space) do you or your church have?

The intersection between the three factors would be the sweet spot for you and your church.[426]

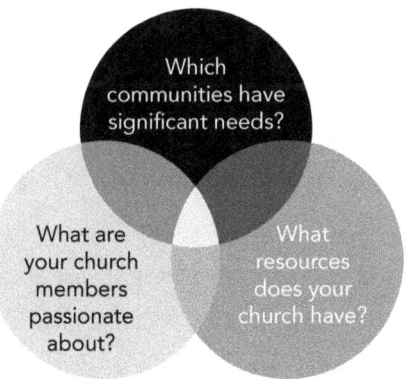

God's Invitation to the Needy

On the first factor, the parable in Luke 14:15-24 is instructive. Jesus specifically told this parable in response to a remark about who may

---

426 This is of course subject to prayerful consideration and the Holy Spirit's leading. See also generally, Jim Martin, *The Just Church: Becoming a Risk-Taking, Justice-Seeking, Disciple-Making Congregation* (Tyndale Momentum, 2012).

enter the Kingdom of God. The parable reveals to us that while God's invitation to the Kingdom is made to all, the reality is that only certain types of people will accept the invitation. Those who have much, who have little needs, who are satisfied with life, who are occupied by worldly distractions—these will likely turn down God's invitation. Who then will likely enter the Kingdom? The poor, the crippled, the blind and the lame. Though they were initially not invited, they were later invited. And others who were not initially invited will be "compelled" to enter the Kingdom. One of the truths to be gleaned from this parable is that *it is the needy who will seek the Kingdom of God, not those who are already satisfied with the world.*

Indeed, during His earthly public ministry, Jesus predominantly drew a certain type of people to himself—the sick, poor and socially marginalised. It is because they were all in such dire need, and self-aware of their need, that they went out of their way to seek Him. To satisfy their needs in Him.

And if our local churches look hard enough, there are such communities around in Singapore. It is important to do our research to identify such communities, which are often hidden. In this regard, it's also important to find out if there are other groups which are already serving those communities, whether Christian or otherwise. This would then affect whether your ministry would duplicate, compete or ally with those groups.

Of course, the challenge in today's context is that we will be 'competing' with many other VWOs and government-based organisations. For example, I think some Residents' Committees (RC), the People's Association and the Community Development Councils actually do a much better job than our local churches. Some such RCs have had legal clinics, medical clinics, tuition programmes, enrichment and hobby classes, elderly care programmes, etc., for years. I spoke to an RC member in the neighbourhood of my church. He said his RC had various assistance programmes. They even give out free wheelchairs to those in need of one. Even so, he said honestly, the take-up rate of their programmes is not high. And these are good programmes, at least on the surface. I realised that the problem is superficiality. Some programmes simply do not meet the real deep needs of people. They just try to cast a wide net in hope they will benefit as many people as possible.

Case Studies

Let's consider examples of other paradigms and models. Bethesda Church Bukit Arang has a special ministry for the intellectually challenged. It aims to teach and disciple the intellectually challenged in the knowledge of the Gospel.

Several churches have special ethno-language-centric outreach ministries. For instance, churches like Chen Li Presbyterian Church, Good News Centre, Grace Thai Fellowship, Santiphap Church (Glory Presbyterian Church), Trinity Christian Centre, True Way Presbyterian Church and Victory Family Centre have Thai ministries or fellowships.[427] Cornerstone Community Church and Judson Baptist Church have Burmese fellowships.

Some churches like Gospel Light Christian Church reach out to the local poor in the Jalan Kukoh/York Hill area, providing drop-in care centres for the children of poor families and a food distribution programme. Their parents are so busy working they hardly have time with their children. So the church provides a bus service to pick the children up from the neighbourhood and send them to the drop-in centre. The volunteers with the food distribution programme develop friendships with the needy families and take them out for dinners regularly.

---

427 Rev Dr Kim Chong Pae, "The Ethnic Church: Catalyst for a Caring Community" in *Ethnic Rhythms: Life in the Global City* (Singapore Centre for Global Missions, 2015), 75.

Some young adults from Gospel Light Christian Church started a literacy and tuition programme for the kids (ReadAble). Their mission is to bring education to the doorsteps of economically disadvantaged children through fun, innovative and customised learning; and to form close partnerships with their parents and the wider community. They conduct weekly English classes in the children's homes, teaching through a combination of play, speech and drama sessions, and reading exercises. This programme has since attracted several young adults from other churches to volunteer with them.

> **It is the needy who will seek the Kingdom of God, not those who are already satisfied with the world.**

Fairfield Methodist Church has a long-established outreach ministry to the elderly in Chinatown and more recently, to Chinese migrant workers. They have a synergistic partnership with a certain NGO that serves migrant workers. Specialised and in-depth services such as those involving legal- or medical-related issues may be provided by the NGO. Community, fellowship and befriending would be provided by the church.

Redemption Hill Church has a Mercy and Justice ministry where its members gather together to pray, study the Word, do outreach activities, and encourage one another. They come up with ways to pray for and support justice ministries and organisations in the region. Some members are volunteers with voluntary welfare organisations (VWOs) and non-governmental organisations (NGOs). The ministry partners a VWO to participate monthly in a food distribution programme in Chinatown, and in the process, builds relationship with the beneficiaries.

Consider also the Geylang Bless God (GBG) ministry that has been going out to the streets to minister to transient sex workers for years. As these transient sex workers are here for short periods of time, there is little time and opportunity for meaningful connections and life transformation. So if you talk about the number of people who have had 'significant visible life change', it is very low. I understand that there's been one or two individuals who 'escaped' the trade and have become advocates against trafficking. So the numbers may be low, but those who have been impacted have themselves become impactful. I consider some other examples in later chapters.

Service to What Extent?—The Power of Passion
My own belief is that real impact, both spiritual and socioeconomic, comes about only with the pursuit of deep justice and mercy. And it's such deep justice and mercy that draws people to the Gospel, to the Kingdom, to Jesus Christ. The question is whether we are prepared to go all the way like the Good Samaritan or Job. Then we can build deep relationships, out of which deep faith can form.

This is where the second factor comes in: The passion of individual church members drives the ministry. When that passion comes from the grassroots, the ministry will be powerful because every individual is a potential Good Samaritan who is willing to go out of his or her way to love people.

How can such passion be inculcated? I believe it comes about from intentional discipleship. No amount of top-down vision casting can replace the power of discipling people into God-loving, neighbour-loving individuals. Indeed, too often, in many organisations and churches I have heard about, it is the leadership who is trying to drag its members along on projects. There is often little buy-in from the grassroots. And yet unfortunately, in a story I've heard, when at the grassroots level, a cell group became passionate about starting a justice and mercy ministry, the church leadership was sceptical about supporting it. This suspicion carried on for a long time. Thankfully, this did not discourage the cell group, who went on to start the ministry. It has since become a reputable shelter and service provider for women with certain needs. Biblical discipleship produces holy passion. And holy passion should be stoked to bear good fruit.

What Type of Justice and Mercy Work Should a Local Church Do?
A church ministry has to also consider whether it wants to only be a service provider meeting immediate needs, or go further. What about development and capacity-building work? What about advocacy work in relation to systemic and structural injustices? This is where the third factor comes in. The types of services and work that the ministry should do are necessarily related to the types of resources the church has.

For instance, if the church has a large number of medical care professionals, it could consider running a free medical clinic. For instance, Pasir Panjang Hill Brethren Church's VWO, PPH Community Services Centre, runs a *pro bono* medical clinic (charging a nominal fee of $5) at Penjuru Dormitory for migrant workers. As a result of this work, the church has also started a Telugu ministry for the migrant workers. If the church has people who are equipped to nurture and educate young children, it could set up early childhood literacy or education programmes.

Where Does Evangelism Come in?
First, church members can share their faith within the mid- to long-term relationships formed with the beneficiaries. One testimony of this is a client of a legal clinic run jointly by Lawyers Christian Fellowship (LCF) and

Boscombe Life Church (BLC). The approach of this legal clinic is unique because it is coupled with counselling. The client who attended the clinic was not represented by a lawyer and had to represent herself in divorce proceedings. Over the next few months, she reconciled with her husband, and had the interim divorce order (decree *nisi*) reversed. She came to know Jesus. Her husband came to know Jesus a year later. So did her three adult children subsequently. Today, her husband and her lead in the Chinese ministry in the church.

To be honest, the number of such stories is few. From a human perspective, the efforts of the volunteers, who have invested a lot of time, energy, emotions and resources over the years, may appear rather fruitless. However, even though such stories may be few, they are immensely heartening.

Second, the ministry is a platform for evangelism to non-Christians who work alongside the Christians. Non-Christian volunteers or activists may join the activities or programmes individually upon the invitation of their Christians friends who are already actively participating in the ministry. Or, they may join the programmes as representatives of partnering organisations, which may or may not be religious-based. There is nothing peculiar or novel about this. It is about Christians being Jesus disciples wherever they are, whatever they do, whoever they are with. That is how some Christian individuals express their faith in secular organisations doing social justice work.

Finally, it is important for a church ministry seeking to do justice and mercy work to be clear about its ethos, ethics and principles of seeking justice and mercy. We turn now to consider the principles of biblical justice.

Chapter Summary

- The relationship between social justice and evangelism is this:
  - ❖ Social justice and evangelism are both expressions of Christian faith;
  - ❖ Social justice and evangelism need not always go together;
  - ❖ Social justice and evangelism may be expressed in different ways and to different extents for each individual;
  - ❖ Evangelism and discipleship are paramount in priority;
  - ❖ Social justice is the result and purpose of evangelism and discipleship;
  - ❖ Social justice is the bridge to evangelism and discipleship;
  - ❖ Social justice and evangelism are partners: They are the demonstration and proclamation of the Gospel of the Kingdom of God.
- Biblical social justice is not to be confused with the social gospel, liberal theology or liberation theology.
- Whether a local church should have social justice ministries is a matter of wisdom rather than principle or doctrine.
- When we meet the deep needs of people, deep relationships can be formed in which a deep Gospel can be sown.
- When considering which communities to serve, the three factors to consider are:
  - ❖ Which communities have significant needs?
  - ❖ What are you or your church members passionate about?
  - ❖ What resources do you or your church have?
- It is the needy who will seek the Kingdom of God, not those who are already satisfied with the world.

Discussion Questions

1. What do you think is the right dynamic between evangelism and social justice? What would the practical expression of this dynamic look like?
2. How do you think evangelism and social justice should be pursued in the lives of an individual Christian and in a local faith community respectively? Should they be different?
3. Share stories, testimonies or experiences you know relating to the pursuit of evangelism and social justice in the lives of individual Christians and in faith communities.
4. How would the dynamic between evangelism and social justice be manifested in your life and your faith community?
5. What is your response to God in the light of what you have gleaned from these thoughts?

INTERVIEW:
Crystal Goh

● ● ●

Crystal Goh is a singer-songwriter based in Singapore. She has been singing and writing songs since 2007. Crystal was mentored by Don Richmond under the National Arts Council's NOISE programme in 2009. In 2010, Crystal performed regular live acoustic sets at OverTime @ Holland Village. From 2010 to 2011, Crystal performed in various World Vision Singapore events, including the organisation's most major campaign, the 30-Hour Famine. In 2013, in collaboration with World Vision, she did a local tour with the Mongolian Kids Choir, performing a self-penned song with the children in several venues across Singapore. Crystal has also sung in numerous events and wedding gigs in the past five years.

In 2011, Crystal was diagnosed with spasmodic dysphonia. This caused distress to her vocal chords, and she struggled to sing. During this time, Crystal chose to focus on songwriting instead. In 2013, she collaborated

> with two vulnerable communities—at-risk youth and children of incarcerated parents—to write, record and perform four original songs. The project, known as Diamonds on the Street (DOTS), gave Crystal the opportunity to bring friendship and hope to the communities through music. DOTS culminated in two live performances and a five-track album.
>
> Although she has not completely recovered, her vocals have since improved, and she is currently exploring ways to tap into the new voice that had risen from her condition. Check out DOTS' website at: http://www.diamondsonthestreet.com/.

1. Do you think that social justice is a key expression of Christian discipleship and witness? Why or why not?

Yes, I do. I believe that God is especially tender and close to the poor (in health, spirit, finances and more) and that His Spirit lives tangibly among them. When we serve the poor, we experience a communion with His Spirit and a divine sense of awe and love.

2. Tell me in particular about DOTS. What do you do there? Why do you do this work? What got you started on it?

Through DOTS, I work with marginalised youths to make meaning out of their crises and to form new and hopeful perspectives for their future through the process of creating art. These youths often face self- or societal stigmatisation, as they are brought up in circumstances or environments that label them as "bad" or even "hopeless".

These youths are rarely or never asked about their goals or dreams for the future and often experience trauma in their formative years. This guided process of identifying difficult emotions, finding meaning in their crises and learning to see themselves as individuals who have the ability to achieve their goals allows them to value themselves and their experiences, and empowers them to face their future with courage.

Through our workshops, we provide a platform for participants to practise interpersonal skills and learn a creative way to communicate difficult thoughts and emotions. We have designed our activities to facilitate the process of reframing our life narratives through meaning-making. Our workshops, which are very reflective in nature, also open up spaces for befrienders to build relationships with the youths.

I do this work because I understand how our perspectives of ourselves can shape how we live our lives. I want to open up creative pathways for the youths to see themselves as valuable, inherently good and with the ability to achieve their goals.

I started DOTS because of a personal crisis, where as a singer-songwriter, I lost my voice and eventually isolated myself from people. The experience convinced me of the necessity of hope and the need to share it with others who, like me, might feel victimised by pain.

During that painful season, the craft of songwriting allowed me to discover new perspectives to my journey and helped me to move from feeling like a victim to identifying myself as someone who would be able to overcome this painful season. The artistic process has a way of allowing us to take risks in imagining new futures and to eventually live out this future.

3. How do you ground the work in or relate it to in your faith?
I see my work as a way to worship God.

4. Do you evangelise to the people you work with?
We believe in creating safe spaces for both befrienders and youths to share one another's pain and to build positive relationships. Great relationships,

to me, are powerful channels to share God's love and to eventually win souls.

One of the truths I hold close to my heart is a quote by Henri Nouwen:

> When we honestly ask ourselves which person in our lives means the most to us, we often find that it is those who, instead of giving advice, solutions, or cures, have chosen rather to share our pain and touch our wounds with a warm and tender hand.

I have always felt that it is very healing to share someone's pain and sit with them. Our beliefs speak through our actions and others can often feel a strong draw towards the Christ who lives in us through our loving acts. The youths we work with are free to respond to this love in their own time.

5. Is your work/organisation tied to any local church? Why or why not?

Our work is not tied to a specific church, but we have had incredible support from the Christian community. We have chosen to see our work as a way that everyone (including those who are not affiliated with churches) can experience the transcendent and divine force of love, goodness and beauty at work.

6. What do you think should be the role of the local church in relation to organisations like yours?

The local church has been effective in its teachings on building strong and healthy relationships.

DOTS would love to learn from local churches how to facilitate strong relationships and to even work together with churches to provide platforms for relationship-building between believers and at-risk youths.

For many of the youths, this could be the first time that they get a taste of a healthy and loving relationship.

7. How does your local church view or support you in your ministry?
I am currently exploring churches as I feel drawn in this season to churches which give more room for quietness and contemplation. I came from a slightly more Pentecostal background.

My previous church was very supportive of me as an individual and has been actively providing opportunities for church members to get involved in social justice in and beyond Singapore.

This has encouraged me deeply and I am grateful for the great examples that many churches have modelled in serving marginalised communities beyond their walls.

INTERVIEW:
Melissa Ong

• • •

As A Rocha's (AR) filmmaker since 2005, Melissa helps to give voice to the people and places that AR is serving and to bring their stories to a wider audience. She works with the international communications team and is based in Singapore. From 2006–2008, she and her husband Daniel served with the AR Canada team in British Columbia, where they lived and worked in community at the environmental centre. In Singapore, Melissa is also involved in sharing the creation care message, and encouraging the growth of the movement in Southeast Asia. She is working on a practical conservation project involving citizen science and is helping people appreciate wildlife in their own backyard. She is passionate about walking with people as they seek to live out creation care in the city and in their vocation. Before AR, she worked in the local television industry as an executive producer/director/writer. She is a member of Zion Bishan Bible-Presbyterian Church.

1. What is A Rocha (AR)? What does AR do?

A Rocha (AR) is an inter-denominational Christian organisation which, inspired by God's love, engages in community-based conservation, scientific research, environmental education and theological training. Our first initiative was a field study centre in Portugal, and so our name is Portuguese and means "The Rock". It was founded in 1983 by Anglican minister Peter Harris and his wife Miranda. AR is now working in 19 countries and has community groups around the world and in Singapore.

2. What do you do at AR?

I serve as a filmmaker in AR International. The majority of the team are in the UK, but I'm based in Singapore and work from home. It's been a real privilege to tell the stories from the ground, to connect with people and places where the teams are working, and to bear witness to beauty, suffering, loss, and God's faithful presence and continued renewal of the earth. We know creation tells of God's glory, but the psalmist also says, "Their words aren't heard, their voices aren't recorded, but their silence fills the earth: unspoken truth is spoken everywhere" (Psalm 19:3-4, MSG). This resonates with me. Part of my calling as a filmmaker involves giving creation an amplified voice, as well as truth telling. My other role is focused on supporting the creation care movement in Southeast Asia, but primarily in Singapore. I help organise a local AR community group called "Friends of A Rocha in Singapore". Giving practical expression to creation care is important for us, so we are excited about starting our two-year citizen science project here—an amphibian survey in urban parks. It's a small contribution to local biodiversity data and we want to help people cultivate wonder again as they reconnect with creation right here in the city.

3. How did you get involved with AR?

Before AR, I was working crazy hours in the television industry as an executive producer, writing and directing programmes mostly about nature, the environment and culture. My passion for nature was quite disconnected from faith. All I knew was that God was the Creator and that was it. I had believed nature was set on autopilot after the first bit of Genesis. I also grew up assuming that this world was going to be abandoned, burnt up, and that heaven was a disembodied state somewhere up there. Part of me was really attracted to missions having grown up in Zion Bishan Bible-Presbyterian Church which was and still is missions-focused.

In 2003, I was involved in an NHK TV series for young people called "Voyage to the Future" which was about youths doing something for the environment. I spent three weeks in Japan, and met Japanese environmental activists and practitioners who poured out their lives to steward the earth. I was very moved by their love and the transformation I saw. I was also sad that Christians who professed love for the Creator were missing. Someone describes it like this: You can't say, "I love Rembrandt" and then proceed to destroy his masterpieces. We do this all the time with creation. I could not help thinking, "Why aren't Christians doing this kind of work? Where are they?"

So I made a decision in Japan that I would really research to find out what the Bible says about environmental issues, to understand eschatology and tricky texts on "a new heaven and new earth". I felt alone as a Christian concerned about environmental issues. Surely there had to be others out there?

When I got back to Singapore I Googled Christian, conservation, environment, and this very foreign phrase "A Rocha" kept coming up, but I checked out other hits first. They were pretty reactive. The webpages said environmentalism was New Age, and that the Church should not be distracted from evangelism and saving souls. Not what I was looking for! I finally clicked on "A Rocha": What I found was an authentic Christian community that was doing real science and real conservation! And I wanted in!

4. How do you ground your work with AR in or relate it to your faith? Do you consider your work with AR an expression of your Christian faith and/or Christian social justice?

AR has helped me to integrate missions and conservation, in longing for ecological justice and in how I live my everyday life. AR is theologically-driven and love-driven in its motivation as a conservation organisation. We do conservation not because we think we are going to save the planet—we cannot. Only God can. Instead of a fear-driven activism, it's more sustainable: We do what we do as a response to the Creator, as worship. In caring for creation we reflect God in his own care of the world; in caring we express what it means to be human as we serve and keep the garden ("*abad*" and "*shamar*", Genesis 2:15), and that includes other image bearers who are in the garden as well. Yes, our world is broken.

The root of the environmental crisis is sin and our broken relationship with God. So it doesn't even matter if one denies that climate is anthropogenic or not. Environmental degradation is a driver for human conflict and war. Pursuing social justice calls us to look holistically. Social justice without ecological justice makes it incomplete. In our projects around the world, it's about participating in Christ's reconciliation, "all the broken and dislocated pieces of the universe—people and things, animals and atoms—get properly fixed and fit together in vibrant harmonies, all because of his death, his blood that poured down from the cross" (Colossians 1:15-20, MSG).

In 2005, I was filming at AR Kenya which has a community conservation programme called ASSETS (Arabuko-Sokoke Schools and Ecotourism Scheme). It combines forest conservation and poverty alleviation. People were cutting down trees illegally to sell because they couldn't afford secondary school fees for their children. Through dialogues, AR learnt of this driver and came up with ASSETS, an eco-bursary scheme. We trained nature guides, built bird hides for the mangrove and forest, worked with hotels, the ministry of education, the wildlife service, tour agencies, community elders and churches. Tourists pay some money for the facilities and that goes into paying school fees for the students who live adjacent to the forest and mangrove. They and their families pledge to take care of creation and practise Farming God's Way, a conservation-friendly and very productive way to grow food. Many places in Kenya have become deserts after the forests were cut, leaving people destitute. But when a forest and mangrove flourish, human communities flourish too. This is what *shalom* looks like.

5. What should the role of the local church be in relation to organisations like AR?
The local church can do so much. If we open our hearts and see what we are doing to the earth, to each other—or even not doing—we will feel we are at a *kairos* moment. Support, send, teach and model creation care. I'm grateful to Zion Bishan Bible-Presbyterian Church for their love, financial support and prayer. I'm proud of our partnership with AR, and of the fact that Zion is probably the first church in the world to have an environmental filmmaker as a missionary!

It is not easy for the Church to understand the missional aspect of AR's work. So why not come and see? Send your pastors, your young people, environmental studies majors to volunteer at our field study centres in Canada, Kenya, France and Portugal. I have met so many young people who love creation and are in the relevant studies, and feel completely alone and unsupported in their passion for creation. They feel disconnected from their faith community. They may feel judged by the secular environmental discourse for being associated with a religion known as the root of the ecological crisis! So support and equip young adults especially to embrace their calling and fit it within God's story of redemption for the whole earth, not just people.

The local church has a great role too in challenging its members to live out their vocation—especially those who are in finance, investment and banking—in alignment with biblical values. Are you in banking? Great! Make money in a way that blesses creation and leaves it in a better state.

With regards to theology, how we treat the world depends on what we believe. What are the filters we put on? If we believe and perpetuate the kind of unbiblical eschatology such as "the earth will be burned up anyway, so why bother?" then Christians will be bad news for creation. Could we examine hymns and songs that have bad theology such as, "This world is not my home I'm just a-passing through"? Also consider the last verse of "Amazing Grace": "The earth shall soon dissolve like snow; the sun forbear to shine. But God who called me here below, will be forever mine." Is this really true? The earth will be renewed and continue forever. In passages that speak about the "new heavens and new earth" (2 Peter 3:13, Revelation 21:1), the Greek word for "new" is "*kainos*", denoting a transformation and renovation. It's not "*neos*" which means "new in time and reality", entirely new from scratch. God will make "all things new", not "all new things".

Katong Presbyterian Church (KPC) is a fine example of a church that is faithful in nurturing human community and creation care. They have a community garden that invites people to have a closer relationship with creation, and they are intentionally implementing things like doing away with styrofoam and plastics at Christmas. This is what Keegan Gan, Creation Care Interest Group Coordinator at KPC, told me about their church:

> Katong Presbyterian Church's value statements include being caretakers of the earth and upholders of justice and mercy. Therefore we always consider the environmental and socioeconomic impact of our activities and purchasing decisions. One of our initiatives includes putting a stop to the use of disposable products. We also hold reflective sessions, which we call dinners and dialogues, to empower the congregation with biblical knowledge about creation care and issues on social justice. By starting a church garden, we are also beginning to see rare species of birds and insects in our premises. We certainly hope to do more in landscaping our compound to provide a much needed green lung in our city.

I also want to applaud Deputy Senior Pastor Alvin Tan from Bartley Christian Church. He was on sabbatical at Regent College and attended their 2015 Pastors Conference, "Holy Ground: Answering God's Call to Creation Care", which AR co-hosted. He was stirred and visited the AR Brooksdale Environmental Centre an hour from Vancouver. When he got back to Singapore, the first message he preached was on creation care!

A useful resource for churches is AR UK's Eco Church programme (formerly "Eco-Congregation") which will equip churches practically.

6. What do you think is the relationship between creation care and evangelism? Many people seem to take the view that creation care is quite a few rungs below evangelism and social justice for people in terms of priority. What would you say to that?

We humans love setting things in hierarchy. It makes life so neat and tidy! Perhaps it is more helpful to ask, "Who is Jesus? What is the Gospel?" I find Chris Wright's summary in *The Mission of God* very helpful. He answers the question, "What establishes ecological concern and specific environmental action as legitimate integral dimensions of biblical mission?" this way:

- They are responding to an urgent global issue.
- They are expressions of our love and obedience towards God the Creator.
- They restore our proper priestly and kingly role in relation to the earth.
- They expose and expand our motivation for holistic mission.
- They constitute a contemporary prophetic opportunity for the Church.
- They embody the core biblical values of compassion and justice.

7. What do you think Christian individuals should do with regard to creation care?

Firstly, we can work to restore our relationship with creation. We can ask questions. What is our relationship with technology? Fossil fuel? Palm oil? Do we make money in a way that blesses creation or harms it and human communities? Wendell Berry says, "To live, we must daily break the body and shed the blood of Creation. When we do this knowingly, lovingly, skillfully, reverently, it is a sacrament. When we do it ignorantly, greedily, clumsily, destructively, it is a desecration. In such desecration we condemn ourselves to spiritual and moral loneliness, and others to want." If we don't know the impact of how we live, it's a good place to start learning.

Secondly, we can educate ourselves and our children to be eco-literate instead of succumbing to "Nature Deficit Disorder" (see Richard Louv's *Last Child in the Woods*).

Thirdly, we can celebrate Sabbath. Get unplugged, get out of the malls and air-conditioned places. Go outside, observe, pay attention, learn the names of the wildlife we have right here in the city. Have you ever seen a colugo?

8. Any other thoughts or comments on the topic?

If Christians feel a resistance, an instinct to hold back, pass negative judgment or shut down when they hear words like environment, climate change, creation care, I think it would be revealing to sit with the feeling and ask why. People do have a visceral reaction to these issues. Perhaps there is the fear of having to change or give up something. As an AR friend Tom Rowley says, it is not like "we have to", as though it is a chore or onerous duty, but it is a "we get to!" This is what being truly human is, being keepers of the Garden and keepers of other image bearers. It is not easy, but our hope is in Christ. "Behold, I make all things *kainos*" (Revelation 21:5).

7

What's Distinctive About the Christian View of Justice: Principles of Biblical Justice

First they came for the Socialists, and I did not speak out—
Because I was not a Socialist.
Then they came for the Trade Unionists,
and I did not speak out—
Because I was not a Trade Unionist.
Then they came for the Jews, and I did not speak out—
Because I was not a Jew.
Then they came for me—and there was
no one left to speak for me.

—Martin Niemöller (1892–1984),
prominent Protestant pastor persecuted in Nazi Germany

We have considered that the Micah Mandate to seek justice, love mercy and walk humbly with God is a call meant for every Christian disciple. We have also considered that evangelism and social justice should be interwoven into the ministry of the individual Christian and the local church. It is important now to consider the ethics and posture of seeking justice and mercy. Why? Because these would determine how we ought to love our neighbours.

A. Causes of Injustice and Suffering

The Bible refers to various sources of injustice and suffering and also the principles by which they should be addressed. Generally, one may observe from the Bible many different causes of hardship: (i) Interpersonal; (ii) vicissitudes of life; (iii) systemic and cultural; and (iv) poor personal choices. Often hardship is multi-causal and complex.[428]

First, hardship may be caused by interpersonal injustice. For instance, in the Parable of the Good Samaritan,[429] the victim suffered injustice from robbers "who stripped him and beat him and departed, leaving him half dead". Other examples are oppression, unfair treatment, withholding of wages, robbery[430] and extortion.[431] In one *pro bono* case I handled, a PRC worker was not paid additional salary for overtime work and work on rest days and public holidays, which he was properly entitled to under the law.[432] In another case, not only was a worker not paid his salary and medical expenses, he was punched on two occasions by his employer when he asked for payment.

Second, hardship may occur due to the vicissitudes of life. For instance, sickness or death of the family breadwinner, natural disasters and job retrenchment.[433] In one story I was told, a pastor's wife was widowed with four children to care for. They had not been financially well off even when the pastor had been alive. The widow had to undergo much hardship to provide for the family and care for the children as a single parent.

Third, systemic and cultural factors may result in injustice and hardship. In Old Testament Israel, a child may be born to parents who are debt slaves. Or, a debtor may commit himself and his entire family to his creditor as debt slaves. Families may then be stuck in an intergenerational poverty trap. Modern systemic or cultural factors resulting in hardship include

---

428 In the Singapore context, an in-depth report on causes of poverty is the Lien Centre for Social Innovation Social Insight Research Series, "A Handbook on Inequality, Poverty and Unmet Social Needs in Singapore" (March 2015).
429 Luke 10:29-37.
430 Jeremiah 22:13; James 5:1-6; Ezekiel 22:28; Micah 2:2.
431 Ezekiel 22:29.
432 See Aw Cheng Wei, "More foreign workers seek help over wage woes", *The Straits Times* (14 June 2015), http://news.asiaone.com/news/singapore/more-foreign-workers-seek-help-over-wage-woes.
433 Genesis 47.

state policies, poor socioeconomic familial background, corruption and bribery,[434] and changes in demography and economy, e.g., technological advances. An example of systemic and cultural factors resulting in injustice and hardship is unmarried single mothers. Legal, social and economic policies produce hardship for them over and above the difficulty of being single parents. While the Government's interest in incentivising marriage is understood, in many cases, women who choose to keep their children do so for a variety of legitimate reasons. Consider that one alternative would have been for the women to abort their children, which could hardly be a preferable outcome. Another example of systemic injustice is a recent research report done by NUS Centre For Culture-Centered Approach To Research And Evaluation (CARE) and HealthServe, in which it was found that 86.2 per cent of the migrant workers surveyed shared that the food they received from food caterers had caused them to fall ill. About 94 per cent noted that the food received was unclean or unhygienic.[435] Underlying this phenomenon is (arguably) society's attitude towards foreign workers. Little or no thought is given to the infrastructure or other means to provide for such basic needs to foreign workers as daily food.[436] Such is an example of both systemic and cultural factors resulting in hardship to a marginalised group of people.

Fourth, poor decision-making may result in personal hardship. The lack of discipline, diligence and determination is likely to result in poverty for the individual and his family.[437] Also, addictions like drugs,

---

434 Amos 5:12; Ezekiel 22:29.
435 Valerie Koh and Marissa Yeo, "Catered food for foreign workers needs more regulation: Researchers", *TODAY* (12 June 2015), http://www.channelnewsasia.com/news/singapore/catered-foodfor-foreign/1909666.html.
436 Alex Au, "Poor deals over meals uncovering regulatory attitudinal and social shortcomings", *TWC2* (12 May 2015), http://twc2.org.sg/2015/05/12/poor-deals-over-meals-uncovering-regulatory-attitudinaland-social-shortcomings/.
437 Proverbs 6:6-11; 12:11; 13:4; 14:23; 19:24.

alcohol and gambling.[438] In a story from One Hope Centre,[439] a VWO that helps people with their gambling problems, a multi-millionaire suffered severe losses in his company but continued to gamble heavily, turning to theft, fraud and loan sharks for money to fuel his gambling addiction. Meanwhile, his father became ill, his wife suffered clinical depression, and his oldest son also got hooked on gambling. The oldest son turned to loan sharks, theft and embezzling his employer's money. Father and son both nearly ended their own lives. Thankfully the father turned to One Hope Centre for help. He persuaded his son to do likewise. They have since managed to quit gambling and their family has been restored.

In a survey conducted by the National Council on Problem Gambling in 2011,[440] it was found that 47 per cent of Singapore residents aged 18 and above participated in some form of gambling. Fifty-nine per cent of the respondents stated that they started gambling at the age of 24 or younger. On drugs, the Central Narcotics Bureau noted in 2014 that two-thirds of new drug abusers were below 30 years of age.[441] This has become a source of concern, so much so that a government taskforce is being set up to tackle this problem.[442]

---

438 Proverbs 23:21.
439 Woon Wei Jong, "Broken By Gambling, Reconciled in Hope" (One Hope Centre, 2010).
440 National Council on Problem Gambling, "Report Of Survey On Participation In Gambling Activities Among Singapore Residents 2011" (23 February 2012).
441 Central Narcotics Bureau, Press Release (26 January 2015).
442 "Task force to tackle youth drug problem", *The Straits Times* (8 November 2014).

B. Didn't God Allow the Suffering?

You may be wondering about this point: Is it not the case that God allowed suffering and hardship to happen to people in the first place? There are many good books written on the theological problem of pain,[443] and there is little else I can offer here. But this issue certainly deserves some attention given the nature and purpose of this book.

Over the years, I have increasingly found that it is almost meaningless to ask, why did God allow that suffering? That question with regard to an event is too abstract. Why did God allow the earthquake? Because creation is broken. Why did God take the man's life? Because physical death remains a present reality. Why did God not prevent it? Because that brings about absurdity in the world. These are all abstract questions with abstract answers.

Such questions can only be asked by the person undergoing suffering. And he must ask in the light of his life story in the hands of God. Because God's hand is moving in each individual life story. Hence it is impossible to ask at such a general level, why allow the earthquake? Yet, consider this: Why did some people survive the earthquake, and some not? Because God is at work in each individual's life story. History, after all, is not a systematic computer programme working itself out based on a series of causative events. History is a whole myriad of individual life stories and choices. It is true that in many cases, the individual may never have the answer to why they had to suffer. For some, they may eventually have the privilege of having the answer revealed to them in their lifetime. At the end of the day, each has to grapple with pain, loss, disappointment,

---

443 E.g., CS Lewis' *The Problem of Pain* and *A Grief Observed*; Phillip Yancey's *Where Is God When It Hurts?*; Ravi Zacharias and Vince Vitale, *Why Suffering?*; Timothy Keller's *Walking with God through Pain and Suffering*. Historically, many theologians have also offered their views on it. E.g., Thomas Aquinas, Augustine of Hippo, John Bunyan, John Donne, John Calvin.

fear and so on. And it is a pastoral, real, tangible problem, which requires pastoral, real, tangible responses, not abstract ones.

My wife's grandfather passed away at the height of his ministry work in missions and evangelism. Why did God take him away at that time? As someone who was not present during the time of his passing, I can see why. His death prompted each family member to pursue their God-given destinies and establish their own spiritual legacies. For Jesus said in John 12:24, "unless a grain of wheat falls into the earth and dies, it remains alone; but if it dies, it bears much fruit". Why did William Borden die before reaching China to fulfil his desire to evangelise to the Muslims in China? Because God had another plan in store to achieve his desire. Why did Jim Elliot and his friends die so early? Because God had a beautiful plan in store. Why did Chuck Colson get sent to prison for Watergate? Because God wanted him to start Prison Fellowship. So I think each life story has to be read in its own light, and in the light of God's hand in it. Ultimately each story is unique. Through the suffering, which He did not cause but allowed, He invites us to weave with him a beautiful story and ending.

It may sound morbid or sadistic to some people, but *suffering is the setting for beauty*. A particular incident in John 9:1-7 reveals this. God allowed a blind man from birth to undergo suffering and hardship not as a form of judgment on the man or his parents for their sins. Instead, Jesus said that His Father had allowed that so that "the works of God might be displayed in him". So that God could write a beautiful story of salvation. A similar incident occurred in Acts 3:1-10. The apostles Peter and John were going into the temple. They passed a gate where a lame man was begging for alms. What did Peter and John do? They did what Jesus did. They healed the lame man in Jesus' name. But Luke, the author of Acts, does not want us to miss anything. The name of the gate was "Beautiful".

Everyone nearby was "filled with wonder and amazement". Peter and John then followed in Acts 3:11-26 to preach the Gospel at Solomon's portico.

Suffering that people or Satan, who is ruler of this world in this age,[444] meant for evil, God allowed so that He can use it to accomplish good,[445] so that He can use it to author beauty.

That to me is also how I make sense of the Fall. He obviously allowed it to happen. God did not mess up. He did not forget to debug a potential virus in the system. In Genesis 1, God repeatedly said it was "good". Some people think it means "perfect". But the Hebrew word "*towb*" is associated with "beautiful" and "whole". The story He began at creation was beautiful. He allowed that beauty to be tarnished so that the grand story, in which each of our life stories are a part of, can descend into crisis. And only with a crisis can there be climax and resolution.

The late Christopher Hitchens once posed the question: How can God create you sick and command you to be well? But all the suffering and brokenness cannot be divorced from God's redemption plan in Jesus Christ. In Christ, we have a God who personally experienced suffering and brokenness with us. In Christ, we have a God who wept with us when He witnessed loss and grief.[446] In Christ, we have a hope of an eternal Kingdom where there will be no suffering, no grief, no death, no mourning and no pain.[447] And God allowed suffering and brokenness so that people can choose their own destiny: Choose to surrender life on earth to enter into an eternal Kingdom or choose life on earth to give up a beautiful eternity.

---

444 John 12:31; 2 Corinthians 4:4; Ephesians 2:2.
445 Genesis 5:20.
446 John 11:35.
447 Revelation 21:4.

Hence, God authored the story of human history to descend into crisis, only to rise in hope in Jesus Christ, and then climax and resolve in beauty.[448] The story cannot be complete and beautiful without the crisis. It would be meaningless. So I think *the answer to the problem of pain is this: Because God is working in our lives, pain will ultimately unfold into a story of hope and beauty.* But it would also be meaningless if we had no role to play, no choices to make in the story. And I think that's the most important matter we have to grapple with in the grand scheme of things.

In suffering and brokenness, there are two possible decisions we may make. The first decision concerns the self: Do we choose hope and look to a good God who is writing a beautiful story, or do we choose to believe that there is no God or He is an evil one? The second decision we may make concerns another person's suffering and hardship. Assuming you choose to hope in God, as God's human agent, what are you going to do about another person's suffering and hardship? God uses His people to be agents of His comfort. In 2 Corinthians 7:6-7, the Apostle Paul said: "... God, who comforts the downcast, comforted us by the coming of Titus and not only by his coming but also by the comfort with which he was comforted by you, as he told us of your longing, your mourning, your zeal for me, so that I rejoiced still more". This is God's response to suffering and hardship. Just as Christ, God Incarnate, came to us to respond to the world's suffering, you are

> **The question we must ask is this: Will I be God's response to injustice, suffering and brokenness?**

---

448 Revelation 21; see NT. Wright, *Surprised by Scripture: Engaging Contemporary Issues* (HarperOne, 2014), Ch. 11 at 197-206 where he discusses the Apocalypse and the beauty of God.

that response as representative of Christ. Hence, in the face of injustice, suffering and brokenness, the question we must ask is this: *Will I be God's response to injustice, suffering and brokenness?*

C. Principles of Biblical Justice

Cognizant of the causes of hardship and suffering, and fuelled by a motivation to respond to the world's suffering and hardship, it is then appropriate for us to consider the ethics and posture of seeking justice and mercy. We now turn to consider this in the light of what the Bible has to say about justice and mercy. As we have considered earlier in this book, biblical justice has an especial concern for the marginalised and weak.[449] But it is not necessarily only confined to these groups of people. The following principles are applicable to various situations. I have sought to non-exhaustively draw out key principles of biblical justice. For some of these principles, they are not derived solely from the biblical passages on *social* justice. It is important to bear in mind that biblical justice and righteousness are not *only* about social economic justice. They are situated within a larger framework of God's character, of the Gospel of God's Kingdom as well as of His design and determination of what is good and right, of *shalom*. Another important point is that while there may be biblical principles of justice, they are not meant to replace, but complement or circumscribe, practical wisdom and sound economics.[450]

Justice as Rights

Biblical justice has to be understood as a matter of rights. The "rights" I refer to includes *moral* and *legal* rights. In terms of God's justice, both

---

449 Zechariah 7:9-10; Matthew 25:31-46; Galatians 2:10; Luke 14:13; James 2:15-17.
450 Kevin DeYoung and Greg Gilbert, *What Is the Mission of the Church? Making Sense of Social Justice, Shalom and the Great Commission* (Crossway, 2011), 186-192.

are obligations, both are sin-and-righteousness issues. Legal rights are enforceable in human legal *systems*; moral ethical rights are not so enforceable, but God Himself ensures them. As I have sought to show in Chapter 3, God's enactment of justice, whether social justice or legal-adjudicative justice, was through the Mosaic Law in the Old Covenant. Justice was not a matter of "it would be good of you to do so". Justice was "you shall do this". It's significant that the same word "*mishpat*" not only translates as "justice" in the Old Testament, but also "judgment", "ordinance", "decision" and "rights", among others. For instance, Proverbs expresses the right treatment expected to be given to the poor, afflicted and destitute as "rights".[451] Likewise in Jeremiah 5:28, God rebukes His people for failing to "defend the *rights* of the needy".

Christian philosopher Nicholas Wolterstorff has sought in his books, *Justice: Rights and Wrongs*[452] and *Justice in Love*,[453] to conceive "justice as inherent rights".[454] Rights are "normative social bonds" situated within relationships between people, between people and God, within community.[455] Contrary to criticism that rights-talk "expresses... possessive individualism",[456] rights are intrinsically *social*.[457] Further, he refutes the false view that natural rights were an invention of 14th Century nominalist

---

451 Proverbs 29:7; 31:5; 31:8, 9.
452 Nicholas Wolterstorff, *Justice: Rights and Wrongs* (Princeton, NJ and Oxford: Princeton University Press, 2008).
453 Nicholas Wolterstorff, *Justice in Love* (William B Eerdman's Publishing Company, 2011).
454 Nicholas Wolterstorff, *Justice: Rights and Wrongs* (Princeton, NJ and Oxford: Princeton University Press, 2008),10-11.
455 Nicholas Wolterstorff, *Justice: Rights and Wrongs* (Princeton, NJ and Oxford: Princeton University Press, 2008), 5-6. Nicholas Wolterstorff, *Justice in Love* (William B Eerdman's Publishing Company, 2011), 86.
456 Nicholas Wolterstorff, *Justice in Love* (William B Eerdman's Publishing Company, 2011), 90-91.
457 Alasdair MacIntyre, *After Virtue* (Duckworth, 1981), 64-67, cited in Roger Ruston, *Human Rights and the Image of God* (SCM Press, 2004), 11-15.

philosophers or 17th-18th Century Enlightenment philosophers (and presumably justifies the Christian's aversion). Instead, natural rights were already found in the language of the 12th Century canon lawyers, the Church Fathers and in the Old Testament.[458]

The Church Fathers since the 4th Century had already articulated the language of *obligation* to the poor and needy. This view was premised on the notion that God created the whole earth as a common store for *all* human beings to share in. Ambrose of Milan wrote, "[e]verything belongs to God... It is God, therefore, who gives these things, and God himself who orders them to be shared with those who need them... This is justice: that one restore to the needy, because it is God who gives".[459] Thomas Aquinas, too, articulated, "[t]he temporal goods which God grants us, are ours as to the ownership, but as to the use of them, they belong not to us alone but also to such others to whom we are able to bring relief out of the things we have over and above our needs", then quoting Basil, "[i]t is the hungry man's bread that you withhold, the naked man's cloak that you have stored away, the shoe of the barefoot that you have left to rot, the money of the needy that you have buried underground: and so you injure as many as you might help".[460] Obligations have correlative rights. It followed in due course that the language of rights emerged as a matter of justice within the Christian tradition.

---

[458] Nicholas Wolterstorff, *Justice in Love* (William B Eerdman's Publishing Company, 2011), 91-92, referring to Brian Tierney, *The Idea of Natural Rights* (Atlanta: Scholars Press, 1997); Nicholas Wolterstorff, *Justice: Rights and Wrongs* (Princeton, NJ and Oxford: Princeton University Press, 2008), 44-90. See also Roger Ruston, *Human Rights and the Image of God* (SCM Press, 2004), 40-45.

[459] Commentary on 2 Corinthians, 9.9, (PL 17:313-314), Avila, Ownership, at 77 cited in Roger Ruston, *Human Rights and the Image of God* (SCM Press, 2004), 42.

[460] ST, 2a 2ae, Q. 32, art. 5 ad 2 (translation modified from the 1929 edn by the Fathers of the English Dominican Province), vol. 9, cited in Roger Ruston, *Human Rights and the Image of God* (SCM Press, 2004), 43.

The normative foundation for rights is the inherent worth of human beings grounded in them carrying the image of God (*imago Dei*).[461] It was the explicit rationale given by God for decreeing that no human being should suffer violation of the person.[462] To wound a human being is to wound God Himself.[463] This therefore distinguishes between on the one hand, good things which people may desire or deserve, and on the other hand, good things which must be guaranteed to the person regardless of the features he possesses. John Calvin also relied on the *imago Dei* as the basis for just treatment of every person. He wrote:[464]

> ... The Lord enjoins us to do good to all without exception, though the greater part, if estimated by their own merit, are most unworthy of it. *But Scripture subjoins a most excellent reason, when it tells us that we are not to look to what men in themselves deserve, but to attend to the image of God, which exists in all, and to which we owe all honour and love.* But in those who are of the household of faith, the same rule is to be more carefully observed, inasmuch as that image is renewed and restored in them by the Spirit of Christ. Therefore, whoever be the man that is presented to you as needing your assistance, you have no ground for declining to give it to him. Say he is a stranger. The Lord has given him a mark which ought to be familiar to you: For which reason he forbids you to despise your own flesh (Galatians 6:10). Say he is mean and

---

461 Genesis 1:27; Nicholas Wolterstorff, *Justice in Love* (William B Eerdman's Publishing Company, 2011), 150-157.
462 Genesis 9:6.
463 John Calvin, *Commentary on Genesis*, trans. John King, M.D (Calvin Translation Society, 1975).
464 John Calvin, *Institutes of the Christian Religion* (1536), Book III, Chapter VII, Section 6, http://www.ccel.org/c/calvin/institutes/institutes.html.

of no consideration. The Lord points him out as one whom he has distinguished by the lustre of his own image (Isaiah 58:7). Say that you are bound to him by no ties of duty. The Lord has substituted him as it were into his own place, that in him you may recognise the many great obligations under which the Lord has laid you to himself. Say that he is unworthy of your least exertion on his account; but the image of God, by which he is recommended to you, is worthy of yourself and all your exertions. But if he not only merits no good, but has provoked you by injury and mischief, still this is no good reason why you should not embrace him in love, and visit him with offices of love. He has deserved very differently from me, you will say. But what has the Lord deserved? Whatever injury he has done you, when he enjoins you to forgive him, he certainly means that it should be imputed to himself. *In this way only we attain to what is not to say difficult but altogether against nature, to love those that hate us, render good for evil, and blessing for cursing, remembering that we are not to reflect on the wickedness of men, but look to the image of God in them, an image which, covering and obliterating their faults, should by its beauty and dignity allure us to love and embrace them.* (Emphasis added)

On the basis of the *imago Dei*, and the view that all human beings are loved by God,[465] some have gone as far as to say that only Christianity provides a solid philosophical foundation for *universal* human rights,[466]

---

465 Nicholas Wolterstorff, *Justice in Love* (William B Eerdman's Publishing Company, 2011), 352-353.
466 Dawn Tan, "Christian Reflections on Universal Human Rights and Religious Values: Uneasy Bedfellows?", *Singapore Law Review 18* (1997): 217.

while others suggest that only certain religious worldviews provide such a foundation but not others, particularly non-religious worldviews.[467] Why? Because all other attempts to rationalise human rights involve grounding human worth on the basis of people's capacity. For instance, Immanuel Kant in *The Groundwork of the Metaphysics of Morals* posited that all humans have equal worth because they all have the capacity for rational autonomy. This is problematic because it follows that people who lose that capacity, for instance due to some infirmity, no longer possess inherent human rights.[468] What is notoriously difficult, however, is to agree on what constitutes inherent natural or human rights. I cannot deal with this issue here because it would require an extensive treatment. Suffice to say, most people today do not dispute the existence of natural or human rights. The contestation lies in the type, content and scope of rights.

Our discussion above leads us to a few implications. Firstly, if we have not already established this by now, I should make it clear that as Christians, we should understand justice as a matter of rights and obligations, as between us and God, and us and people. Justice is not a good-to-have.

---

[467] Michael J Perry, "The Morality Of Human Rights: A Nonreligious Ground?", Emory University School of Law, *Public Law & Legal Theory Research Paper Series, Research Paper No. 05-6*. Even atheists admit as such: Raimond Gaita, *A Common Humanity: Thinking About Love and Truth and Justice* (Routledge, 2000), 23-34; Arthur Allen Leff, Unspeakable Ethics, Unnatural Law, *Duke Law Journal (1997)*: 1129, 1149; Jeffrie Murphy, "Afterword: Constitutionalism, Moral Skepticism, and Religious Belief", in *Constitutionalism: The Philosophical Dimension*, ed. Alan S Rosenbaum (Praeger, 1988), 239, 248. Related to this idea is that historically, the edifice of civil political liberalism originated from, and was founded on, Judeo-Christian beliefs, principles and thought: See Harold Berman, *The Interaction of Law and Religion* (Abingdon Press, 1974); see also Norman Doe and Anthony Jeremy, "Justifications for Religious Autonomy" in Richard O'Dair, Andrew Lewis, eds., *Law and Religion: Current Legal Issues* vol. 4 (2001): 421.

[468] Nicholas Wolterstorff, *Justice in Love* (William B Eerdman's Publishing Company, 2011), 320-353.

Secondly, rights and obligations are never abstract or individualistic. They are necessarily grounded in context and they are social. If I were the only human being in this world, it would be irrelevant and meaningless to say that I have natural or human rights. The shape and texture of these rights and obligations are necessarily determined by the specific context of the community and its members.

Justice is Justly Seeking Moral Good
This principle of biblical justice is derived deductively rather than based on the exegesis of any biblical passages. In short, the principle is that justice must be sought justly and to obtain moral good. The deductive logic is as follows.

The reason why Christians should seek justice is because we are called by God to do so, as an expression of covenantal faithfulness, as an expression of our Kingdom citizenship. Justice-seeking is therefore merely a form of *living* justly. It should follow then that living justly should be our priority. It would be contradictory to seek justice unjustly because it would undermine the very duty of living justly. What then is the content of living justly or unjustly? It is the justice and righteousness of God as His Word reveals.

And seeking justice must be for the purpose of obtaining what is objectively morally good in people's lives. In other words, to love a person, to seek the *shalom* of a person, requires that we seek what is objectively good and right for the person, not what that person subjectively believes to be good and right for him. If a needy person requests you to chop off his arm for absolutely no reason at all, believing it to be good for him, it is unfathomable that justice requires you to do so. As Christians, our understanding of what is good and right must necessarily be informed by revelation from God's Word and divinely bestowed practical wisdom.[469] This is not to say that there will never be ethical conflicts. Given the fallen state of the world, it is inevitable that some form of harm could entail from attempting to pursue good. I do not profess to offer any comprehensive treatment of Christian ethics here.[470] However, I believe that ethical problems are never to be grappled with in the abstract. In actual situations of ethical conflict, I believe that our wise and loving God will enable us to make good and right decisions if we ask, or if not, He Himself will do what is good and right for us.

> **Justice must be sought justly and to obtain moral good.**

Justice is Personal Care

Jesus highlighted the Good Samaritan to show us that we must exhibit personal care. Christians have displayed such personal care for victims of hardship since the early Church. During the first two centuries, plagues were common, many victims died, and cities and provinces were abandoned and fell into ruin. The non-Christians would throw the sick out before they were even dead and treated their unburied corpses as dirt. In contrast, the Church nursed the sick and dying.[471]

In Singapore, many local churches and individual Christians set up voluntary welfare organisations (VWOs) which provide such personal care to meet immediate needs. Apart from VWOs, such personal care ministry often takes place at an informal personal level. Recently, an elderly man in

---

469 James 1:5.
470 See Normal L Geisler, *Christian Ethics: Contemporary Issues & Options* (Baker Academic, 2010).
471 Rodney Stark, *The Rise of Christianity* (Princeton University Press & Harper, 1996), 76, 83. Michael Nai-Chiu Poon, ed., *Pilgrims and Citizens: Christian Social Engagement in East Asia Today* (ATF Press, 2006), 96.

my church was beset with medical problems and had to be hospitalised. His wife suffered from the deteriorating condition of dementia. Their children were derelict in their filial responsibilities. Various individuals in my church took turns to send the wife to the hospital and prepare home-cooked meals for her and the children. The deacons raised the necessary funds for medical care and other expenses. The pastoral staff and deacons looked into finding a nursing home for the couple. Also, being concerned about the long-term financial sustainability for the couple, they explored various options to obtain passive income for the couple. They also arranged for the wife to execute a Lasting Power of Attorney (LPA) while she still had mental capacity. I was heartened to witness Matthew 25:35-36 and the Church as a community of justice and righteousness being practised. Biblical justice is personal care.

Justice Prohibits Exploitation and Protects Livelihood

Biblical justice prohibits exploitation, and protects livelihood and basic necessities. The Mosaic Law prohibits lenders from taking the borrower's means of livelihood as security,[472] or taking from the poor, the migrant workers, the widows and the orphans basic necessities of life such as clothes as security.[473]

The Mosaic Law obliges lenders to enforce debt (by taking possession of the loan security) in a dignified manner.[474] It also obliges employers (including employers of one-time service contractors) punctual payment of wages for poor hired labourers.[475]

---

472 Deuteronomy 24:6.
473 Deuteronomy 24:12-13, 17-18.
474 Deuteronomy 24:10-11.
475 Deuteronomy 24:14-15.

Justice is Generous Giving

Biblical justice is the generous giving of material provisions and money. The Christian's paradigm with regard to material wealth is that it is a gift from God.[476] Indeed, "For all things come from [God], and of [His] own have we given [Him]".[477] Wealth is given to us for proper stewardship to serve God and serve others.[478] The Christian can be generous in giving because he can trust in a God who provides.[479] Hence in Deuteronomy 15:4, God declares through Moses, "But there will be no poor among you; for the LORD will bless you in the land that the LORD your God is giving you for an inheritance to possess".

Generous giving may be by way of lending without interest.[480] The richer and more powerful are obliged to be generous to lend to the poor at no interest to the extent that the poor needs.[481] In Deuteronomy 15:7-8, it is declared: "If among you, one of your brothers should become poor, in any of your towns within your land that the LORD your God is giving you, you shall not harden your heart or shut your hand against your poor brother, but you shall open your hand to him and lend him sufficient for his need, whatever it may be." Recall also that the gleaning laws required landowners to reduce their own profits for the poor to work to pick up the leftover harvest.[482]

Biblical justice is also concerned with charitable donations, e.g., the triennial release of storehouses of tithe for the economically vulnerable,[483]

---

476 Leviticus 25:23; 1 Chronicles 29:12, 14.
477 1 Chronicles 29:14.
478 Recall the Parable of Talents; also 1 Peter 4:10.
479 2 Corinthians 9:6-15.
480 Deuteronomy 23:19; Exodus 22:25; Leviticus 25:36; Nehemiah 5:7; Psalm 15:5; Ezekiel 18:13.
481 1 Timothy 6:17-19.
482 Deuteronomy 24:19-21; Kevin DeYoung and Greg Gilbert, *What Is the Mission of the Church? Making Sense of Social Justice, Shalom and the Great Commission* (Crossway, 2011), 143-144.
483 Deuteronomy 14:28-29, Deuteronomy 26:12-15; Malachi 3.

alms giving or works of charity[484] and giving of financial relief.[485] It also involves redistribution[486] and communal sharing of property.[487] For the individual Christian, the amount to give is a matter of personal conviction,[488] bearing in mind that "it is more blessed to give than to receive"[489] and that "[w]hoever sows sparingly will also reap sparingly, and whoever sows generously will also reap generously".[490] The Christian is also to remember that he cannot serve both God and Mammon; he will hate one and love the other.[491] It is also significant that the apostle Paul considered that one purpose for work is that the Christian may have "something to share with anyone in need".[492]

A friend of mine shared with me a life-changing insight he received when serving as a deacon of his church and various church ministries had to present their budgets to the board of deacons. When the foreign missions ministry presented, he was shocked to realise that his monthly salary could fund the expenses of boarding and providing training and education for more than a dozen indigenous pastors in a neighbouring country. He realised then how much financial resources Singapore Christians have which can be used to bless the Church in neighbouring countries. Ever since then, he has actively organised gatherings to connect wealthy Christian individuals with Christian ministries and individuals. These relationships are to forge financial support partnerships for the

---

484   Matthew 6:2; Acts 9:36; Luke 11:40-42.
485   Acts 11:29; 1 Corinthians 16:1-2.
486   2 Corinthians 8:13-14.
487   Acts 4:32.
488   1 Corinthians 16:2; 2 Corinthians 9:6-15.
489   Acts 20:35; Luke 6:38.
490   2 Corinthians 9:6; Psalm 112:5; Proverbs 3:9-10; 11:24-25; Malachi 3:10. For a better treatment of godly stewardship of money, see David Wong, *Making Money Sense: God's Truth* (Armour Publishing, 2008).
491   Matthew 6:24; Luke 6:13; 1 Timothy 6:9-11.
492   Ephesians 4:28.

ministries or individuals in need. It only takes S$35 a month to support a child in Cambodia through World Vision. That's the cost of a meal for two persons at a casual dining restaurant. So while most of us may not consider ourselves rich, this perspective should prompt us to consider whether the verses discussed above pertaining to the richer and the poorer should apply to us.

Justice is Dignifying and Responsible

Biblical justice is dignifying and responsible. This has several facets. In summary, biblical justice empowers and builds capacity in people to work for themselves, take ownership of their circumstances, thereby encouraging them to live dignified and fulfilling lives.[493]

At an individual level, biblical justice encourages those who can work to provide for themselves. The gleaning laws illustrate this.[494] The laws could simply have obliged landowners to pick the harvest and set a portion aside for needy persons to take and go, but they did not. Instead, the laws specifically provided for needy persons to go to the fields to pick the harvest themselves.

At an interpersonal level, Deuteronomy 15:13-14 requires former creditors and masters to "furnish liberally" their liberated debt slaves with means of production and tools for livelihood.[495] In this sense, biblical justice is about capacity building.

At a structural level, biblical justice facilitates work by providing a way for otherwise socioeconomically disenfranchised families to

---

493 Michael Schluter, "Welfare" in Michael Schluter and John Ashcroft, *Jubilee Manifesto: A framework, agenda & strategy for Christian reform* (IVP, 2005) Ch. 10, p. 179; Kevin DeYoung and Greg Gilbert, *What Is the Mission of the Church? Making Sense of Social Justice, Shalom and the Great Commission* (Crossway, 2011), 151.
494 Deuteronomy 24:19-22, Leviticus 19:9-10 and 23:22; Kevin DeYoung and Greg Gilbert, *What Is the Mission of the Church? Making Sense of Social Justice, Shalom and the Great Commission* (Crossway, 2011), 143-144.
495 Trent C Butler, ed., *Holman Bible Dictionary* (Holman Bible Publishers, 1991), 828.

obtain a means of economic production. The families are then to apply their own diligent efforts to utilise these economic resources and provide for themselves. The Jubilee Law in Leviticus 25 illustrates this. The law provides for a reset of land distribution to the original allocation for families and clans and for debt slaves to be set free. This means that the families that would otherwise have been debt slaves would be free to work the land.

Biblical justice also encourages people to take responsibility of their circumstances and learn to exercise stewardship over assistance granted to them. For instance, lending rather than outright giving is the preferred mode of financial support in the Bible. Deuteronomy 15:7-8 provides that the Israelites were to "lend" to a poor Israelite "sufficient for his need, whatever it may be". Yet, the lending is to be at no interest.[496] Jesus went further to exhort us to do good by lending to even our enemies and expect no repayment.[497] This suggests that although the Christian lender is to be prepared that he will get nothing back in return, lending is generally still preferable to an outright donation. Lending ensures that the assistance is sustainable for the lender,[498] and also for the borrower in that it prevents dependency,[499] and encourages him to take ownership of his circumstances and work towards financial sustainability.

The above principles about dignified work and empowerment must be understood within a broader theology of work.[500] It should be understood

---

496 Leviticus 25:36-37; Exodus 22:24; Deuteronomy 23:20.
497 Luke 6:34-35.
498 David Wong, *Making Money Sense: God's Truth* (Armour Publishing, 2008), 82.
499 Paul Mills, "Finance" in Michael Schluter and John Ashcroft, *Jubilee Manifesto: A framework, agenda & strategy for Christian reform* (IVP, 2005) Ch. 11, p. 201.
500 See R Paul Stevens, *The Other Six Days* (Regent College Publishing, 1999); Timothy Keller, *Every Good Endeavor: Connecting Your Work to God's Work* (Riverhead Books, 2014).

that humans were made to work[501] and find fulfilment in work.[502] Being made in the image of God,[503] we would be like God just as God was and is a worker[504] who delighted in His work.[505] In Genesis 1:28-30, God calls humanity to "co-creativity", to work with Him in shaping the world, to "keep" or steward creation as God "keeps" us.[506] In fact, the biblical prophetic literature suggests that we will also be working in the new heavens and the new earth.[507] Unfortunately, when sin occurred in Genesis 3, the curse of sin is that work became painful[508]—it would most certainly be so since work often entails participation with other human beings who are sinful, flawed and therefore, quite literally, painful to work with. Despite the potential pain of work, it remains however that work is intrinsically "good for us, good for the world and good for God".[509] Further, work enables us to earn money to "share with anyone in need".[510] Dietrich Bonhoeffer suggests that work has a therapeutic value of freeing us from ourselves:[511]

> Work plunges men into the world of things. The Christian steps out of the world of brotherly encounter into the world of impersonal things, the 'it'; and this new encounter frees him for objectivity; for the 'it'-world is only an instrument in

---

501 Genesis 1:28; 2:15.
502 Ecclesiastes 3:13; 5:18.
503 Genesis 1:26-27.
504 Genesis 1-2; John 5:17; Revelation 21:5.
505 Genesis 1:31.
506 Genesis 2:15; Numbers 6:24; R Paul Stevens, *The Other Six Days* (Regent College Publishing, 1999) at 100, 113.
507 Isaiah 65:21-22.
508 Genesis 3:17-19.
509 R Paul Stevens, *The Other Six Days* (Regent College Publishing, 1999), 100, 124.
510 Ephesians 4:28.
511 Dietrich Bonhoeffer, *Life Together*, trans. JW Doberstein (New York: Harper & Row, 1954), 70.

the hand of God for the purification of Christians from all self-centredness and self-seeking. The work of the world can be done only where a person forgets himself, where he loses himself in a cause, in reality, the task, the 'it'. In work the Christian learns to allow himself to be limited by the task, and thus for him the work becomes a remedy against the indolence and sloth of the flesh. The passions of the flesh die in the world of things. But this can happen only where the Christian breaks through the 'it' to the 'Thou', which is God, who bids him work and makes that work a means of liberation from himself.

In short, work is dignifying, brings fulfilment, liberates the individual, and enables the individual to serve God and the world. It is no wonder then that biblical justice promotes work.

Dignifying justice can take shape in simple ways. For instance, purchasing products or services from a charity as opposed to making outright donations. A friend of mine wanted to support a social enterprise in Nepal which supports and empowers single mothers and trafficked women (Touch Nature Nepal). At the same time, she wanted to bless my wife and I for our wedding. She purchased a large batch of candles produced by the ladies at Touch Nature and arranged to have it delivered to us for use as our wedding door gifts. My friend could have simply made a donation. Some may argue that it would have been more sensible because the full sum of money would have been available to the social enterprise and perhaps more money could have been distributed to the ladies. But the ladies would not have had the satisfaction of putting the skills which they had painstakingly acquired to work and the thought that their work was valued.

I have so far used the terms "empower" and "capacity building". Of course, the Bible does not actually use these terms. To that end the biblical passages cited above are drawn based on an intersection of the deductive and the inductive, rather than pure exegesis. These concepts are in fact very modern concepts. But that is not to say that these concepts and frameworks are therefore unhelpful for the Christian pursuing social justice. Many Christian ministries and organisations have historically often adopted the best practices of doing good from their secular counterparts. This is, after all, consequent to the common grace which God blesses one and all with.

Further, there is arguably a theological basis for the Christian in empowering others. First, God empowers His people to do His will. This was the very *modus operandi* which Jesus had taken with His disciples during His earthly ministry.[512] And empowerment is intrinsic to the Great Commission[513] as it involves delegation of authority and the consequent enabling of the disciples to fulfil that mission. The Holy Spirit empowers and equips believers to do His work.[514] This is really an extension of God's creation mandate to humanity to participate in His creation work by stewarding the earth.[515]

Second, this same *modus operandi* of delegating, authorising and empowering was adopted subsequently by the apostle Paul. Paul did this with his two protégés, Timothy and Titus, leaving them to take charge of the churches at Ephesus and Crete respectively.[516]

This brief reflection on empowerment gleaned from the Bible also suggests to me that empowerment is not equated with independence.

---

512   Luke 10:19-20.
513   Matthew 28:18-20.
514   Acts 1:8; Ephesians 4:11-13; 1 Corinthians 12:7-11.
515   Genesis 1:28-30.
516   Titus 1:5; 1 Timothy 1:13.

Indeed, God empowers and commissions us but also desires us to *depend on Him*. Similarly, in apostle Paul's relationship with Timothy and Titus, they were empowered and delegated by Paul but nevertheless remained both dependent on God and also on Paul as a mentor and source of support. I think the practical implication is that *in empowering others, we should also point them vertically to dependence on God and horizontally to mutual support in their communities of care.*[517]

Justice and mercy require *respect* for the individuals and communities involved. They are after all fellow human beings made in the image of God. Over the years, I have learnt that respecting the individuals and communities we work with requires: A two-way street of learning; using the appropriate language and terminology in the appropriate context (for instance, "beneficiaries" as opposed to "partners"); listening more rather than offering one's own ideas and solutions; finding the best in the individuals and elevating that.[518]

One amazing initiative (not a Christian ministry) I came to know of which taught me much about relationship and empowerment is Diamonds on the Street (DOTS). The ministry was started by Crystal Goh, whose interview has been included in this book. I attended a performance organised by DOTS involving at-risk youths from a particular girls' residence. DOTS had

> **In empowering others, we should also point them vertically to dependence on God and horizontally to mutual support in their communities of care.**

---

517   For an elaboration on what empowerment and capacity building entail, visit the book's website section on "Empowerment and Capacity Building".
518   See also Micah Network, "Micah Network Declaration on Integral Mission" (2001).

been journeying with the girls over the prior six months, empowering them with the skills to write their own songs and stage their dramatic performances. They got professional recording engineers to record the girls' songs. The girls performed songs incorporated into a dramatic sketch reflecting their stories and aspirations. It was truly a beautiful performance. The girls' families, friends and probation officers were invited to the performance. DOTS curated the performance in a way that the audience members could participate in the performance. Tears were shed. Families embraced. Hope abounded.

Justice is Relational and Empathetic
Biblical justice is relational. It is contextualised in relationships, promotes relationship, and is grounded in compassion and empathy. The Mosaic Law provided for inclusion of the socially, economically and politically marginalised to participate in communal worship, e.g., celebration feasts before God's presence.[519]

The prohibition of charging interest on loans or profits on the provision of food effectively means that loans are charitable.[520] Or, the provision of money is a financial investment in a joint venture enterprise.[521] This means that the lender and borrower, or co-investors, share common interests, risks and profits. It is therefore a more equitable commercial relationship and arguably better for the overall economy as extremely risky enterprises would be discouraged.[522] This therefore incentivises the parties to maintain a good accountable relationship.

The example of Jesus' ministry also shows us the emphasis He placed

---

519   Deuteronomy 14:28-29; Deuteronomy 16:13-15; see also Galatians 3:26-29.
520   Exodus 22:25, Deuteronomy 23:19-20, Leviticus 25:35-37; see also Luke 6:34-35.
521   Paul Mills, "Finance" in Michael Schluter and John Ashcroft, *Jubilee Manifesto: A framework, agenda & strategy for Christian reform* (IVP, 2005) Ch. 11, pp. 204-207.
522   Paul Mills, "Finance" in Michael Schluter and John Ashcroft, *Jubilee Manifesto: A framework, agenda & strategy for Christian reform* (IVP, 2005) Ch. 11, pp. 204-207.

on developing relationships with socially marginalised persons. He was often found to have dined with tax collectors and other "sinners".[523] These people were social outcasts. Jesus specifically went to them because He said these were the ones who needed His healing.[524] Understanding the passages in context, He appears to mean that these were the persons who recognised their own need for Him. Why? Because they were the marginalised. This was in contradistinction to the religious teachers, who were way up there in the social hierarchy of the time. The example of Jesus dining with the tax collectors and sinners at their homes also suggests that Jesus was intentional about entering their social context. In a sense, a lesson can also be drawn from Jesus' Incarnation, being the Word made flesh,[525] as a fully divine yet fully human person.[526] John Stott says this teaches us that "we cannot stand aloof from those to whom we speak the gospel, or ignore their situation, their context. We have to enter into their social reality and share in their sufferings and their struggles".[527]

The triune community of love within the Holy Trinity is also a model of relational justice.[528] The notion of the Holy Trinity—the one essence and three persons of God the Father, God the Son and God the Holy Spirit—is central to the orthodox evangelical Christian faith, finding its heritage in the Nicene Creed of AD 325. The triune community of perfect fellowship and love justifies the theological declaration made by the apostle John that "God is love".[529] God is not merely *loving*; God is love itself. Since love necessarily involves a relationship between at least two persons, the notion

---

523 Mark 2:13-17; Luke 5:27-32; Matthew 9:10-13; Luke 19:1-10.
524 Mark 2:17; Luke 5:32; Matthew 9:13.
525 John 1:14.
526 Cf., Kevin DeYoung and Greg Gilbert, *What Is the Mission of the Church? Making Sense of Social Justice, Shalom and the Great Commission* (Crossway, 2011), 54.
527 John Stott, *The Contemporary Christian* (IVP, 1992), 349.
528 Thanks to Ng Zhi Wen and Jonathan Cho for highlighting this insight about the Holy Trinity and social justice.
529 1 John 4:8.

that God is love is only logically possible if God exists as a community of love. And since love necessarily requires right relationships and right conduct between persons, love necessarily requires social justice, that is, just conduct and egalitarian participation in a just community. Thus, the Holy Trinity is the embodiment of perfect relational, social justice which results in perfect *shalom* within the triune community of love.

What does this mean for us? First, the perfect triune community is a model for us in our relations of love and justice with one another. Hence the apostle John's bold assertion: "Anyone who does not love does not know God, because God is love". This is a huge statement. Anyone who does not love, who does not act justly, does not know God. Justice is therefore necessarily social and relational. Second, the perfect triune community is the source of our love and justice. In John 15, Jesus declares that as we abide in Him, He will abide in us. As the Father has loved the Son, so will the Son love us. And so shall we love the Son. And the Holy Spirit who comes from the Father will come to us and bear witness to the Son. So that we may bear witness to the Son. The triune community is therefore at work in empowering us to bear fruit—the fruit of the Gospel, the fruit of love and justice. Without this, we can do nothing.

The example of God the Father and God the Son, and the teachings of the apostles, also teach us that justice and mercy must be grounded in empathy and compassion. When God commanded the Israelites in the Mosaic Law to do justice, He reminded them first that the reason why they must give proper treatment to the orphans, widows or foreigners is because they themselves were once slaves and foreigners, oppressed in Egypt.[530] God was calling on the Israelites to first have empathy with the 'other' so that they were motivated by the emotional and moral

---

[530] Deuteronomy 24:17-18; Leviticus 19:33-35; Exodus 23:9. See Ken Wytsma, *Pursuing Justice: The Call To Live and Die For Bigger Things* (Thomas Nelson, 2013), 115.

compulsion of empathy and compassion to do justice. Empathy and compassion compel us to action. Even God Himself was moved by the cries of the Israelites enslaved in Egypt to concern and then to action.[531] The Scriptures paint the image of God stretching out His hands or extending His holy arm to act because of His compassion.[532] In the gospels, we see that on many occasions, Jesus was moved with compassion so much so that He took action.[533] Hebrews describes Jesus as one who empathises with our human weaknesses even as our great High Priest in heaven.[534] In Romans, the apostle Paul exhorts believers to rejoice with those who rejoice and weep with those who weep.[535] This is after all to reflect the character of God, who heals the brokenhearted and binds up their wounds.[536]

A particular ministry (which shall not be named) comes to mind. It has been ministering to local sex workers in Geylang for the past five years. They go out every week to walk the streets, praying and talking to the ladies. Over time, they have developed a close friendship with the ladies, getting to know their families, their personal spaces and their work places. They have invited the ladies to try an alternative route by learning skills such as baking and jewellery making, and other life skills, such as, communicating in English and social etiquette. It has been a long and tiring journey for the core volunteers (they are all volunteers) at the ministry. There were many instances of the ladies leaving and returning and leaving again. There were many complex social, emotional and relationship issues. But over time, the investments have paid off. The ladies are beginning to see alternative futures for themselves and their

---

531 Exodus 2:23-25.
532 Exodus 3:20, 7:5, 15:12; Isaiah 52:10.
533 Luke 7:13; Matthew 9:36, 14:14, 15:32, 20:34; Mark 6:34; John 11:34-38.
534 Hebrews 4:15.
535 Romans 12:15.
536 Psalm 147:3.

families. They send their children to a partner ministry for nurturing and education. They are working together with the ministry to build their family relationships. Their ministry illustrates the need to understand justice and mercy as primarily about journeying with the people we seek to love.

Another example relates to a friend of mine who has a ministry to homeless persons. He and other volunteers would go out weekly to hang out with the homeless persons. Recently, my friend shared about a homeless man who had been friendly but was staunch in his own religious beliefs. My friend had been reaching out to him for several months. The man pulled my friend aside and told him that he felt his life was nothing because he was a drunkard. My friend shared with him the Parable of the Prodigal Son. The man leaned forward and whispered, "Now I want to be a Christian." My friend then prayed with him, after which he said, "Now I feel very peaceful." He shared that he felt so much power that evening that he simply had to believe in Jesus. Praise God! This was the work of months of relationship with this homeless man, the work of much prayer support, and the work of God.

Justice is Restorative and Reconciliatory
Biblical justice is about restoration and reconciliation. An illustration of this is Exodus 21:18-19: A person who physically assaults another is obliged to ensure that his victim is "thoroughly healed". Also, people charged with certain crimes are to make restitution to the victim.[537] The Jubilee Law in Leviticus 25 also promotes restoration and reconciliation of familial relationships.

---

537   Leviticus 6:1-7; Exodus 20:16; 22.

The Kingdom Gospel itself also presents a view of restoration and reconciliation of relationships.[538] Those who believe in Christ are reconciled with God.[539] Christ also tore down all prior hostilities and reconciled all divided factions, ethno-national groups and did away with all distinctions, to draw the whole world to Him.[540] Christians and the Church are thus to seek the reconciliation and redemption of the world with God,[541] bringing people into the Kingdom of God. In the Corinthian church, the apostle Paul implored the church to restore, "forgive and comfort", and "reaffirm [their] love" for a man who had been disciplined for sin but had been sufficiently punished and come to repentance.[542] In the Beatitudes, Jesus said: "Blessed are the peacemakers, for they shall be called sons of God".[543]

The Christian tradition of peacemaking has been one of the foundations for restorative justice initiatives (both Christian and secular) in many countries and in various spheres, including criminal justice (e.g., Church Council on Justice and Corrections in Canada), family justice, Truth and Reconciliation Commissions (TRCs) in war-torn nations (e.g., South Africa's TRC headed by Desmond Tutu), and bridging marginalised communities (e.g., Maori communities in New Zealand).[544] Restorative justice seeks to restore victims, offenders and communities. This takes place through

---

538   Christopher Townsend, "Believing in Justice" in Jonathan Burnside and Nicola Baker, eds., *Relational Justice: Repairing the Breach* (Waterside Press, 1994), Ch. 11; Pierce Allard and Wayne Northey, "Christianity: The Rediscovery of Restorative Justice" in Harold Coward, ed., *The Spiritual Roots of Restorative Justice* (Albany, New York, State University of New York Press, 2001), 119-141.
539   2 Corinthians 5:18.
540   Ephesians 2:14-18.
541   Colossians 1:15-20; 2 Corinthians 5:18-21.
542   2 Corinthians 2:5-11.
543   Matthew 5:9.
544   See generally John Braithwaite, "Restorative Justice: Assessing Optimistic and Pessimistic Accounts", *Crime & Justice* 25.1, 1999; Jonathan Burnside and Nicola Baker, eds., *Relational Justice: Repairing the Breach* (Waterside Press, 1994).

various processes including mediation, healing circles (bringing an entire community with an offender and victim to discuss restoration of relationships and address broader underlying issues), restorative probation and family group conferences (offender and victim along with their respective families come together to work out ways to deal with the harms caused). The verdict on such processes remains tentative as they produce significant advantages and also disadvantages.[545] Nevertheless, restorative justice processes are viable options and approaches to respond to social justice issues.

Justice is Deliverance: It Destroys the Tools and Systems of Oppression
Biblical justice exhorts the indictment of oppressors, the dismantling of tools and systems of oppression, and the rescuing of victims from oppression.[546] Stephen Mott and Ronald Sider observe that biblical justice is "not a mere mitigation of suffering in oppression, it is a deliverance. Justice involves rectifying the gross social inequities of the disadvantaged".[547]

The International Justice Mission (IJM) exemplifies this. A Christian global non-governmental organisation (NGO), it serves victims of violence: Human trafficking, sexual violence, police brutality, property grabbing, and citizen rights abuse.[548] IJM employs the following four-fold methodology to seeking justice.[549]

---

545 See John Braithwaite, "Restorative Justice: Assessing Optimistic and Pessimistic Accounts", *Crime & Justice* vol. 25, 1999:1.
546 Job 29:17; Psalm 10:15; Luke 4:18-20; Jeremiah 22:3.
547 Stephen Mott and Ronald Sider, "Economic justice: A biblical paradigm", *Transformation* 17.2 (2000): 50-63, 54.
548 For anyone who wants to learn more about various practical strategies of addressing injustice and oppression, I would commend the following books by the founder of IJM, Gary Haugen: *Good News About Injustice* and *Just Courage: God's Great Expedition for the Restless Christian*.
549 Gary Haugen, *Good News About Injustice: A Witness Of Courage In a Hurting World* (IVP, 2009), 172-186.

Victim rescue: The IJM Kenya team helped prove the innocence of a man who was tortured by the police to confess to a bank robbery he did not commit. He was released after three-and-a-half years in prison, went to university and after graduation, joined IJM as staff.

Perpetrator accountability: In another case in Kenya, IJM worked with a mother of a six-year-old girl who was raped by a man from their village. The police did not want to press charges. The community had experienced several such incidents, so this was a deep wound for them. The IJM worked to bring the matter to justice. The man was eventually sentenced to 12 years in prison. This has brought hope for justice and a safer community. Perpetrator accountability is not just delivering a single victim from oppression. It is also removing a source of oppression for many others. It also allows the perpetrator to face up to his wrongs and hopefully repent of them. Romans 13:4 makes it clear that the purpose of state power is precisely to punish evil and wrongdoing. This is the manner by which God enacts order in society.

Victim aftercare: Departing from the IJM examples, Hagar International Singapore operates a Trauma Recovery and Safe Transit and Resettlement Programme for victims of trafficking and abuse. Hagar supports the victims by facilitating trauma-focused socio-medical intervention, equipping them with life skills and job skills for potential employment, and arranging for safe transit and resettlement back in their home countries.

Structural transformation: Perpetrator accountability is one form of structural transformation because it removes the source of oppression. Building capacity and political will in communities and government agencies is also structural transformation, e.g., IJM provides training to police forces in various countries on professional ethics, victim treatment and best practices. In some African communities, IJM has trained local pastors to protect widows and orphans from property-grabbing by others in the community. These pastors would stand up for the widows and ensure that they are able to obtain the inheritance they are entitled to and not be thrown out of their own homes or land. They are also taught to help teach their congregation to do up wills to prevent such property-grabbing interlopers. Another form of structural transformation work is advocacy, to which we turn next.

Justice is Advocacy: Being a Voice for the Voiceless

Biblical justice involves advocating for the weak. It is about being a voice for the voiceless.[550] Advocacy is precisely what the Holy Spirit does on our behalf.[551] Prayer is in itself a form of advocacy. We pray to God *on behalf of others*, and in so doing love them and love God. In this respect, the Bible uses the word "intercession" to describe prayer and also advocacy. Jesus is described as interceding for us as our High Priest before the Father.[552] Moses interceded on behalf of the Israelites to petition God to take away the serpents harming them.[553] In Genesis 18:22-33, Abraham interceded on behalf of Sodom to seek God's mercy upon the city. Jeremiah, in Jeremiah 29:17, urged the exiled Jews to

> **Biblical justice exhorts the indictment of oppressors, the dismantling of tools and systems of oppression, and the rescuing of victims from oppression.**

---

550 In Isaiah 1:17, God demanded His people to "plead the widow's cause". In Proverbs 31:8-9, the King was instructed to "Open your mouth for the mute, for the rights of all who are destitute. Open your mouth, judge righteously, defend the rights of the poor and needy". And Job declared that he "took up the case of the stranger": Job 29:16.
551 Romans 8:26.
552 Hebrews 7:25; Romans 8:34.
553 Numbers 21:7.

"pray to the Lord on… behalf" of Babylon, the city they were subjugated in.

Advocacy can take many forms. There is advocacy for structural and systemic transformation, involving legislative, policy or cultural change. Advocacy need not be public, loud or brash. Various VWOs and NGOs in Singapore engage in advocacy work through both private and public consultations with the Government, e.g., One Hope Centre worked with the Government in a committee to look at policies relating to moneylenders. HealthServe provides the Government with feedback and engages in private consultations on various issues relating to migrant workers, including issues of public health, dormitory conditions and work safety, etc. I discuss more on advocacy in the public square in Chapter 8.

Advocacy can also be through cultural change. My wife, a professional theatre actress, acted in a play titled *Tribes* staged by Pangdemonium. The play centred on a deaf young man with hearing, i.e., non-deaf, family members. In the course of her preparation for the show, she invested much time researching on the deaf community, deaf persons and children of deaf adults (CODA). She also learnt sign language from an inspiring deaf lady. The production was not only deemed a success by critics and reviewers, it was also lauded for raising awareness about the deaf community. During the show's run, my wife got to befriend members of the local deaf community. Many people who watched the show expressed how through the show they learnt about the struggles deaf people go through, which they would otherwise have never known about. Cultural advocacy takes place in all forms. Art and journalism are two powerful means of such cultural advocacy because they are often non-didactic but, if done well, can grip the imagination and rouse the empathy of people.

Then there is also interpersonal advocacy. We need not be lawyers or civic activists to do interpersonal advocacy. All we need to do is to listen to the people we serve and understand their social and economic reality.

Then we are able to help them to explain their needs and context to the relevant stakeholders. The very act of translating and communicating their needs, issues, thoughts and feelings, is in itself a form of advocacy An example would be accompanying a person to seek help at a government agency and explaining the person's needs to the agency.

There is, also, of course legal advocacy. Legal advocacy has especial significance in the Christian faith because the Bible uses legal language to describe Jesus' role as our advocate before God the Father.[554] Who is the prosecutor? None other than Satan, the accuser.[555] And the saints who are accused (this is probably all of us Christians) overcome the accuser by the blood of the Lamb, Jesus Christ, and the word of their testimony.[556]

To deny access to *legal* justice is a form of *social* injustice. That is not to say that "justice" is "law".[557] But in the modern context where the bureaucratic State regulates most of our lives through the law, *de facto* disability to access the law breeds injustice. Hence the need for *pro bono* legal services.[558]

Justice is Responsible Stewardship of Creation

Biblical justice entails responsible stewardship of creation.[559] In Leviticus 25, the Lord emphasises that all the land which the Israelites possessed belonged to Him. They were only stewards of the land. This harks back

---

554 1 John 2:1; Romans 8:34.
555 Revelation 12:10.
556 Revelation 12:11.
557 For the different aspects of the 'access to justice' movement, see: Ronald Sackville, "Some Thoughts on Access to Justice" (2004) 2 *New Zealand Journal of Public and International Law* 85; Christine Parker, "Access to Justice" in *Just Lawyers: Regulation and Access to Justice* (Oxford: Oxford University Press, 1999), Ch. 3; Stephen Bottomley and Simon Bronitt, *Law in Context*, 4th edn (NSW, Sydney: The Federation Press, 2012) Ch. 5.
558 For an elaboration, see book's website section on "History of Pro Bono Legal Advocacy".
559 See Pope Francis's "Encyclical Letter Laudato Si of the Holy Father Francis on Care for our Common Home" (2015).

to the creation stewardship mandate—God gave the whole earth to humanity for their stewardship, and to work the garden of Eden and to "keep it".[560] The Psalmist declares rightly that the whole earth is the Lord's.[561]

God's laws regarding creation reveal not only His concern for creation but also His expectation that His people share this same concern.[562] In Jesus' teachings, he referred to God's provision and care for the sparrows and the birds of the air.[563] God's love for creation has been described by Dante Alighieri as "love that moves the sun and the stars".[564] Stewardship of God's creation is a direct expression of loving the Creator God.[565]

On one level, biblical justice requires that people treat creation fairly and equitably. The mandatory Sabbath years are for the land to have "solemn rest".[566] Mind you, *not only* rest for the *people*. But rest for the *land*. Similarly, the Sabbath rest is intended for the "ox and donkey".[567]

It would be presumptuous to think that because animals and plants cannot communicate verbally with humans, they can be treated *unjustly*. On the contrary, the fact that God made covenants with the animals suggests that they are capable of receiving and reciprocating justice.[568]

Further, the ultimate destiny of humanity and creation are interwoven. Humanity's sins have a profound spiritual and physical effect

---

[560] Genesis 1:28-30; Genesis 2:15.
[561] Psalm 24:1; Deuteronomy 10:14.
[562] Deuteronomy 22:4, 6.
[563] Luke 12:6; Matthew 6:26.
[564] *The Divine Comedy*, Paradiso, Canto XXXIII, 145.
[565] See Francis A Schaeffer, *Pollution and the Death of Man* (Crossway Books, 1992).
[566] Leviticus 25:4-5.
[567] Exodus 23:12.
[568] Genesis 9:8-10; Hosea 2:18.

on creation.[569] The bondage and futility which creation is subjected to was the result of Adam's sin, and God's consequential curse in Genesis 3.[570] Yet, as the destiny of humanity is glory in God's perfected Kingdom, so also is creation's destiny.[571] Creation is not destined for destruction but for redemption, as human bodies are destined for resurrection and glorification.[572] In Isaiah's prophetic vision of the perfected Kingdom, he sees creation and humanity living in *shalom*.[573] Isaiah's prophetic vision of the New Heaven and New Earth is repeated again in the Revelation to John.[574] In Revelation 21:5, God declares, "Behold, I am making all things new". The references in the passage to the original creation suggests that the state of creation in Revelation is a reversal of the curse on creation.[575] So in the perfected Kingdom, creation will be renewed, and the relationship between creation and humanity will be reconciled into a state of *shalom*.[576] Creation will rightly honour and glorify God.[577]

But what has this discussion on creation got to do with social justice? Irresponsible stewardship of creation has a direct impact on people. As mentioned earlier, the poor are vulnerable to environmental degradation because they often do not have the means to mitigate any suffering or injustice caused by environmental changes. In a November 2015 World

---

569   Romans 8:19-22.
570   Genesis 3:17–19. See also Isaiah 24:4-6.
571   Douglas Moo, "Nature In the New Creation: New Testament Eschatology and the Environment", *Journal of the Evangelical Theological Society* 49/3 (September 2006) 449, pp. 461-462.
572   1 Corinthians 15:42-53.
573   Isaiah 11:6-9; Isaiah 65:25-26.
574   Revelation 21. See also 2 Peter 3:13.
575   Douglas Moo, "Nature In the New Creation: New Testament Eschatology and the Environment", *Journal of the Evangelical Theological Society*, 49.3 (September 2006): 466.
576   See also Colossians 1:19-20.
577   Isaiah 43:18-21; Psalm 148:3-5.

Bank report,[578] it was estimated that if climate change continues at present levels, about another 100 million people will be pushed into poverty within 15 years. This is due to the likely impact of climate change on the increase in frequency of natural disasters, losses in agricultural yield and rising food insecurity, and increased prevalence of diseases. The report estimates that food prices may rise by 12 per cent due to climate change by 2030, severely affecting poor households in Sub-Saharan Africa who spend as much as 60 per cent of household income on food.

Conversely, humanity's proper care of creation in the present world will result in a harmonious relationship which not only pleases God,[579] but also blesses humanity. One amazing story with regard to humanity's relationship with creation is the story of Christian the Lion.[580]

Christian was a lion acquired by Harrods department store in London. He was then sold to John Rendall and Anthony "Ace" Bourke in 1969 (yes, in the past, department stores stocked lions for sale). When Christian grew too big for them to manage, they arranged for Christian to be reintegrated back into the wild. In 1971, John and Ace travelled to Kenya to visit Christian. They were warned that Christian might not remember them. He could therefore be dangerous. When John and Ace arrived in Christian's territory, Christian was initially cautious but as he recognised his former owners, he leapt playfully onto the two men, nuzzling their faces. Christian's two lionesses and a cub also welcomed the two men. In 1973,

---

578 Stephane Hallegatte, Mook Bangalore, Laura Bonzanigo, Marianne Fay, Tamaro Kane, Ulf Narloch, Julie Rozenberg, David Treguer, and Adrien Vogt-Schilb. *Shock Waves: Managing the Impacts of Climate Change on Poverty*. Climate Change and Development Series (Washington, DC: World Bank, 2016).

579 Douglas Moo, "Nature In The New Creation: New Testament Eschatology and the Environment", *Journal of the Evangelical Theological Society* 49/3 (September 2006): 449, pp. 481-482.

580 Victoria Moore, "Christian, the lion who lived in my London living room", *The Daily Mail* (4 May 2007); Mike Celizic, "'Hugging' lion's ex-owners reflect on his legacy", *Today* (30 July 2008); URL to Youtube video of documentary recording the men's first reunion: https://www.youtube.com/watch?v=cvCjyWp3rEk.

the two men returned to look for Christian. By this time, Christian was full grown, leading his own pride, and had several cubs of his own. At the reunion, Christian knocked the men over and embraced them.

This story of human beings expressing such love for animals and receiving love in this manner is a glimpse of the renewed state of creation as depicted in Isaiah 11 and 65, deepening our conviction about our future shared destiny in the New Heaven and New Earth, and about the blessing of love which we will enjoy in companionship with creation.

> **In the perfected Kingdom, creation will rightly honour and glorify God.**

Further, the interconnectedness of every inhabitant of this world mediated through the environment, and the possible impact of any small, seemingly insignificant variable in the environment, means that our individual personal actions may contribute to a significant impact on our neighbours living across the globe (think Butterfly Effect). This takes the second Greatest Commandment to "love our neighbour" to a global and yet microscopic dimension. While our personal actions may appear to have insignificant impact on the environment, such attitudes should be placed in perspective—if entire communities and cities of people change their lifestyles, significant change could happen.[581]

Care for creation is also a means of pursuing intergenerational justice. If nature and natural resources are seen as a common gift for all of humanity, including past, present and future generations, ensuring the

---

[581] It is reported in 2011 that Singapore has the 27th largest carbon footprint per capita, possibly the 2nd largest in South-East Asia: "CO2 Emissions from Fuel Combustion - 2011 Highlights", OECD/International Energy Agency, 2011. In 2014, the World Wide Fund for Nature found that Singapore had the 7th largest ecological footprint, i.e., the population's demands on natural resources, in the world: Laura Elizabeth Philomin, "Lion City's green ranking worsens", *Today Online* (7 October 2014).

sustainability of nature's resources is a form of doing justice and passing on equity to future generations. It is important to also recognise that when I refer to nature's "resources", I do not *only* mean resources as instrumental for humanity's use or exploitation. Instead, nature's resources must be appreciated for its own value. Nature's biodiversity and beauty are inherently valuable as God's creation, and as resources for humanity.[582]

Responsible stewardship of creation has a direct bearing on humans, especially those who are made vulnerable because of poverty and unfulfilled basic material needs. Responsible stewardship and the application of biblical social justice principles necessarily results in sustainable lifestyles and practices, a sustainable economy, and consequently, fair and equitable access to basic provisions made available to the poor and needy.[583]

Justice is Practical Wisdom and Virtue

Biblical justice is also chiefly practical wisdom and virtue.[584] Wisdom is given by God for "guarding the paths of justice".[585] Justice is not only about statutes and precedents but also practical wisdom, as illustrated by King Solomon's split-the-baby decision.[586] Jethro's advice to Moses on establishing a legal adjudication system and selecting delegated judges also shows that not only is justice a matter of wisdom, it is also a matter of virtuous character.[587]

---

582   Pope Francis's "Encyclical Letter Laudato Si of the Holy Father Francis on Care for our Common Home" (2015) at paras. 33-34.
583   See Alex Evans and Richard Gower, "The Restorative Economy", *Tearfund*, "Theology: For a Just and Sustainable Economy", 2015.
584   Jonathan Burnside, *God, Justice and Society* (Oxford University Press, 2011), 111; Daniel Koh, "Justice: A Christian Social Ethical Perspective" in Daniel Koh and Kiem-Kiok Kwa, *Issues of Law and Justice in Singapore* (Armour Publishing, 2009), 17-18; Robert F Cochran, David VanDrunen, *Law and the Bible: Justice, Mercy and Legal Institutions* (IVP, 2013), 111-119.
585   Proverbs 2:6-8; Proverbs 8:15-16.
586   1 Kings 3:16-28.
587   Exodus 18:13-27.

D. Biblical Justice and Contemporary Theories of Justice

Evident from the superficial survey above, biblical justice contains certain values, ethics and principles. I do not think they necessitate that we adopt a particular economic or political philosophy.[588] Others have attempted to at least extrapolate these principles to a larger normative vision for contemporary society.[589] Whether the Bible compels Christians to adopt a *comprehensive* normative vision for society today, I think it is up to the individual Christian's interpretation and convictions. However, it is worth considering how some of these biblical principles of justice interface with significant contemporary theories of justice. The reason is that many of these contemporary theories of justice do influence how social justice is understood and practised in the world today. I have discussed these contemporary theories of justice in relation to biblical social justice on the book's website's section on "Biblical Justice and Contemporary Theories of Justice". Philosophers covered include John Rawls, Ronald Dworkin, Amartya Sen, Martha Nussbaum, Peter Singer and Michael Walzer.

It is important, I think, to be acquainted with other contemporary theories of justice because as Christians engage in social justice, we will inevitably encounter, engage, partner or challenge people who hold different religious and ideological convictions. This is most acute when the Christian pursues social justice in the public square. To that we now turn.

---

[588] See Robert F Cochran, David VanDrunen, *Law and the Bible: Justice, Mercy and Legal Institutions* (IVP, 2013), 111-119.

[589] Michael Schluter and John Ashcroft, *Jubilee Manifesto: A framework, agenda and strategy for Christian reform* (IVP, 2005).

Chapter Summary

- The Bible shows different causes of hardship: (i) Interpersonal; (ii) vicissitudes of life; (iii) systemic and cultural; and (iv) poor personal choices. Often hardship is multi-causal and complex.
- Suffering is the setting for beauty.
- The answer to the problem of pain is this: God allows suffering because He is writing in our lives through suffering a story of hope and beauty.
- The question we must ask is this: Will I be God's response to injustice, suffering and brokenness?
- The principles of biblical justice are:
  - Justice is rights;
  - Justice is justly seeking moral good;
  - Justice is personal care;
  - Justice is generous giving;
  - Justice is dignifying and responsible;
  - Justice is relational and empathetic;
  - Justice is restorative and reconciliatory;
  - Justice is deliverance: It destroys the tools and systems of oppression;
  - Justice is advocacy: Being a voice for the voiceless;
  - Justice is responsible stewardship of creation;
  - Justice is practical wisdom and virtue.

Discussion Questions

1. Which Bible passages caught your attention? What did you learn from those passages? What implications would those biblical truths have on your life?
2. What did you learn about biblical justice? How would these lessons affect your life and worldview?
3. How are the above biblical principles of justice being expressed in your life and your faith community? Which of them are missing in your life or faith community?
4. What is your response to God in the light of what you have gleaned from these truths?

INTERVIEW:
Associate Professor Irene YH Ng

● ● ●

Irene YH Ng is an Associate Professor of Social Work in the National University of Singapore and Director of the Social Service Research Centre. She holds a joint PhD in Social Work and Economics from the University of Michigan. Her research areas include poverty and inequality, intergenerational mobility, youth crime, and social welfare policy. She is Principal Investigator of an evaluation of a national Work Support programme and Co-Principal Investigator of National Youth Surveys 2010 and 2013. She is engaged in various committees, for instance, in the National Youth Council, the Chinese Development Assistance Council, Ministry of Social and Family Development, National Council of Social Service and Ministry of Manpower. Her teaching areas include poverty, policy, youth work and programme planning.

1. Do you think that social justice is a key expression of the Christian faith? Why or why not?

Yes, because God is love and God is just. When we say "God is just", people tend to think of God punishing individual sins, such as theft, murder and sexual immorality. But at the heart of God's justice is His love. A just God cares that those who are oppressed, marginalised and vulnerable are not being unjustly treated. Thus, God's justice is ultimately about social justice. Even the laws in the Bible that on the surface seem to be about individual sins are ultimately about how we relate to others; they are "social". Therefore, the greatest commandment is to love the Lord our God with all our heart, soul and mind; and to love others as ourselves (Luke 10:27). If God's main command is to love Him (who is loving and just) with our whole being, and to love others as ourselves, how can social justice not be the key expression of a follower of Jesus?

2. What is the distinctiveness (if any) of Christian social justice, as opposed to secular social justice?

God's redemptive love, mercy and sovereignty. Based on the principles of love and mercy, Christian social justice shows more grace and generosity than secular social justice. Because of His sovereignty, we can do so unconditionally and with the hope that God will prevail. We do not hold back from loving the oppressed for fear that they will take us for a ride. Instead, we keep loving just as God keeps loving and forgiving us.

3. What do you personally do as an expression of social justice?

My goal in life is to live simply and invest in the poor. I make purchases and lifestyle choices that keep life simple and expenses low so that the money I save can be used to bless the poor and people who work with the poor. I try to base decisions on relationships: How does my decision affect my loved ones, those around me, or others who might be affected by my decision, e.g., the poor? For example, I try not to patronise organisations that I know treat workers unfairly, and I choose to live in an HDB neighbourhood that gives me closer access to community with others.

4. How do you ground or relate your work and research in or with your faith?
Prayer is key, seeking God each day and asking Him to lead me to do the right thing in terms of relationships and the larger good, not self-gain (many times I fail). I see my work as a calling, a vocation from God. My research is on poverty, so I constantly seek God on how my research can "defend the poor" by revealing truths based on data, and not based on my own biased judgment. I teach social work, and my prayer as a teacher is that He leads me to inspire and equip my students to do good well. In all, I pray that I bring Him glory, which is not easy in a secular setting.

5. What do you think is the individual Christian's role in relation to social justice?
If social justice is a key expression of the Christian faith, then every Christian has a responsibility to play his part. We must live counterculturally. We must talk about the vulnerable differently from others, emphasising grace and not deservingness. We must show generosity in the giving of our money, time and other resources, and confess our tendency to hoard for self-gain.

I once attended a workshop in a missions conference where the speaker said that in today's capitalist society, it is not just "the love of money that is the root of all evil" (1 Timothy 6:10), but that money is the root of all evil. I kind of agree with that. The proliferation of wealth and material comfort in a society like Singapore makes it difficult for us to free ourselves from the need to keep up with the Joneses. In such a context, we almost need to treat money as harmful. That's the starting point, I think. As Hebrews 13:5,6 says: "Keep your lives free from the love of money and be content with what you have, because God has said, "Never will I leave you; never will I forsake you", so we say with confidence, "The Lord is my helper; I will not be afraid. What can man do to me?" (NIV)

6. How do you think Singapore Christians have fared in relation to social justice?

The Singapore Church is mainly middle class and rich. We live such segregated lives from the vulnerable in Singapore society. Unfortunately, Protestants have been the ones who have over-emphasised individual responsibility and deservingness. But I think churches have practised social responsibility. Corporately, churches have been one of the most generous in terms of funding and providing social services. The challenge is to get Christians to be passionate about, and involved in, social responsibility other than by monetary support.

8

Should Our Ideas of Social Justice be Brought into Society? Justice and Righteousness in the Public Square

... not just to bandage the victims under the wheel but to put a spoke in the wheel.

—Dietrich Bonhoeffer[590]

A. The Anti-Trafficking Advocacy Experience

In Singapore, there is this unspoken sentiment that ordinary citizens should stay out of politics. We might get into trouble with the authorities if we dabble in politics, or so we think. Many of us are therefore afraid to raise *policy* issues for debate. I myself, perhaps being risk-averse in personality, was afraid of discussing policy issues in public. However, my perspective changed when I began to get involved in efforts against one of the major social ills in the world today: Human trafficking.

In battling the scourge of human trafficking, it is not feasible to depend solely on individuals or civil society organisations. This is because human trafficking involves dealing with organised crime, gangs, triads and so on. Rescuing victims is a highly dangerous activity. In one

---

[590] Edwin H Robertson and John Bowden, eds., *No rusty swords; letters, lectures and notes, 1928-1936, From the Collected works of Dietrich Bonhoeffer* (Collins, 1965), 225.

story recounted by Bridget Tan, founder of Humanitarian Organisation for Migration Economics (HOME), she had to stealthily meet with a young sex worker who had been trapped in makeshift brothels in forested areas. It was dangerous terrain. It was therefore crucial for government policy changes to be made so as to specifically address such enforcement issues. Further, fighting human trafficking cannot only involve victim rescue. It requires prosecution of the perpetrators. Before 2014, Singapore had no legislation that sufficiently dealt with the heinous act of human trafficking. Convinced that this was a gaping hole in our legal system, I wrote an article published in a local legal academic journal highlighting this, arguing for a specific omnibus statute which addresses human trafficking.[591] I was not the only one advocating this. There were many activists from various civil society groups, such as HOME, Transient Works Count Too (TWC2) and Singapore Committee for United Nations (UN) Women, who were doing their part to engage with the Inter-Agency Taskforce for Trafficking-in-Persons set up by the Singapore Government. In the end, constructive change came about in 2013. Member of Parliament Christopher de Souza, who is a professing Roman Catholic, announced that he would be introducing a Private Member's Bill on human trafficking. How did this come about? In an interview, he revealed that a lady came up to him at a wake and asked him, "What are you doing about human trafficking?"[592] That started an exploratory journey for him. He shared that in his journey, he visited a shelter run by Catholic nuns who selflessly take care of trafficking victims. That for him was the ethos behind the Bill on trafficking: "If

---

591 Ronald JJ Wong, "A Critique of International and Singapore Legal Treatments of Trafficking in Persons", *Singapore Journal of Legal Studies* 179, July 2014.
592 Rachel Au-Yong, "Christopher de Souza: If I can save one person, it will be worth it", *Singapolitics* (18 October 2014) at http://www.singapolitics.sg/supperclub/christopher-de-souza-if-i-can-save-one-person-it-will-be-worth-it.

it could save just one person, deter a syndicate from bringing in just one person, it would be worth all the effort." On 3 November 2014, the Prevention of Human Trafficking Act (POHTA) was successfully passed as law in Singapore. The POHTA is only the beginning of a long road against trafficking, but perhaps it has already served to deter perpetrators from trafficking.

This short account of how POHTA was enacted exemplifies for me a very simple idea. If we truly want to bring about justice and righteousness, we must inevitably engage at all levels: Providing personal care for victims of injustice, and lending a voice to victims in advocating for policy and legislative changes to protect them, ensure their wellbeing, and deter future wrongdoing. This short account also exemplifies for me that advocacy need not be *political*, in the sense that one need not be a *politician* or join a political party, to bring about change. We could be like that lady who went up to Christopher de Souza and asked him a searching question, "What are you doing about... ?" We could be like the Catholic nuns running a shelter for victims of injustice, and through that work, highlighting the needs and issues that the victims face to the people who can bring about policy and legislative changes. We could write papers or articles that propose policy and legislative changes. Or, we could be like the civil society activists who engage with the Government in private consultations and public forums. By doing so, we would not be getting involved in partisan politics. Instead, we would merely be fulfilling our roles as citizens in dialoguing about policy. This is one form of engagement in the public square. Is there justification in our Christian faith for us to engage in the public square? I believe so.

In this chapter, I reflect on how Christians are to be salt and light of the world in the public square as a means of loving God and loving neighbour. In pursuing this aim, I believe that civil dialogue should be the procedure, process and point of public square engagement. Such a paradigm is grounded in, and motivated by, a respect for the *imago Dei* in every person.

B. Salt and Light in the Public Square

Jesus instructed His disciples to be salt and light of the earth.[593] I have often heard it bandied around in Christian circles and rhetoric. It has been used to justify everything from American exceptionalism and her participation in war to picketing outside abortion clinics. Surely this salt and light goal cannot be so limitlessly broad? Hence, I resolved to investigate this matter. What did Jesus mean by being salt and light of the earth?

Salt is a curious mineral. In the Bible, it was used to preserve[594] and to add taste.[595] It was required for Israelite offerings to God.[596] It was used to make a conquered land lie in waste.[597] It was a figurative symbol of barrenness[598] and given its preservative nature, a metaphor for perpetuity, a promise of fidelity; hence the term, a "covenant of salt" between God and His people.[599] Related to that is an old Middle Eastern notion of salt covenants as covenants of friendship. Also, the disinfectant nature of salt is associated with the notion of purification.[600] Hence Jesus said in Mark 9:49 that "everyone will be salted with fire". And in the same

---

593 Matthew 5:13-16.
594 Exodus 30:35.
595 Job 6:6.
596 Leviticus 2:13; Ezekiel 43:24.
597 Exodus 9:45.
598 Deuteronomy 29:23; Zephaniah 2:9; Psalm 107:34; Jeremiah 17:6; Ezekiel 47:11.
599 Numbers 18:19; 2 Chronicles 13:5.
600 Ezekiel 43:24.

passage, Jesus said in Mark 9:49, "[h]ave salt in yourselves, and be at peace with one another". There are so many different associations and usages for salt! Suffice to say, trying to understand what Jesus meant by salt based on the biblical-historical usage of salt is going to be a frustrating exercise.

Reading Jesus' usage of the word "salt" in context, however, gives us a clue. In Matthew 5:13, Jesus said, "You are the salt of the earth, but if salt has lost its taste, how shall its saltiness be restored? It is no longer good for anything except to be thrown out and trampled under people's feet." A few observations are worth highlighting.

First, although some commentators suggest that reference to "the earth" is reference to salt as a fertiliser for the soil,[601] I do not think this makes sense given the reference to "taste". If salt is used as fertiliser, taste is irrelevant. Instead, I think Jesus meant "the earth" as "the world". Jesus was likely using the rhetorical device of parallelism in verse 13 and verse 14, "you are the light of the world".

Second, it appears then that Jesus was referring to salt as a taste enhancer. This is congruent with Paul's exhortation in Colossians 4:6 to "[l]et your speech always be gracious, *seasoned with salt*, so that you may know how you ought to answer each person".

Third, it is likely that Jesus' reference to salt was not meant to explicate what His disciples were supposed *to be*, but rather, what they were *not supposed to be*. And if we take Matthew 5:13 to dovetail with Luke 14:34-35, then this reading makes sense. In Luke 14:34-35, Jesus was effectively saying, if you are not salty, you will not only be rejected as a taste enhancer; you will not even be used as a fertiliser. What were Jesus' disciples not supposed to be? As salt, they were not supposed to

---

[601] Norman Hillyer, "Salt" in Colin Brown, ed., *The New International Dictionary of New Testament Theology* (Paternoster Press, 1978); Eugene P Deatrick, "Salt, Soil, Saviour", in *The Biblical Archaeologist* 25 (1962).

lose their saltiness. As Jesus' disciples, they were not supposed to lose their essential characteristic of being Christians. Apparently, in the ancient Middle East, salt would be diluted with other compounds and therefore lose its saltiness. What does it mean to not be diluted in faith? Reading the Matthew 5 and Luke 14 passages together, this becomes clearer. In both passages, Jesus' exhortation about salt is preceded by a teaching on the expectations for Jesus' disciples in God's Kingdom: In Matthew 5, the Beatitudes; in Luke 14, bearing one's own cross. Therefore, as Jesus' disciples, we are not to be diluted in our faith, or else we would be useless to the world. This was the nub of Jesus' exhortation here.

What about light? Jesus said in Matthew 5:14-16: "You are the light of the world. A city set on a hill cannot be hidden. Nor do people light a lamp and put it under a basket, but on a stand, and it gives light to all in the house. In the same way, let your light shine before others, so that they may see your good works and give glory to your Father who is in heaven." Jesus' instructions reveal two aspects about the light which His disciples are supposed to be: (i) Verses 14-15: The obviousness of its presence; (ii) verse 16: Its nature and purpose.

We'll begin with (ii) nature and purpose. The light of Jesus' disciples is reflected in their "good works" (nature) for people to see so that the world may praise the glory of God (purpose). Indeed, Jesus Himself declared in John 8:12 that He is the light of the world. He epitomises, and is the perfect paradigm of, what it means to be God's people—to do good works that all the world may see and give glory to the Father. For Jesus called His own ministry work "good works".[602] What are "good works"? They are acts which benefit others in love and in a morally good way. Tabitha or Dorcas was "full of good works and acts of charity".[603] Good

---
602   John 10:32.
603   Acts 9:36.

works is to bring up children, show hospitality, wash the feet of saints, and care for the afflicted.[604] It is to be generous and ready to share our wealth.[605] It is to do as Jesus did—to heal, to love, to include, to teach, to preach, to give worth, to honour, and so on. The imperative to do "good works" cannot be understated. We are God's creative masterpiece, created in Christ Jesus to do, walk in, immerse in, the good works which God prepared beforehand for us to do.[606] We are called to be *zealous* to do good works.[607]

> ●●●
> **To be salt and light of the world is to live such good lives, in moral conduct and good works, that we are obviously distinctive and have impact on the world.**

The result is that the goodness of Jesus' disciples, as reflected in their moral conduct and "good works" cannot possibly be hidden.[608] It's not about being showy or about personal vainglory, as prohibited by Jesus.[609] Instead, to be salt and light of the world is to live such good lives, in moral conduct and good works, that we are obviously distinctive and have impact on the world.

So why did Jesus tie salt and light together in the same instruction? One might suppose it is because loving neighbours by being salt and by being light, by speaking truth and by living truth,[610] by proclaiming righteousness and

---

604 1 Timothy 5:10.
605 1 Timothy 6:18.
606 Ephesians 2:10.
607 Titus 2:14; see also 1 Timothy 2:10; 5:25; Titus 2:7; 3:8; 3:14; Hebrews 10:24.
608 See also 1 Timothy 5:25.
609 Matthew 6:1-4.
610 Soren Kierkegaard, "Truth is the Way" in Charles E Moore, *Provocations, Spiritual Writings of Kierkegaard* (Plough Publishing, 2002).

by demonstrating righteousness, must be intrinsically bound together in a disciple for the glory of God. One without the other is hypocrisy at worst. Even at best, a Christian would have no credibility, no legitimacy, to speak in the public square. The world is watching. The world is judging. Are we salty enough and bright enough in the public square for the world to declare praises to our God?

C. What is the Public Square?

Most human settlements have some form of public square, e.g., town halls, city halls and marketplaces, which often forms the central locus of communal activity. In Chinese clan villages, a house containing the clan's ancestral urns often constitutes the town hall. In the Bible, the *agora* translated in the NLT as "public square"[611] is generally referred to as the "market" or "marketplace" in other translations (ESV and NIV). It is where economic transactions took place;[612] where labourers waited for hire;[613] where children played;[614] where food was sold;[615] where the governing authorities presided.[616] During the Old Testament times, the elders of the town would sit at the city gates at the public square.[617] The "public square" in the Bible is also a physical space freely accessible to the public, where the local community could gather.[618] Hence, there were so many people at the marketplace whom Jesus could heal.[619]

---

611 Acts 17:17.
612 Ezekiel 27:24.
613 Matthew 20:3.
614 Matthew 11:16-17.
615 1 Corinthians 10:25.
616 Acts 16:19.
617 Job 29:7; Proverbs 8:3-5.
618 Deuteronomy 13:16; 2 Samuel 21:12; Job 30:28; Proverbs 1:20; Matthew 11:16; 20:3; Mark 12:38; Matthew 23:7.
619 Mark 6:56.

Two points on the public square are worth our attention. First, *the public square was a space where people could dialogue or debate with one another.*[620] Second, *truth and wisdom must prevail in the public square for there to be justice and righteousness in the community.*[621]

The public square is the space freely accessible to the local community in which the life of the community occurs—where members of the community dialogue, and where truth and wisdom ought to prevail for justice and righteousness to flourish in the community. In our present time, such spaces are not merely physical-geographical, e.g., literal public places. They may be platforms for public dialogue e.g., public lectures, public consultations, and in Parliament. They may also be intangible and mediated through various media, e.g., the Internet, newspapers, social media, books, music and films. The latter part of the aforesaid definition of public square is intuitively common sense to me. If truth and wisdom are not present in Parliament, for instance, Singapore would be in danger of passing senseless and unjust laws.

D. The Christian's Mandate: Express God's Love and Truth Through Word and Deed in the Public Square to the Glory of God

How then should Christians relate to the public square? Should Christians bother to participate in the public square? If so, how should Christians engage?

---

620 Acts 17:17.
621 Isaiah 59:14; Proverbs 1:20.

A Platform to Love by Communicating the Gospel

In Acts 17:16-17, Paul saw the idol-worship going on in Athens and he was "provoked" in "his spirit" to share the Gospel with people in the synagogue and the marketplace/public square "every day". The philosophers there heard Paul's preaching in the public square and summoned him to the Council of Areopagus so as to determine whether to add Paul's deity to their pantheon of gods. There, Paul engaged the Council and shared the Christian worldview adopting the language of the Athenians, using cultural references to two works of Greek literature.[622] Several persons who heard Paul, including a Council member, became convinced of the Gospel.[623] Paul loved the people of Athens so much so that he went every day to the public square to share the Gospel. Yet, one must be cognizant of the *manner* in which Paul engaged the Athenians; I elaborate on this below.

Also, Bruce Winter suggests that the apostle Peter had exhorted his audience to do good deeds among non-believers in the *public sphere* as *citizens* so that they too may acknowledge and glorify God and so that the foolish ones would be silenced.[624]

By presenting the Christian worldview in the public square in a winsome manner, we are pursuing the Great Commission and the Great Commandments.

---

622 Epimenides of Crete and Aratus's poem "Phainomena", http://spindleworks.com/library/rfaber/aratus.htm.
623 Acts 17:34.
624 1 Peter 2:12, 15. Bruce Winter, "Pilgrims and Citizens: The Paradox for the First Christians" in Michael Nai-Chiu Poon, ed., *Pilgrims and Citizens: Christian Social Engagement in East Asia Today* (ATF Press, 2006), 30-31.

A Platform to Love Neighbours and Love Ourselves by Shaping Public Matters Informed by God's Loving Truth

Loving neighbours as ourselves

To the Judeans exiled to Babylon after they had been conquered by King Nebuchadnezzar, God gave them a word which must have been puzzling given the circumstances. In Jeremiah 29, they were told to settle down in Babylon—build homes, plant gardens, start families; they would be there for 70 years. And in Jeremiah 29:7, God told them: "Seek the welfare [*shalom*] of the city where I have sent you into exile, and pray to the Lord on its behalf, for in its welfare you will find your welfare".[625]

The context in Jeremiah 29 and our context today are similar. The Jews were transient residents in a foreign kingdom. We are transient residents or 'resident aliens' in an earthly kingdom. The Christians in the early Church also recognised this. In an anonymous Epistle to Diognetus, a 2nd Century letter, the author wrote that Christians "reside in their respective countries, but only as aliens. They take part in everything as citizens and put up with everything as foreigners. Every foreign land is their home, and every home a foreign land".[626] Similarly to the subjugated Jews in Babylon, our beliefs and values are sometimes in opposition to the beliefs and values of the state or the people around us. In that context, the Jeremiah 29:7 principle tells us: If you seek the *shalom* of the city, if you contribute to public matters that which accrues benefit to the city, you will benefit. Therein lies the principle of mutual benefit. Although we live as exiles, as subjugated peoples, as transient sojourners, *seek the* shalom *of the city because therein we will find our shalom.*

---

[625] Paul Barnett, "Jesus, Paul and Peter and the Roman State" in Michael Nai-Chiu Poon, ed., *Pilgrims and Citizens: Christian Social Engagement in East Asia Today* (ATF Press, 2006), 72-73.

[626] Daniel KS Koh, "Resident Aliens and Alienated Residents" in Michael Nai-Chiu Poon, ed., *Pilgrims and Citizens: Christian Social Engagement in East Asia Today* (ATF Press, 2006), 126-127.

Public matters informed by God's loving truth

In the case study at the start of this chapter, I mentioned how various people and groups were advocating for anti-human trafficking policies and legislation. Why? Because they believe that it was good and right to benefit the victims of human trafficking. And this was a matter of public policy and importance. I believe that promoting good and right public policies, programmes and cultural norms is to love others. The question is: What are good and right policies?

I believe that the truth revealed by the Sovereign Creator God is good and right. A digital preservation technician I met recently told me about how in the 1990s a NASA scientist wanted to review data from soil samples collected on Mars in 1975. To his horror, the data had been misplaced and backed up in huge magnetic tapes in a format so old that the programmers who were familiar with it had died. So the scientist could not access the data on the magnetic tape. God designed and programmed the world. But He is not dead. Who better to know how to operate the world, to know what is good for the world, than the all-knowing designer Himself? It would follow that ethical, social, economic or political views informed by God's truth would also be good and right for the world. This would be the case even if the world may not accept its source or moral authority. Hence, I believe that *contributing to public matters as informed by biblical truth is loving our neighbours.* Jeremiah 29:7 therefore contains a specific application of the Second Greatest Commandment to love our neighbours as ourselves.

Christ and culture, God's Kingdom and earthly kingdoms

Yet, contribute to public matters to what end? Surely not to build utopia on earth? There are nuances to this general proposition, which I will not go into detail here. But they are important nuances. We need to think biblically, rigorously and comprehensively about the role of civil government when thinking of public policy. And when one considers political theology, it is inevitable that one would have to consider the relationship between God's Kingdom and earthly kingdoms. One might think of Richard Niebuhr's *Christ and Culture* (1951) which DA Carson has attempted to evaluate from a purportedly Bible-centric lens in *Christ and Culture Revisited* (2008). One might think of Augustine's *De Civitate Dei, City of God* (5th Century AD), Martin Luther's Two Kingdoms/Governments doctrine in *On Secular Authority—To What Extent We Owe It Obedience* (1523), John Calvin's Two Kingdoms doctrine as reflected in, among others works, *The Institutes of the Christian Religion* (1536). The limitations of this book prevent me from elaborating further.[627] But allow me to sketch a superficial picture of the possible views which political theology present to us.[628] In the Lord's Prayer, Jesus taught His disciples to pray, "Your kingdom come, your will be done, on earth as it is in heaven". The unanswered question is: How was God's Kingdom to come on earth?[629]

The first possible view is that God's Kingdom is wholly distinct and separate from earthly kingdoms such that God's Kingdom people should have nothing to do with earthly kingdoms at all.[630] Simply evangelise to

---

[627] These monumental works, no matter how great they are for their time, must be parsed through the Word of God and the Holy Spirit. It is a simplistic anecdote but it is worth remembering that the German Christian National Socialists sought to fuse Nazi ideology with Christian theology, relying on Martin Luther's work as precedent, justifying heinous wrongs.

[628] See Elizabeth Phillips, *Political Theology: A Guide for the Perplexed* (T&T Clark International, 2012).

[629] This is a different issue of how the State should relate with the Church. In summary on this issue, there have been 4 main models: (1) Erastianism: The State controls the Church; (2) Theocracy: The Church controls the State; (3) Constantinianism: The State favours the Church and the Church accommodates to the State to receive that favour; (4) Partnership: Church and State recognise each other's distinct spheres in constructive collaboration: See John Stott, *The Message of Romans* (IVP, 1994), 339.

[630] Martin Luther's two kingdoms doctrine is an example of such a view: Elizabeth Phillips, *Political Theology: A Guide for the Perplexed* (T&T Clark International, 2012), 57-71.

people and then make them live in separation from the world. On this view, it does not even matter that there is injustice in earthly governments and societies.[631] Instead, Christians are to live their own lives of faith in their own isolated communities. The problem with this is that it appears to be unbiblical and unfeasible.[632] Even the Quakers, who in the early 17th Century initially held firmly to the view that they should have nothing to do with politics of the world, ultimately embraced politics, beginning with politician William Penn in the later half of the 17th Century and culminating in US President Richard Nixon in the 20th Century.[633] The Quakers were pacifist abolitionists who participated in the Civil War and the anti-slavery cause surreptitiously by assisting in the Underground Railroad for emancipated black slaves to escape to safety. This illustrates how separatism is inevitably contradictory to the biblical injunction to love our neighbours.

The second possible view is that God's Kingdom is to be expressed through earthly kingdoms, though not necessarily replace them. On this view, Christians are supposed to seek to transform earthly institutions into conformity with Kingdom principles and values. This might be done by way of imposing cultural preferences of certain Christian groups through legislative, judicial and ecclesiastical processes to transform society, what TM Moore described as "culture triumphalism".[634] The problem with this is that one would be hardpressed to find support in the Bible

---

631 Indeed, Martin Luther's two kingdoms doctrine has been criticised to have justified the German Church's silence and passivity in the face of the totalitarian Nazi regime: Elizabeth Phillips, *Political Theology: A Guide for the Perplexed* (T&T Clark International, 2012), 59.
632 In 1 Corinthians 5:9-10, the Apostle Paul clarified to the Corinth church that he did not mean for them to disassociate with immoral people of the world because then they "would need to go out of the world". Implicit in Paul's reasoning was that it was not tenable at all for Christians to live in complete isolation from the world.
633 See Frederick B Tolles, "Quakerism and Politics", The Ward Lecture, 1956.
634 TM Moore, *Culture Matters: A Call for Consensus on Christian Cultural Engagement* (BrazoPress, 2007), 14.

for such a duty on Christians. It may be an *outcome* arising from Christian faithfulness, but it does not appear to be an intended *goal* of faithfulness. Examples of God's people in positions of power and influence in earthly kingdoms who could have possibly achieved this are Joseph in Egypt and Daniel in Babylon. In both cases, the biblical writers did not describe them as seeking to transform the institutions of the empire they served in. Indeed, they did not even seek to dismantle the dominant religious institutions of those empires, let alone transform the wider societal culture. Instead, the themes that the biblical writers emphasised in their stories were their faithfulness in their worship of God, their faithfulness in carrying out their duties as servants of their earthly kings, and how the sovereign God carried out His divine purposes as regards Israel through these individuals.

The third possible view is a more extreme version of the second, which is that God's Kingdom is to altogether replace earthly kingdoms. The closest that came to this, though not completely accurate, was the Christianisation of the Roman Empire post-Constantine in the 4th Century. This is not only unbiblical, it is also contradictory to Jesus' remarks about rendering unto Caesar what is Caesar's and rendering unto God what is God's,[635] and that His Kingdom is not of this world.[636] Furthermore, the history of God's covenant people as recorded in the Bible suggests that as a matter of fact (not as a norm), God's people have almost always been a minority in pluralistic earthly kingdoms. As a matter of feasibility, even ancient Israel's theocratic system of governance instituted through Moses ultimately failed. In Acts 1:6, the apostles appeared to still miss the big picture when they asked Jesus, "Lord, will you at this time restore the kingdom to Israel?" They were still thinking that Jesus came to establish

---

635 Mark 12:17; Matthew 22:21.
636 John 18:36.

an earthly kingdom of Israel. Jesus' answer appears enigmatic but the latter events in the New Testament show that the apostles subsequently understood His words to mean that His Kingdom was hardly one which resembled any earthly kingdom or empire.

A fourth possible view is that the focus should be on the individual person, who is both a citizen in God's Kingdom as well as a citizen in the earthly kingdom. God's Kingdom is at once separate from, but also overlaps in different spheres with, earthly kingdoms.[637] However, for the individual Christian, God's Kingdom is over and above earthly kingdoms, even though the latter may seek to limit or persecute the former.[638] As a citizen of the earthly kingdom, the Christian pays his dues to the state in accordance with his citizenship obligations, to the extent that there is no contradictory obligation or principle in God's Kingdom.[639] Indeed, a contextual exegesis of certain Scriptural passages suggests that Christians should voluntarily subject themselves to state authority *even despite persecution* and suffering caused by the state,[640] but never when compelled to do anything contrary to God's standards of righteousness. So while the Gospel is subversive, it does not promote civil anarchy.[641] As a citizen of God's Kingdom, the Christian expresses his faithfulness to God

---

637 This could be seen as grounded in Augustine's two cities doctrine in his monumental work, *City of God*.

638 The earthly kingdoms are all subject to the sovereignty of God, and are in fact servants of God: Romans 13:4, 6; Isaiah 45:1; Daniel 4:17; John 19:11.

639 Mark 12:17; Matthew 22:21; Romans 13:1-7; Acts 4:18, 5:29; 1 Peter 2:13, 17; Exodus 1:17; Daniel 3; Daniel 6; see John Stott, *The Message of Romans* (IVP, 1994) at 338-347.

640 Michael F Bird, "One Who Will Arise To Rule Over The Nations: Paul's Letter to the Romans and the Roman Empire" in Scot McKnight and Joseph B Modica, eds., *Jesus is Lord Caesar is Not: Evaluating Empire in New Testament Studies* (InterVarsity Press, 2013), 158-160, citing Romans 5:3-5, 8:18, 31-39, 12:14, 17, 13:1-7; Judith A Diehl, "Anti-Imperial Rhetoric in the New Testament" in Scot McKnight and Joseph B Modica, eds., *Jesus is Lord Caesar is Not: Evaluating Empire in New Testament Studies* (InterVarsity Press, 2013), 57.

641 Judith A Diehl, "Anti-Imperial Rhetoric in the New Testament" in Scot McKnight and Joseph B Modica, eds., *Jesus is Lord Caesar is Not: Evaluating Empire in New Testament Studies* (InterVarsity Press, 2013) at 57.

by seeking to live out and express what is of the Kingdom. He would also seek to love others by seeking to express Kingdom values and principles in earthly institutions. But it is motivated by love. His motivation is not to seek to convert every earthly institution into what he thinks to be Kingdom ones. This is not to say that the latter outcome is not supposed to happen. It might happen. But that is not the point. The Christian pursues this aim while fully aware that before Christ's return to consummate God's Kingdom,[642] he will not be able to, nor even hope to, transform all earthly institutions to Kingdom ones.[643]

Having grappled with these views for some time, I am personally inclined to the fourth view above. I think it is the most biblically coherent and supported.[644] First, the Bible speaks of God as the one who creates a new heaven and a new earth;[645] Jesus Christ as the one who makes all things new.[646] It is neither the Church nor humanity. Secondly, an exegetical study of the verbs and adjectives relating to the Kingdom reveals that it is God who establishes and ushers in His Kingdom, not us.[647] Our primary response to the Kingdom is to enter it and then manifest it.

> **It is God who establishes and ushers in His Kingdom, not us.**

Irrespective of which of the above views one takes, if injustice is passed off as justice and human laws that contravene

---

642 Matthew 24:30-31.
643 See generally Oliver O'Donovan, *The Desire of the Nations: Rediscovering the Roots of Political Theology* (Cambridge University Press, 1999); John Howard Yoder, *The Politics of Jesus* (Eerdmans, 1994); Elizabeth Phillips, *Political Theology: A Guide for the Perplexed* (T&T Clark International, 2012) at 13-23.
644 Kevin DeYoung and Greg Gilbert, *What Is the Mission of the Church? Making Sense of Social Justice, Shalom and the Great Commission* (Crossway, 2011), 128-134.
645 Isaiah 65:17.
646 Revelation 21:5.
647 George Eldon Ladd, *The Presence of the Future* (Eerdmans, 1996), 193.

Natural Law[648] are administered in the earthly kingdoms, there will inevitably be harm. As discussed in Chapter 4, if a person of God stands by and does nothing in the face of injustice, he has sinned. And it violates the Second Greatest Commandment to love our neighbour. On this view then, the reason why God's Kingdom people should rectify injustice and advocate what is good and right in the public square is *out of love* and an *expression of covenantal faithfulness* to do justice. It suffices also for us to remember that neither the State nor the Church is absolute, which many theologians in the Church's history such as Augustine, Luther, Calvin, Bonhoeffer and others have been consistently clear about. Only God is absolute. That has to be the chief qualification to all our political theology. As Andy Crouch observes:[649]

> [T]he question is really not whether we will have empires (we will) or whether they will endure (they will not), but what *kind* of empires we will have in this time between the times. Will our empires succumb entirely to the idolatry of power and the lust for domination that comes when human beings explicitly cast off their accountability to the Creator God? Or will they be chastened by the vision of [the] tree [in Daniel 4:20-21]? … It is only when the Most High is scorned or forgotten that judgment comes, 'until you have learned that the Most High has sovereignty over the kingdom of mortals, and gives it to whom he will' (Daniel 4:25)…
>
> The ethicist Oliver O'Donovan makes the perceptive observation that the resurrection of Jesus, vindicating him as

---

648 Romans 2:14-15.
649 Andy Crouch, "Foreword" in Scot McKnight and Joseph B Modica, eds., *Jesus is Lord Caesar is Not: Evaluating Empire in New Testament Studies* (InterVarsity Press, 2013), 12-13.

King of kings and Lord of lords, does not spell the end of political rule in history—and we might add that, empirically at least... it has not spelled the end of empires. But it *has* put an end to the claim of rulers to provide *salvation*—rescue from the conditions of sin and death. And none too soon, because these claims were always faintly pathetic and frequently became frighteningly demonic—there is a reason the world cheers at the fall of 'Babylon the Great'. We no longer need to invest our political structures with hopes of eternal rescue from the abyss of chaos—that has been done and dealt with by Christ. Instead, we grant them humbler status, befitting mere creatures—indeed, creatures of creatures, our own cultural creations meant to serve the purpose of image-bearing. They are meant to secure certain kinds of liberty and to provide, as in Daniel's vision, for the flourishing of all. They can only do so when they are chastened by the proclamation of the world's true Ruler, the one who truly is the Beginning and the End, who has triumphed over death and hell.

And if one were to adopt the Reformers' theology of calling and vocation, if one believes that the station of life he is in is what the Lord has called him to or assigned to him,[650] if one believes that all our earthly roles, offices or functions should be submitted to the lordship of Christ so as to fulfil them "as to the Lord" or "in the Lord",[651] then one must inevitably grapple with how one ought to live out one's own vocation in the Lord.

Lord Shaftesbury or Anthony Ashley Cooper, the 7th Earl of Shaftesbury, also known as the Poor Man's Earl, understood this. He was a zealous

---

650 1 Corinthians 7:17, 24.
651 Ephesians 5:17, 22; 6:1, 7; Colossians 3:18-24.

evangelical British politician who sought many social reforms to benefit the lower socioeconomic classes. On his vocational calling as a politician, he once said, "Every one chooses a career, and it is well if he chooses that which is best suited to his talents. I have taken political life because I have, by God's blessing, many advantages of birth and situation which, although of trifling value if unsupported, are yet very powerful aids if joined to zeal and honesty. It is here, therefore, that I have the chief way of being useful to my generation".[652]

One 'vocation' which many, if not all of us have, is the earthly role of citizenship in a modern democratic state. It is no surprise that Calvin considered that the calling as a civil magistrate, i.e., the modern equivalent of a state leader, was one of the noblest callings. Just as Paul legitimately exercised his citizenship rights in Acts 22:25, modern Christians too can exercise their citizenship rights of participating in the democratic process. Bruce Winter suggests that when Peter exhorted his audience to "[k]eep [their] conduct among the Gentiles honourable… [so that] they may see [their] good deeds and glorify God on the day of visitation", it included, perhaps primarily, doing good in the public sphere as *citizens*.[653]

In a speech in 2004, Prime Minister Lee Hsien Loong (then Deputy Prime Minister) articulated that "[p]eople should debate issues with reason, passion and conviction, and not be passive bystanders in their own fate. Disagreement does not necessarily imply rebellion, and nor should unity of purpose and vision mean sameness in views and ideas".[654] Indeed, as citizens we should not be passive but actively debate issues

---

[652] Edwin Hodder, *The life and work of the seventh Earl of Shaftesbury* (London, Cassell & Company, 1886), I:105.
[653] 1 Peter 2:12, 15. Bruce Winter, "Pilgrims and Citizens: The Paradox for the First Christians" in Michael Nai-Chiu Poon, ed., *Pilgrims and Citizens: Christian Social Engagement in East Asia Today* (ATF Press, 2006) at 30-31.
[654] Speech by Deputy Prime Minister Lee Hsien Loong at the Harvard Club of Singapore's 35th Anniversary Dinner – Building A Civic Society.

regarding our collective society. How should one be a Singapore *citizen* as to the Lord?[655] How can we as Christian Singapore citizens or residents participate in the public square to contribute to public matters and public policy?[656] How can we as Christians in our respective vocations do this?

An illustration of this would be the public consultation and debate in 2004 over the establishment of casinos in Singapore. Individuals, including Ministers of Parliament and ordinary citizens, as well as religious bodies like the National Council Churches of Singapore (NCCS), MUIS (the Islamic Religious Council of Singapore), Pergas, and civil society organisations like AWARE all contributed to the debate in opposition to the casinos. This was done through public statements and private consultations. Another example is NCCS's engagement with the Bioethics Advisory Committee (BAC) on biomedical research issues, with the Ministry of Health on amendments to the Human Organ Transplant Act, with the Ministry of Law and Ministry of Health on the status of children born through Assisted Reproductive Technology including in-vitro fertilisation.

And if all that sounds too overwhelming, consider the smaller things: Simply writing an email to a government ministry to provide feedback on a policy or even a particular case can have significant impact. When the National Parks Board brought a roving exhibition of old metal swings, see-saws and benches to the grass patches above Raffles Place MRT, it changed the visual and cultural landscape of Raffles Place. People hung around at the lawns and chatted with one another. It became such a beautiful and warm environment. When my friends and I realised that the exhibition

---

655 And on some views, this would extend to local churches as a community of individual citizens, as well as corporate citizens, although on the latter, corporate citizenship does not confer the same citizenship rights under the law as afforded to natural persons. E.g., corporate citizens such as companies, organisations or churches cannot vote.

656 Thio Li-ann, "Attending to the Weightier Matters of the Law: Faith, Hope and Love in the Public Square" in Daniel Koh and Kiem-Kiok Kwa, *Issues of Law and Justice in Singapore* (Armour Publishing, 2009), 175-229.

was reaching its end and was to be torn down, we were disappointed and decided to write to the National Parks Board (NParks) to urge them to keep the swings and benches there. We got friends and friends' friends to affirm our petition. To our pleasant surprise, NParks decided to retain the swings and benches. They remain at the Raffles Place lawns, providing a social haven in an otherwise cold concrete environment.

This is not to say that every moral, social or economic prohibition or exhortation in the Bible must be expressed in the State's civil law and policies. Every issue must be grappled with on its own terms. A proper perspective of law—the function of law, politics and political systems—must inform our approach towards the positions and suggestions we promote in our engagement in the public square.

Individual and societal impact of presenting our Christian worldview in the public square

There is also the impact of presenting our Christian worldview in the public square. People are watching. When Jesus was crucified and the earth shook and boulders split, the Jews there continued to mock Jesus. Who would have known that it would be the Gentile Roman centurion and guards present at Jesus' death who would be "filled with awe and said, 'Truly this was the Son of God!'".[657]

Once, at a secondary school class gathering, I found out that an ex-classmate of mine whom I have not kept in close contact with had become a Christian. I chatted with him about it, and to my surprise, he told me that the notes I had penned and articles I had posted on Facebook had helped him in his struggle towards faith. People become convicted of Christ in the least expected ways and in the least expected places. Do

---

657 Matthew 27:54.

you know how many people are reading your Facebook posts? Your forum letters? Your YouTube videos? Journal articles? Parliamentary speeches? Your (seemingly private) conversations in public? We may not know who is reading what we say or observing what we do in the public square. But there might be someone who is. If there is, *will he feel attracted to Christ, or will he feel repelled from Christ by what we say or do*?

A Platform for Loving Neighbours in Deed
Christians should be in the public square loving their neighbours *in deed* while they love *in word*. As discussed earlier, Jesus instructed His disciples in Matthew 5:13-16 to be light of the earth and do "good works". These good works would be inevitably obvious in public to the world. The salt and light of the earth are to be hearers, talkers *and doers.*[658] Proclaiming truth that is good and right has to be coupled with living and *doing* what is good and right.

E. What is Civil Dialogue and Why Participate in It?

In Germanic customs during the Middle Ages, when two parties had a disagreement but had no witnesses to testify in their case, they would have a trial of a peculiar sort—they would engage in combat. The disputing parties would bear sword and shield, and fight until one of them died (or suffered some nasty debilitating injury). The belief then was that whoever was innocent or entitled to his claim would have been aided by God in the battle. Thank goodness we have done away with such quasi-judicial

---

658   James 1:22-25.

practices. Unfortunately, trial by combat has taken on new forms in the modern context. I have seen how in some heated debates on social-ethical issues, people would descend into incivility, name-calling, vicious speech, hate mail, and even death threats.

How then should public square engagement be done? I believe the answer is civil dialogue. Civil dialogue is conversation between persons in a way that respects every participant and that seeks understanding.

Why civil dialogue? I believe civil dialogue is necessary in our present sociocultural context. In Acts 17, Paul went to the synagogue and public square and proclaimed the Christian worldview. Why did he do that? Why did he not spend time building up a relationship with people first before proclaiming the Gospel to them? Paul knew the context of the time well. Acts 17:21 says (rather sardonically): "Now all the Athenians and the foreigners who lived there would spend their time in nothing except telling or hearing something new". The people of Athens would gather at the public square to discuss or listen to ideas. Paul was capitalising on that. Paul said elsewhere: "For though I am free from all, I have made myself a servant to all, that I might win more of them".[659]

Likewise, we need to exegete not just the Bible but also the ethos and zeitgeist of our present time and society, so that we can respond to it biblically. We need to know not only the accessible public square platforms of the day, but also discern those which allow us to best achieve what we seek to do.

We live in a post-postmodern age. The pop culture notions of postmodernism expressed in the form of negative values such as scepticism, irony and relativism have disenchanted many people. If indeed there were no grand narrative, if any notion can be differently perceived

---

659   1 Corinthians 9:19.

in different contexts, then the response would be to derive meaning only in those things that one can be certain of. Hence, in today's world, people tend to accept authority as legitimate if founded upon things that involve egalitarian, universally accessible participation, and which the individual himself participates in. Under this ethos, people overcome scepticism by authenticity, authenticity achieved by anonymity and avatar. Consider for a moment one of the most important recent revolutions in the way we do things or think about things. Crowdsourcing. Wikipedia. Crowdfunding. Bitcoin. Minecraft. Alternative media. These are manifestations of the post-postmodern ethos. Yet, what has this go to do with civil dialogue?

In a time where individuals feel more and more insignificant, where people are longing for egalitarian respect and worth, where people want to make social connections but are becoming more alienated from one another, dialogue is a necessity. Dialogue that is egalitarian and universally accessible. Dialogue in which people feel that they can be heard. Dialogue in which people seek to understand and are open to changing their own views in response.

One of the most influential philosophers of our time is German philosopher Jürgen Habermas.[660] Habermas offers a theory and ethics of discourse and argues that it is both *through* and *in* discourse that we may find meaning and understanding. He makes important insights about discourse which may resonate with us. For instance, he says that claims asserted through speech-acts may not always be truth claims, but sincerity claims. In essence, he is saying that when making certain views in a dialogue, one issue is whether the participant has integrity with respect

---

660   To be sure, we should not adopt wholesale every attractive theory available and give it a Christian spin. Yet, there are things to be learnt, or perhaps re-learnt from theories like those of Habermas'. After all, John Calvin posited by the doctrine of common grace that if there be any good we could enjoy derived from non-Christians who have received common grace from God, we should gladly do so.

to both his speech and his conduct. Then there are moral rightness and empirical truth claims which must be universally accessible, as opposed to ethical claims which may be addressed only to those who share certain values and norms. He says there are certain presuppositions which participants must make about the dialogue for it to work: Non-exclusion of participants, equal voice, ability to speak honestly, non-coercion in the process and procedures of discourse.

If, as the Reformers ascribed to, belief is internal and cannot be created or compelled by the external; if we believe that every human being has the imprint of the *imago Dei* and therefore has inherent human dignity;[661] if we believe that the consequence of the Fall in Genesis 3 is a relational rupture; if a breakdown in universal communication is the curse of humanity's hubris;[662] and conversely its redemption is for, among other things, evangelism and worship;[663] then dialogue which is universally accessible, participative, egalitarian, would respect every individual's human dignity.

Perhaps such civil dialogue is what apostle Peter meant when he talked about giving an *apologia* (defence) of our faith "with... *respect*".[664] When my wife and I were undergoing pre-marital counselling in view of getting married, we were taught a certain technique to work out our disputes. We were made to take turns to express how we feel or think about the issue in question without saying "you" but only saying "I". The other person was to only listen and not say a single word until it was his or her turn to speak. When we attempted it for ourselves, we found it extremely difficult to keep quiet and only listen. But we also found it extremely powerful in helping us communicate our thoughts and feelings, and to understand

---

661 Genesis 1:27.
662 Genesis 11.
663 Acts 2.
664 1 Peter 3:15-16.

the other person's point of view. Amazingly, I felt that the process—of listening and of communicating without subtly or indirectly accusing the other—was an act of love in itself. Civil dialogue which seeks to truly communicate understanding is an enormously important activity we must partake in to love our neighbours.[665]

It is significant that in every prayer, God respects us and loves us enough to *dialogue with us*. Abraham dialogued with God.[666] Job dialogued with God. Moses dialogued with God.[667] Elijah dialogued with God.[668] Nicodemus dialogued with Christ.[669] The rich young man dialogued with Christ.[670] The Samaritan woman at the well dialogued with Christ.[671] In Isaiah 1:18, God said to Israel, "[c]ome now, let us reason together." Dialogue is everywhere in the Bible. More importantly, it is implicitly deemed to be good and right.

> **It is significant that in every prayer, God respects us and loves us enough to dialogue with us.**

I believe that civil dialogue should be our *procedure, process and point*. Procedure because it is the manner through which we engage. Process because it is a long-term journey and framework we believe to be right and therefore want to commit to. Point because it is not merely the medium but the message itself; by civil dialogue, we

---

665 Rowan Williams, "Relations between the Church and the state today: What is the role of the Christian citizen?", http://rowanwilliams.archbishopofcanterbury.org/articles.php/2009/relations-between-the-church-and-state-today-what-is-the-role-of-the-christian-citizen.
666 Genesis 18.
667 Exodus 22-24, 32.
668 1 Kings 19.
669 John 3.
670 Matthew 19:16-30.
671 John 4.

send the message to our fellow humans that they matter, they have worth, they have the *imago Dei* imprinted on them, *ergo*, the ethics of dialogue is just as important as the subject matter of the dialogue. In that regard, please visit the book's website's section on "Ethics of Civil Dialogue".

F. Application in Singapore

Now that we have considered the what, why and how of civil dialogue in the public square, it bears considering how that is to be applied in Singapore. I conclude with no solutions but only further questions, because the quest for informed understanding, an invitation to include others to participate in the conversation, is in itself a dialogue.

What are the public squares in Singapore? What is happening in these public spaces? What is good and bad about the public square in Singapore today? What is good and bad about Christians engaging in the public square today? How should Christians engage in the public square today? Is there a practical way we can model good Christian public square engagement? What are the greatest needs that should be addressed in the public square? How should we create platforms for civil dialogue in the public square?

I end off with a positive example. Between 15 September and 9 October 2014, two influential thought leaders were invited to participate in an online dialogue or debate organised by Institute of Policy Studies (IPS) Commons on an important issue: "Is it Time for Singapore to Consider a Right-to-Die Bill?"[672] The two leaders were Bishop Emeritus Robert Solomon and Professor Tommy Koh. I will end by echoing a comment in

---

672   "Is It Time to Consider a Right-to-Die Bill?", *Institute of Policy Studies*, http://www.ipscommons.sg/debate/.

a local online news site (non-mainstream media) on the online debate:[673] "How we wish online debates about important issues can be concluded in such a civil and informed manner."

It is my wish too that there will be more examples and models of civil and informed dialogue in the Singapore public square, in order to pursue the common good of our society, to pursue justice and righteousness, to love our neighbours as ourselves, to honour, give weight to, and cherish every individual—every Singapore resident—and the *imago Dei* imbued in him or her.

---

673 "Tommy Koh vs Robert Solomon: Debate suggests S'poreans not too big on right-to-die", *Mothership blog*, http://mothership.sg/2014/10/tommy-koh-vs-robert-solomon-debate-suggests-sporeans-not-too-big-on-right-to-die/.

Chapter Summary

- To be salt and light of the world is to live such good lives, in moral conduct and good works, that we are obviously distinctive and have impact on the world.
- The public square is the space freely accessible to the local community in which the life of the community occurs, where members of the community dialogue, and where truth and wisdom ought to prevail for justice and righteousness to flourish in the community.
- By presenting the Christian worldview in a winsome manner and loving people in deed in the public square, we are pursuing the Great Commission and the Great Commandments.
- Seek the *shalom* of the city because therein you will find your *shalom*.
- Civil dialogue is a conversation between persons in a way which respects every participant and which seeks understanding.
- Civil dialogue should be our procedure, process and point.

Discussion Questions

1. Do you agree with the ideas and principles in this chapter on seeking justice in the public square? Why or why not?
2. What are some ideas or principles you learnt and found helpful? How would you adopt these for yourself?
3. Share stories, testimonies or experiences which positively exemplify a good approach to seeking justice in the public square.
4. What are your thoughts on the dynamic between Christians and culture, and between Christians, the Church and the political state?
5. What is your response to God in the light of what you have gleaned from these thoughts?

INTERVIEW:
Rev Dr Daniel Koh

• • •

Rev Dr Daniel Koh Kah Soon, a Methodist Minister, is a full-time lecturer at Trinity Theological College (TTC). He obtained his PhD in Ethics from Durham University. At TTC he teaches Pastoral Theology, and Ethics, and he is the Director (English) of TTC's Centre for the Development of Christian Ministry that organises mainly evening courses for lay-training. Daniel is active in Christian social outreach where he is a member of the Ethics Committee of a major hospital, a member of a Central Institutional Review Board, and a member of the National Organ Transplant Ethics Panel. He is also the Chairperson of the Methodist Welfare Services, which provides wide-ranging care and social services for the poor and needy; families-in-crisis and youths-at-risk; homes for the destitute and nursing homes for the elderly.

1. Do you think that social justice is a key expression of Christian discipleship and witness? Why or why not?

I wouldn't use the term "social justice". The term *mishpat* used in the Bible is often translated as justice. But it is justice that includes a social dimension. From scriptural teaching, especially found in Psalms, Isaiah and the Minor Prophets, justice is of utmost importance to Christians for a few reasons: It is part of God's character. God is just and He loves justice. It is also God's desire that those who follow Him and worship Him should cultivate justice so that justice becomes a part of our character. In practical terms, justice means being actively concerned about the wellbeing of those who are poor and needy; particularly the ones who are vulnerable and voiceless such as the orphans, widows and sojourners/foreigners. Justice is expressed in attending to those who are often referred to as the last, the least and the lost is clearly taught by our Lord Jesus in Matthew 25. Elsewhere in James, we are told that our religion is worthless unless we also, as part of our Christian witness, care for the orphans and widows, people who are usually seen as the poor and powerless.

2. What do you think is the local church's role in relation to justice and mercy?

The local church is closest to the neighbourhood in which the church is physically located and members gather for regular worship. She is best placed to know and understand the social condition of the ordinary people staying in the vicinity. That proximity to a neighbourhood should challenge members of the church to be aware of issues which common people encounter and offer assistance to alleviate social ills. Sometimes a church may be protected from the wider challenges which beset the people whose plights are hidden from a well-protected privileged class, if the church is found in a district where the rich and successful people tend to reside or socialise. But even in such a sanitised location, if the members of the church are well-taught and guided to assume discipleship that includes caring about social justice issues, they can still be mobilised to attend to societal welfare. Christians in upper-middle class churches are probably better educated and draw a higher income. As such, they should be able to offer expert advice in thinking through challenges from a deeper multidisciplinary perspective. Local churches have much to offer either on their own or through combined efforts with churches in the same location.

However, from my own observation, it would appear that our churches have not quite understood what justice means, why it is an essential component of living a faithful life as a disciple of Christ, and how to engage in works of justice and mercy. Perhaps churches have concentrated too much on issues like evangelism, missions and numerical growth of churches, and neglected what John Wesley refers to as social holiness. We have to reclaim our prophetic voice to speak against societal evil, social inequality and ill-treatment of the marginalised. I am not suggesting that we should ignore evangelism, missions and church growth. These are important parts of the wide range of ministries and concerns for Christians and the church. What I am saying is that while it seems easier to concentrate on such traditional ministries, we must not forget or neglect the social dimension and interest of our faith, expressed in the need for us to be people who love justice and who will work for social justice.

3. How do you think the Singapore local churches have fared historically and recently?

Historically, in Singapore, Christians were at the forefront fighting against social evils, such as the opium trade and drug abuse. At those times in the early history of our country, it was a luxury for boys to receive formal education. Christians started mission schools, not only for boys, but also for girls. When healthcare was not very accessible, churches set up clinics and hospitals to provide healthcare for the poor. We do have some good social outreach projects that promote opportunities for people to be educated, to receive help and to get out of the poverty trap. This is something that we can be proud of.

How about the current situation? Apart from the Roman Catholic Church, most churches in Singapore are either ignorant of or quiet about the need for Christians to be concerned about issues of justice, though there are good examples of churches being actively involved in ministries of mercy expressed through social outreach projects. We can say that there are many churches which have well-organised social outreach agencies that provide tangible care for the poor and needy, the sick and the elderly, the vulnerable youth and children-at-risk. Apart from churches, there have been initiatives driven and supported by groups of Christians, e.g., HealthServe, Prison Fellowship, and St Luke's Hospital and Eldercare Centres. Some of the larger denominations have social outreach arms like the Anglican Community Services, The Presbyterian Community Services, Touch Community Services and the Methodist Welfare Services.

But what we have offered seem to be mainly at the level of what I term as 'ambulance service'. We are good at providing immediate care for people with urgent needs. Of course, 'ambulance service' is essential. When someone meets an accident, we do not waste time discussing the condition of the car, the validity of one's driving licence, the condition of the road, or if the victim wore appropriate clothes. Wounds must be attended to on an urgent basis. There is a need for, 'ambulance service' to take care of urgent needs. While we may excel at the level of 'ambulance service', the church might be lacking at two other levels.

The second level is the need to offer holistic multi-agency care. A person who is trapped in chronic poverty may require not just monthly financial assistance. It is likely that someone at home is ill or incarcerated. It is probable that the person's meals are irregular or unhealthy. If there are children, they may need help with their schoolwork. Multi-agency holistic assistance will demand more people to help and it will take longer to walk with the affected family until, for example, a child or the children have been guided to complete school education, have found decent jobs and have broken the poverty trap. The third level is most difficult. We are lacking in offering in-depth multidisciplinary studies on social issues which affect societal wellbeing. This requires Christians who are experts in different disciplines and professions; pastors and theologians, and ethicists to form special interest groups, and have structured meetings studying social issues, assessing existing policies, and framing improved policies and offering directions in sociopolitical development which will meet basic requirements of social justice for the sake of the common good. An oft-quoted Chinese saying speaks of teaching someone to fish and not just giving that person fish. When a person is hungry, he should be given fish first even if it is a small *ikan kuning*. Concurrently, a multi-agency approach should be in place to help that person to acquire the necessary skills and to finance the purchase of the fishing nets and boat. But someone who is interested in and understands the requirement of social justice must work our policies that will ensure that when a person has learnt how to fish, he is allowed to fish in a lake, perhaps paying an affordable sum for the upkeep of the lake and natural environment. What must not happen is to forbid the person to fish or put up social barriers which make it impossible for the fisherman to catch his fish.

4. What is the relationship between the local church and the individual Christian in relation to justice and mercy?
If the local church is concerned about social justice and this is known to the members of the church, it is likely that the individual Christians who are members of the local church will tend to be drawn to social justice as an integral part of their Christian social witness. It is essential therefore for the church, especially the pastors and lay leadership, to set the tone for the mission of the church which takes social responsibility as something not optional but required for all Christians.

On the other hand, if a local church were to ignore or consider social justice as peripheral to the life, ministry and discipleship of the church, this will also rub off on those who attend that particular church. While it is regrettable for any church to downplay the role of social responsibility, the fortunate thing is that in a place like Singapore there are well-read Christians as well as Christian groups outside of a local church that encourage likeminded Christians to explore ways in which they can be faithful in their social witness and social outreach. These Christians will provide the counter-balance to local churches which seem to be more insular in their outlook and limited in their views of Christian discipleship. I am cautiously optimistic that the informed lay people will help to turn the local church which lacks interest in social justice around, at least in convincing the local church to accept greater social responsibility, even if it is at the 'ambulance' level which I mentioned earlier.

5. How can Singapore local churches disciple and empower believers in relation to justice and mercy?
First, the pastors and lay leaders of the local churches must be convinced that justice and works of mercy are inseparable from a wholesome understanding of Christian discipleship. If this is in place, there must

be committed advocates in the churches who will offer and supervise an intentional discipleship training programme, which should include practicum, for the churches. Since not every local church has the required experience or expertise, it helps to identify resources and people who can assist in training and mentoring more Christians in social outreach and in interpreting social conditions.

At the inter-church level, Christians who share similar interests may meet occasionally for studies and consultations on different social issues which require deeper reflection and attention. Out of such groups, serious papers providing critique to both international and local social problems and policies, and offering possible solutions informed by our understanding of justice can be published and circulated either in printed form or through social media. We should be open to expert opinions from people who are not Christians and are not averse to working with Christians.

6. What do you think is the relationship between social justice and evangelism?

I shall not define social justice and evangelism. There is literature available which would give adequate definitions for the two core requirements of what constitute both biblical and wholesome discipleship. I will say what I first heard in mid-1975 when the late Stanley Mooneyham, former President of World Vision International said at the First Chinese Congress on World Evangelisation held in Hong Kong in 1976. He did not use the term social justice but he used "social responsibility", which would include social justice. At that gathering he reminded some 1,600 delegates that social responsibility and evangelism are the two wings of a plane. For the plane to take off and attain new heights of achievement, we need both wings to be strong and balanced. We need both. Our Christian witness suffers and our growth as disciples will be stunted if we give too much emphasis to one and neglect the other.

7. Any other thoughts or comments on the topic?

It is quite clear that the topic of justice has attracted wide studies and discussions in the past 20 years. Those who are talking about justice are respected scholars from both the Christian traditions and those who may not share the same faith as us. Since the publication of *A Theory of Justice* (revised, 1999) by John Rawls, we now have books written by thinkers like Amartya Sen, *The Idea of Justice* (2011) and Michael Sandel, *Justice: What's the Right Thing to Do?* (2010). Among Christian social ethicists and philosophers, we can easily recall the works of Duncan Forrester: *Christian Justice and Public Policy* (1997), Nicholas Sagovsky: *Christian Tradition and the Practice of Justice* (2008), and Nicholas Wolterstorff's two books, *Justice: Rights and Wrongs* (2008) and *Justice in Love* (2011). See also a local collection of essays, Daniel KS Koh and Kwa Kiem Kiok, eds., *Issues of Law and Justice in Singapore: Some Christian Reflections* (2009).

By mentioning these books, I am saying that justice as a topic is obviously of deep concern to both secular scholars as well as Christian ethicists, philosophers and theologians. At the same time, it should be obvious that for Christians to be well-informed about such a topic, we should be aware of what people outside the church are also saying. This will help us to build bridges with others, and collaborate with likeminded people who are seeking social justice and the common good for the wider community.

It is therefore essential for the church to encourage some of our best and brightest minds, who must be people who love and fear the Lord, to pursue further studies not only in the traditional disciplines of systematic theology, biblical studies, important though they are; but surely the church in Singapore is big-hearted enough to not only encourage but also to support over the long-term some of them to do doctoral studies in Christian ethics. These people must be open to working with other Christians who are experts in other fields like political philosophy, jurisprudence, economics, urban planning and social sciences. When that happens, we will be able to provide more significant and credible leadership in the way we go about observing and assessing social problems, critiquing the dominant ideologies and flawed policies which might foster social inequality, and offering better alternative views and policies for the sake of social justice.

Let me end by quoting what John Stott said in one of his last books. Usually when someone of the stature of John Stott gives advice in the final years of his life, it behoves us to pay undivided attention. [I copy myself by repeating what I wrote for a newsletter.]

John Stott, in his book, *The Living Church: Convictions of a Lifelong Pastor* (2011) shares this observation: "One of the most important questions facing Christians in every age and every place is this: what values and standards are going to dominate our national culture?" (137)

He goes on to pose this question for Christians who should be concerned about our Christian engagement in the plural world:

> Will Christians be able to influence their country so that the values and standards of the kingdom of God permeate the whole national culture—its consensus on moral and bioethical issues, its recognition of human rights, its respect for the sanctity of human life (including that of the unborn, the handicapped and the senile), its concern for the homeless, the unemployed and people trapped in the cycle of poverty, its attitude to dissidents, its stewardship of the environment, its treatment of criminals, and the whole way of life of its citizens? (137-138)

Over the years the Church has benefitted from the guidance of theologians and pastors, Bible scholars and evangelists. But John Stott gets it right when he says, "We need to pray that God will raise up *more ethical thinkers* (emphasis is mine), who will not just climb Mount Sinai and declaim the Ten Commandments, but will argue that God's standards are best" (147). Our Church and society can benefit from having more Christians trained in clear and competent ethical thinking if we want to make significant contribution to Christian social ethical engagement in our complex world.

INTERVIEW: Dr David LT Yap

● ● ●

> David Yap is the Advisory Pastor of Yio Chu Kang Chapel. He served as an elder of this local church from 1977 to 2015. Actively engaged in cross-cultural missions, he is a member of the Board of Governors of SIM International, chairs SIM East Asia Ltd, the Council overseeing the ministry in Asia, and continues in the ongoing encouragement of missions development in his home church. He is also the Chairman of Bless Community Services, a volunteer welfare organisation engaged in community work. David was a banker for 18 years prior to taking up responsibilities in the church's pastoral ministry and in missions.

1. Do you think that social justice is a key expression of Christian discipleship and witness? Why or why not?

I believe that social justice must be an integral expression of Christian discipleship. This is because the Lord whom we worship is a just God. The theme of the Lord's concern for the disadvantaged—the orphans, widows and aliens—rings out loud in Scriptures (e.g., Deuteronomy 10:17-18).

And God expects those who belong to Him to act justly and to love mercy, as expressed in Micah 6:8 (NIV):

> He has shown you, O mortal, what is good.
>   And what does the Lord require of you?
> To act justly and to love mercy
>   and to walk humbly with your God.

The parable of the sheep and the goats as recorded in Matthew 25:31-46 brings to our attention our Lord Jesus' expectations of His disciples. Those who show acts of mercy and compassion to people deprived of basic necessities in life—the hungry, the thirsty, the sick, and those imprisoned—they are counted as righteous in the Lord's sight.

The exhortation given to the church in Galatians 3:26-28 (NIV) reflects God's standard for social relationships:

> So in Christ Jesus you are all children of God through faith, for all of you who were baptized into Christ have clothed yourselves with Christ. There is neither Jew nor Gentile, neither slave nor free, nor is there male and female, for you are all one in Christ Jesus.

All who are children of God need to know that every individual is of equal value in Christ. God's children must therefore seek to uphold this truth.

2. What do you think is the relationship between social justice and evangelism?

I believe the relationship between evangelism and social justice is about loving God and loving neighbour, which Jesus explained by telling the Parable of the Good Samaritan (Luke 10:25-37).

Indeed, the Lord's Great Commission as given in John 20:21 brings to our attention that the mission as entrusted to us is really an extension of His mission on earth. It is significant that at the commencement of Jesus' ministry, He read from Isaiah 61 and identified Himself as the fulfilment of the prophecy given therein (read Luke 4:18-21). The prophecy specifically referred to the proclamation of "good news to the poor", "liberty to the captives" and the setting free of "those who are oppressed". Our Lord was clearly concerned for those who have suffered social injustices. It is also significant that we have been reminded in James 2:14-17 that "faith by itself, if it does not have works, is dead" (v17).

Our responsibility in bringing the Gospel message must be done with recognition that Christ is interested in liberating the whole person.

3. What do you think is the local church's role in relation to social justice? How does the tension (if any) between social justice and evangelism play out in a local church?

The local church must be a faithful witness in the neighbourhood where it is located. Each church will need to consider prayerfully the areas that she can go forth as an assembly and serve together in Christ's name, as He has laid upon our hearts. This will require shared commitment to the cause as placed in the hearts of the assembly of Christians.

Today, we live in a society where most basic human needs are provided for. But there are some who fall in between the cracks, economically and socially. It is noted that in Singapore, the Government and volunteer welfare organisations (many of which have been established by churches) have risen to serve, to meet the needs in the community.

The Lord will use the local church as well as individuals (who are really "the church in the marketplace") whom He has placed in various places in society to fulfil His purpose. The commendable work of William Wilberforce and George Müller come to mind.

Wilberforce was used by the Lord as he tirelessly spoke out and crusaded against slavery in the early 1800s. Müller relied on the Lord for His provisions as he lovingly cared for the orphans in his days.

Indeed, the local church and believers will need to identify the social issues of the day that cause pain, poverty or social injustice, for ministry, while mindful of the priority of the Gospel message of Jesus Christ.

But there is a tension. The tension lies in setting priorities—usually in relation to time and energy to be accorded. In this, the account as recorded in Matthew 26:6-13 is instructive. Jesus' response to the disciples' argument that the cost of the ointment could be better spent brought out two realities that the church will always need to consider:

- The priority of loving and worshipping Him, and
- The reality that there will be many social causes placed before us in this world.

The church must be concerned with issues of social justice in our community. Our response and involvement must be done out of love for Him and as He directs. We can believe that the Lord will provide the needed resources for our engagement when we know that He is leading us for engagement in the issues before us.

4. What do you think is the relationship between social justice and intercultural missions? How does the tension (if any) between social justice and evangelism play out in intercultural missions?

In our commitment to fulfil the mission that Christ has given to us, we must be mindful that it would include evangelising the unreached, ministering to human needs, and discipling believers into churches.

In ministering to human needs, we humbly acknowledge that the ultimate human need is to know God and that He has called us to compassionate, holistic service in this broken world. There will be opportunities to serve to help alleviate suffering, foster development, and effect change in society.

We do recognise that those in the frontline in cross-cultural missions will often be confronted by manifestations of sin and injustices in this broken world. Suffering and disease, violence and conflict, pain and death all have their roots in human sin, the pervasive presence of evil, and ultimately in broken relationships between God and humanity, humanity with each other, and humanity with creation. Sin and the injustices it fosters are essentially relational.

We must be alert to the reality of engaging in spiritual warfare. Prayer and the armour of God are essential for spiritual battle. Evil, sin, the forces of darkness are apparent and emphasised differently across cultures and worldviews, but often we can be blind to their manifestation in our own culture.

Jesus' three parables in Matthew 25 teach us how we should live as Kingdom citizens while awaiting the soon return of our King. The Parable of the Ten Virgins (vv1-13) underlines the importance of being prepared for His return. The Parable of the Talents (vv14-30) emphasises that kingdom citizens must use the resources entrusted to them by the King in service for Him, not for themselves. And the parable of the sheep and the goats inform us that kingdom citizens are identified by their acts of compassion lovingly ministered to those in need, for God's glory.

Being on mission in home country or in a foreign land really should be no different. We are called to be on mission for Christ in this world. And as expressed in Acts 1:8, we are to be witnesses for Christ where we are placed, with the witness radiating outwards in wider circles.

5. What would you say to a church member who tells you, "this local church is not doing enough for the poor and marginalised"?

I would counsel the member as follows:

> a. He should come alongside the church leadership to share the burden in his heart, and to commit to seeking the Lord's will together on this matter. If it is the Lord's will that the particular church be engaged in this ministry, and when God's people seek Him earnestly, I believe He will reveal His will to His people clearly, and He will provide the needed resources. This is where church leadership plays a vital role, as exemplified in the account in Acts 13:1-3.

> b. The member should also be open to the possibility that the Lord may be directing the individual member to be personally involved as a part of his calling, rather than for the whole local church to be mobilised for a particular ministry.

Church leaders will no doubt be mindful of stewarding the Lord's resources as entrusted to the local church—priority of time, talents and finance—among the many possible ministries for engagement. When there is clarity that it is the Lord's will for broader or deeper engagement in a particular ministry by the local church, I believe the church that desires to be obedient and purposeful will respond with commitment and joyful engagement. I am also of the view that very often, when the Lord places a 'stirring' in a member's heart, He will also use that person wonderfully to be engaged in that ministry directly.

6. Is there a difference between the role of the individual and the local church in seeking biblical social justice?

Yes, I believe there is a need to make that distinction. The local church will need to seek the Lord for direction on ministry engagements. As mentioned earlier, the church will need to prayerfully consider the stewarding of the Lord's resources as entrusted to the local church. There can be many ministries that various church members consider to deserve the local church's engagement. It would not be right to move the whole church to do this or that upon every individual's request. So, the church leadership needs to seek the Lord on the kind of ministries to be engaged in.

We are also aware that the Lord uses different individuals to fulfil His purpose for His Kingdom work. The scope of one's ministry engagement may well extend beyond the ministries of the local church. We have seen wonderful examples in church history when God raised individuals to move into new frontiers. We read of the testimony of pioneer missionaries, most of whose ministries extended beyond that of the spheres of the local church's engagement. But the Lord's universal church was there—He may raise people from various local churches for engagement in His Kingdom work! Such individuals would have been nurtured in local churches and have been actively engaged in their churches' ministries. But the Lord may use them beyond the spheres of the local church's ministry engagements.

I would add that as a member of the local church, it is important that the individual is accountable to the local church leadership on what the Lord has placed in his heart. The local church should provide the spiritual support and guidance. The person should be available to serve within the spheres of the local church, but should be open to the Lord's direction for wider ministries, should the Lord so reveal.

7. Any other thoughts or comments on the topic?
There are two key thoughts that come to mind as I reflect on this topic. First, we live in a broken world. Sadly, there are pervasive manifestations of evil and injustice all around us—as seen in the disregard of life, abuse of power, discriminations due to ethnicity, social class or gender, and the undermining of basic human dignity. In reality, all these require more than human solutions.

Second, God graciously invites us to be involved in His mission. God calls us to a dynamic partnership with Him and with each other in His Kingdom work. We need to rely fully on Him as we serve in the areas that He directs, and we need to be open to how we complement one another as members of the body of Christ.

INTERVIEW: Lawrence Ko

• • •

Lawrence Ko, MDiv (TTC), is the National Director of Singapore Centre for Global Missions. He served as a pastor for seven years in a local church and in management of Christian organisations including YMCA, ORTV and TWR-Asia. He is founder-director of Asian Journeys Ltd, a social enterprise involved in Asian social concerns, particularly in environmental work and work among heartland youths and urban poor. Lawrence also serves on the Asian Lausanne Committee Executive Committee, Singapore Lausanne Exco and the Asia Evangelical Alliance Mission Committee (where he served as chair from 2008-2012). Lawrence has been involved in China missions research and environmental missiology over the past 10 years.

1. What are your thoughts on social justice in the Singapore Church?
I was involved in the Asian Lausanne and Singapore Lausanne. The Singapore church has been held hostage by a very conservative theology: Individualised faith, personal salvation, church planting. This is a reaction to the theology debate in Latin America in the 1970s. Our theology is very much influenced by Navigators and Campus Crusade. My theology was very much based on the theology of Campus Crusade. But I realised that [Christianity] is greater than just winning souls.

The evangelicals emerged from the 20th Century in reaction to liberation theology. It started with helping the poor, but it got more socialist and Marxist. Lausanne, over the last 40 years, has been a very important platform. Not many people understand it. It allows for greater laity involvement. If we can broaden the theological basis, moving forward, we need a new theology of God, Christ, and the mission of the church.

Do you know the story of Jim Wallis? He was a preacher's kid in a typical all-white church. Until he went to college. He wondered, why does the church not talk about the liberation of the blacks? He went to ask his church leaders about it. A church senior asked him, "Will you allow your sister to marry the blacks?" He got fed up and left the church. He was very active in campaigning against the Vietnam War. He asked a few Christians, "What is the Christian perspective on the Vietnam War?" Christians answered, "It is not for us to comment." He left the faith. He became involved in different causes, trying different ideologies. Ten years later, frustrated, he read a Bible which had been left on the table. And he got a shock. He realised that this was the revolution leader he had been looking for. He joined the seminary and worked with the homeless poor. Once, it was too late to bring a homeless person to the shelter, so he brought him home. His home became a shelter. He is an adjunct lecturer at Harvard Business School. I am just using this story to show the power of the Gospel. We need to recover our theology. It is very important. Too much of our material is from the West or other contexts.

2. What do you think is the relationship between justice and evangelism?

The Hebrew word for righteousness is *tsadaq*. It means right relations with men and the environment. It comes down to our relationship with God. Boaz and Ruth—how they related to each other. Moses—how he related to his people.

Righteousness, justice and the Bible are all integral. The reality is that the Jubilee has never been practised. How can that be fulfilled? It is only under the lordship of Christ. It comes back to the faith and the Gospel. It is going to be very difficult. But therein lies the challenge.

Evangelism is very important. Because unless you are converted, it is very tough [to practise justice].

3. What would you tell a local church in terms of expressing that? Are you supposed to have both justice and evangelism? Or, do you separate the two?

The Great Commission is not synonymous with evangelism. I talked with Edmund Chan and they have been talking about discipleship at Covenant Evangelical Free Church (CEFC). The Great Commission is about what it means to be disciples. When I was pastoring a church, I wanted to emphasise discipleship. Some of the elders in church came to me and said, "Lawrence, we cannot be disciples any more." They take discipleship to mean memorising verses and scripture reading.

Over the last six months, I have been consulting with the Methodist Missions Society. They asked me to do a strategic review. The Methodist core values must be included. One of the key aspects of Wesley is not just personal holiness, but social holiness. Up to the very end of John Wesley's life, he was still very passionate for the poor. Social holiness saved England from violent revolution, unlike France. If we take discipleship and recover the personal aspect of piety, we can do justice without putting additional burdens on Christians.

4. Should social justice be pursued by individual Christians or directed by church leadership?

The US spent 60 million dollars on the environmental crisis. But look at the haze situation in Singapore now. The big businesses have a bigger influence. I suspect a lot of us cannot articulate the Gospel. The God-man. The incarnate. Once we highlight the incarnate God, we will also become incarnate. So no matter whether we are at work, at Timbuktu, at Geylang—that is your mission already. Beyond a passport to go to church on Sunday or a holy huddle.

So we begin with discipleship. I asked a friend of mine who is a climate scientist. I was very excited to meet him. "How do you use this to serve God?" He said, "At work, I try to be nice and friendly so they can know that I am Christian." There is a lot more he can do. Tim Keller puts it very well. We must recover the theology of work. I have a lot of friends who want to leave teaching and become missionaries. But I say, "Stay there. You are at the frontline of missions." We must make people understand the idea of the priesthood of believers. I was a HR man. The paperwork is important, but the people work is more important. You've got to make every manager a HR manager. The HR people think, "That will take away our rice bowl." No, they will then be your friends and improve on productivity. That's what HR is about. It is not just about payroll and bonuses.

Once we help Christians realise how to be Christian in their daily lives, this is the church at work—in the courts, hospitals, on the stock exchange.

Wherever you go, can you be a force for truth and compassion?

As Christian HR professionals, we also give people second chances. We had to hammer a manager who committed adultery in the office. He broke down and cried and asked for forgiveness. We have to show grace.

5. You mentioned overseas missions. The tension there I suppose is that if you tell everyone to stay where they are and not go to seminaries, then who would go for missions?

First of all, our premise is again that everyone is a missionary. Using the theology of work and business as a mission. In the church hierarchy, we always put missionaries and pastors at the top of the hierarchy. Then businessmen.

(And lawyers below that.)

If you are sent overseas on assignment, if you take up a job that takes you overseas, maybe your church does not have a policy that recognises you as a missionary, but you are a missionary. Maybe SCGM can affirm and recognise you (as a missionary) and create business networks of people who are in sensitive regions. If you are called to be a Wycliffe missionary, go. We need that. If you are called to plant churches, we need that as well. But in the 20th Century, to be effective in the missions setting, we need businessmen, policy makers. At the Earth Summit 2012—they evaluated what had happened since 1992. We can design the future we want. The church needs to be active in this. We have all the expertise in our pews. We need more Nehemiahs, people who realise that we are going there on the Government's expense, but we are actually God's man on the spot.

6. So then what do you think local churches can do to foster all of that?

The key thing is that the theology must change. Then hopefully the pastors and leaders will change. Unfortunately, churches have become so reliant on pastors; we have placed them on pedestals. We need to bear in mind the five-fold ministry. Unless we get the theology right, the church will not think. We need a more dialogical approach rather than a one-way flow. I am a firm believer of the church. We are to be a body of Christ. We need to think about how to act out our ministry.

7. What will you tell a church member who is very convicted about discipleship and justice, but does not receive support from church leaders?

Again, we come back to the theology and the word. John Stott is a good example. He wrote a book on responding to contemporary issues in the modern way. He believes in learning from his members. It's not just about the four spiritual laws or personal pietism. It is deeper than that. Are we even thinking? The young people are growing up to want to live for a cause. The church is teaching about living an easy life. So what happens? The young vote with their feet.

8. What do you think about para-church organisations like SCGM?

Some people are offended by the para-church. For me, it's just about the functionality. The key player is still the church. When I was a pastor in the early days, and wanted to do youth ministry, I went to Youth for Christ (YFC) and asked them, can you devise good programmes for me? They asked for our best leaders. We sent our best youth leaders to YFC. After university our youth had been church-hopping. They had become drifters. If you reach out to foreign students, but don't bring them to church, they will go back without knowing how church life is like. But those who spend time in church will go back home and continue to be rooted. It has to be grounded in the church.

9. This is slightly off-topic. But I am now thinking about technology and how it is replacing cell group and service. Why bother to have cell group when I can have cell group everyday on my Facebook group? That is something we are grappling with. This is why I am drawn to denominational worship. I am drawn to the Anglican Church because of the sense of historical continuity. It is not just based on convenience. I am against the Saturday church; historically the church meets on the 8th day. Christ resurrected on Sunday. The world also follows it. To some, the Anglican liturgy is very boring, but to me it is the power of God. Going inside a concert-like church service, you don't even talk to anyone inside. What does it mean to have an encounter with one another in a transnational context, beyond just virtual interaction? The encounter is very important.

The question to ask is, who is the church? The young people are part of it. I was asked to be a mentor in the young adults ministry in my church. Even though they are in their 20s, they are still thinking like a youth ministry. They should be stepping up as church leaders. They are under-utilised. This generation grew up with parents telling them to pursue your dream. My contention is this. The church has to have very clear views about the public square. We have to identify areas to make statements. If the Gospel is true, we have to declare the truth. Especially in contexts where truth is suppressed. All the more we need to sound the clarion's horn.

9

What's the State of Social Justice in the Singapore Church Today? Challenges and Opportunities for the Singapore Church

> *I see it all perfectly; there are two possible situations—one can either do this or that. My honest opinion and my friendly advice is this: do it or do not do it—you will regret both.*
>
> *If anyone on the verge of action should judge himself according to the outcome, he would never begin.*
>
> —*Søren Kierkegaard*

A. Where are We Now?

Blind spots are dangerous and potentially fatal. Once, I was driving on an expressway chatting with my friend who was seated at the passenger seat next to me. All of a sudden, a black BMW veered towards me from the left. By gut instinct and without even checking the right lane, I swerved to the right lane to avoid the BMW. The BMW drove past us and filtered into my lane. A middle-aged lady with a large hairdo and wearing huge (no doubt, branded) shades was driving the BMW. My friend and I could not help but feel our lives had been preserved by God's grace that day. We could have been killed just because that lady did not check her blind spot before changing lanes. We could have collided into another vehicle.

Having looked at the history of the global and the Singapore Church's views on, and practice of, social justice, this chapter looks at the present. As will be seen from the results of a survey conducted among Singapore Christians below, it appears that social justice is presently still hidden in a *blind spot* of the Singapore Church. While this blind spot is not immediately fatal, it could be potentially dangerous for the health of the Church. What are the prevailing views and attitudes towards social justice in the Singapore Church today? How does the Singapore Church fare in terms of its expression and pursuit of social justice? And what areas of improvement are there in this regard? We consider these issues in the survey.

B. Empirical Survey

The survey was conducted among 117 Christians in Singapore, coming from all the mainline denominations and traditions such as the Methodist, Anglican, Lutheran, Baptist, Brethren, Presbyterian, Bible-Presbyterian, Evangelical Free Church, Pentecostal, as well as smaller independent churches, on their attitudes and views regarding various issues including social justice and their local church. The survey also covered other issues, such as family life, civic consciousness, participation in local church, faith communities or para-church organisations, work and career, and perceptions of Christians in Singapore. The intent of the survey was to provide empirical evidence of the attitudes of Christians in Singapore so that the Singapore Church would be able to reflect on possible challenges and opportunities for the Church in the coming years. Here are various charts setting out key findings relevant to the subject matter of this book.

Demographics of Respondents

Gender

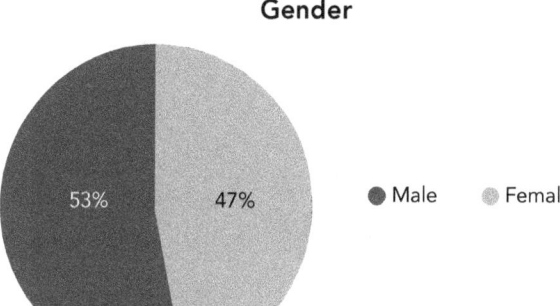

Age Group

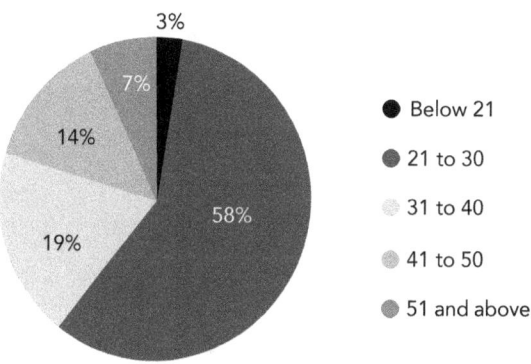

Highest Education Level

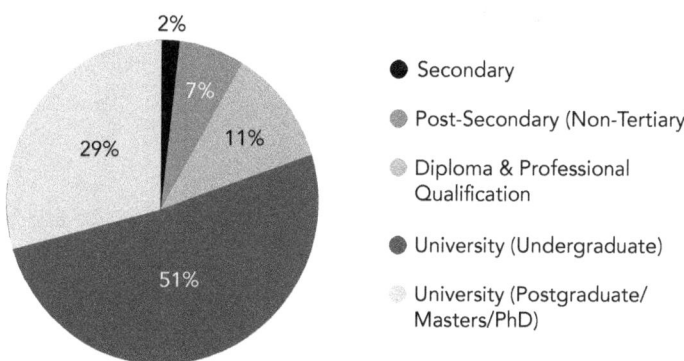

Annual Income

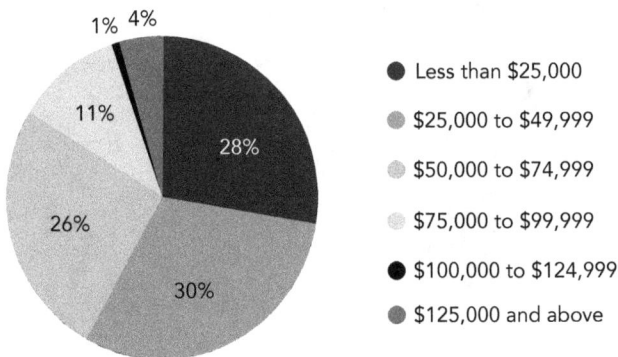

Size of Church

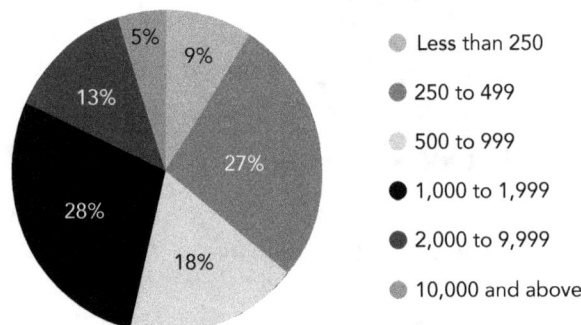

Attitudes and Views on Social Justice and the Local Church

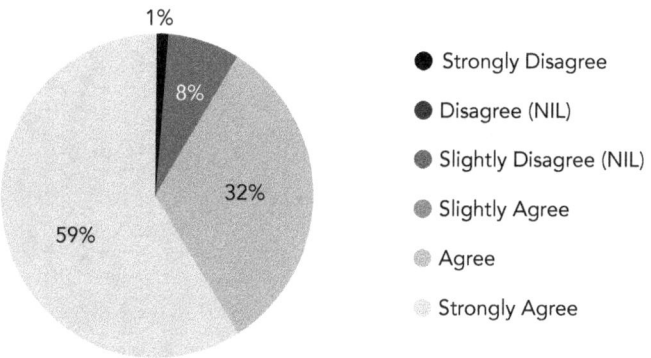

Social justice (defined here as concern and action for the socioeconomically less well-off) is part of the Christian faith

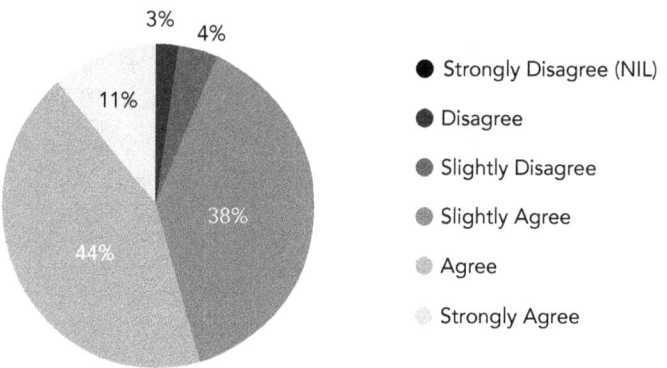

I pursue social justice

Has your church had sermons/workshop/discussions/ministries on social justice?

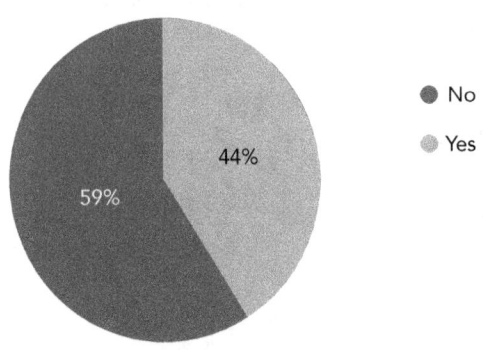

My church leaders understand social justice.

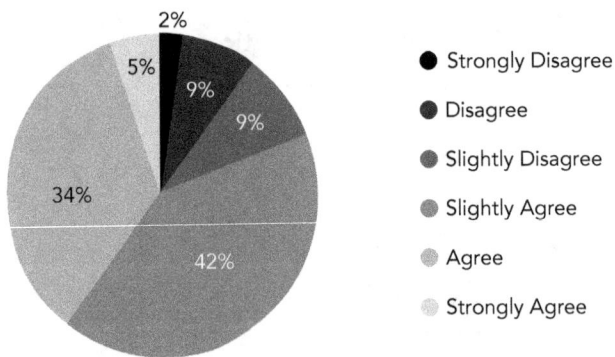

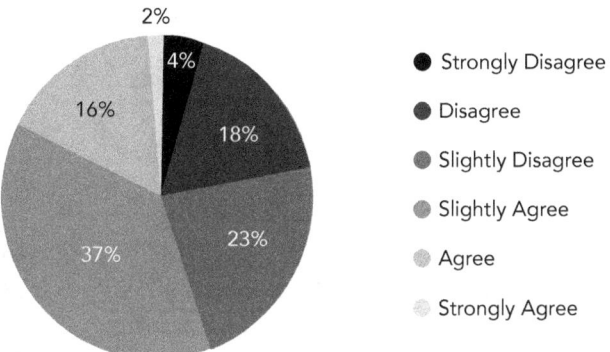

My church is doing enough regarding social justice.

- Strongly Disagree: 2%
- Disagree: 4%
- Slightly Disagree: 18%
- Slightly Agree: 23%
- Agree: 37%
- Strongly Agree: 16%

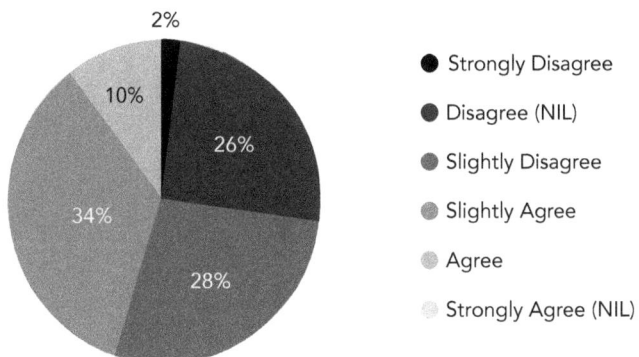

The majority of my church congregation understands biblical social justice.

- Strongly Disagree: 2%
- Disagree (NIL)
- Slightly Disagree: 26%
- Slightly Agree: 28%
- Agree: 34%
- Strongly Agree (NIL)

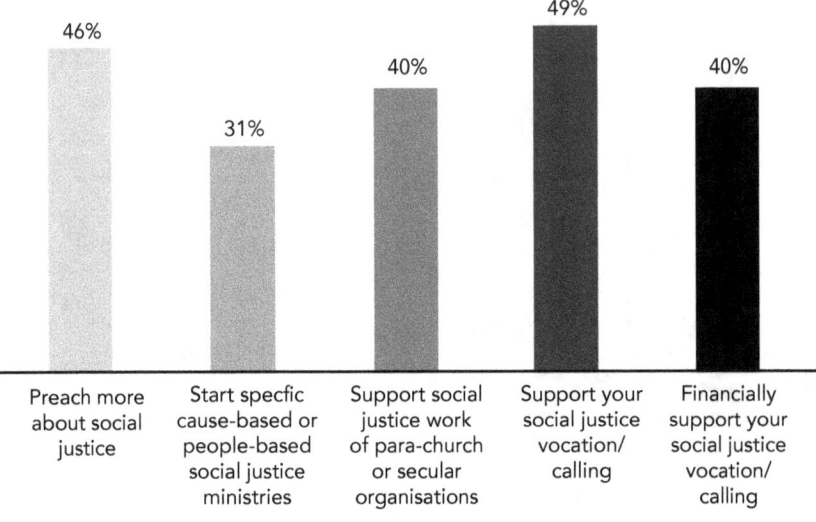

Attitudes and Views on Civil Society

Currently, I volunteer at 1 or more organisation(s).

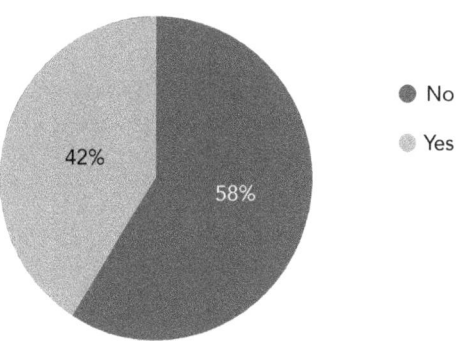

I make regular donations to charitable causes or organisations.

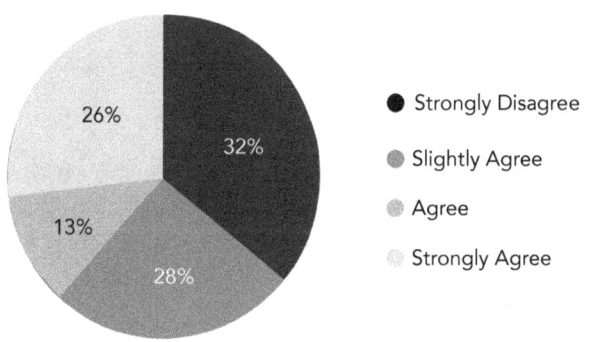

The Singapore Government is doing a good job in furthering the interests of Singapore society and community.

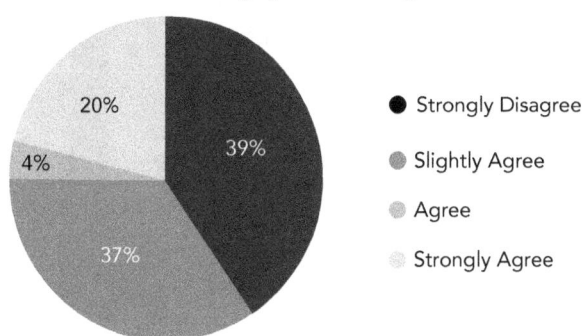

Attitudes and Views on How Non-Christians View Christians in Singapore

Do you think that generally, non-Christians have a negative view of Christians in Singapore?

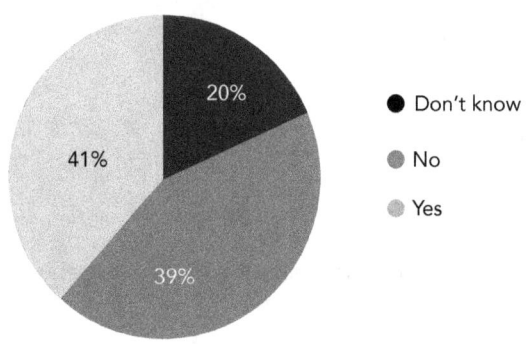

- Don't know: 20%
- No: 39%
- Yes: 41%

What words would you use to describe the attitudes that non-Christians have of Christians in Singapore? (Options under this question are not exclusive.)

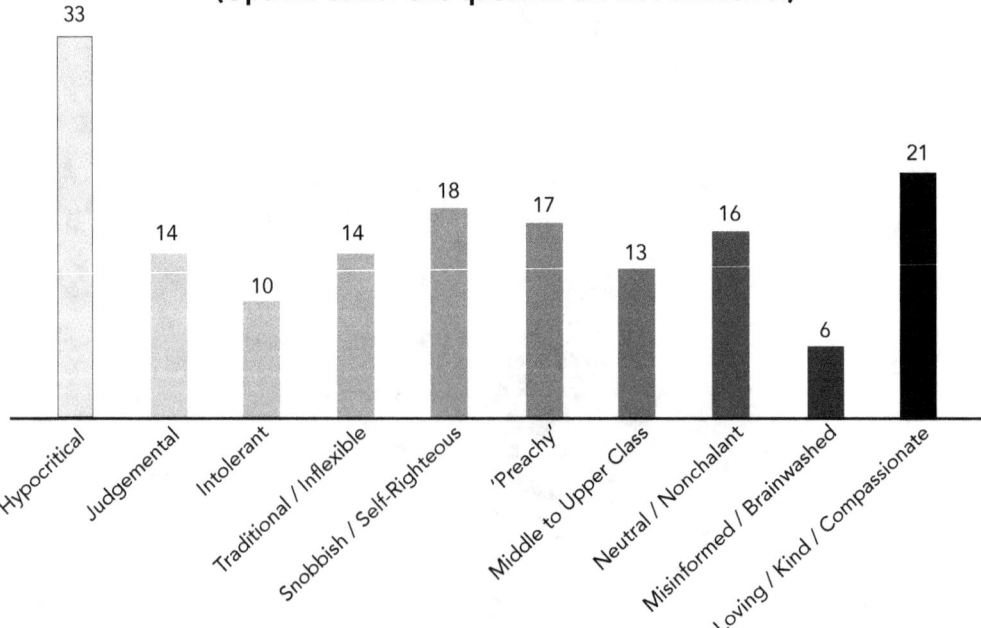

- Hypocritical: 33
- Judgemental: 14
- Intolerant: 10
- Traditional / Inflexible: 14
- Snobbish / Self-Righteous: 18
- 'Preachy': 17
- Middle to Upper Class: 13
- Neutral / Nonchalant: 16
- Misinformed / Brainwashed: 6
- Loving / Kind / Compassionate: 21

C. Trends in the Survey

Qualifications on the survey should be mentioned. First, the survey was conducted online and respondents were contacted primarily through social media and email. This may have led to the significant percentage of respondents being in the age group of 21 to 30 years old. The views of those below 21 and above 51 years old are underrepresented (collectively amounting to only a total of 10 per cent of the respondents). Second, an overwhelming percentage of respondents have had university education (80 per cent). In contrast, another survey suggests that about 32 per cent of Christians in Singapore have had university education.[674] Thus, the results of the survey may not be representative of the wider Singapore Church.

The first significant trend from the survey results is that the practice of social justice among the respondents appears to be prevalent. Ninety-nine per cent of the respondents agree that social justice is a part of their faith, and 93 per cent agree that they are pursuing social justice. This may be the result of a skewed demographic of the respondents due to the social groups which I had tapped on for responses to the survey. Interestingly, 58 per cent of the respondents indicated that they do *not* volunteer at any organisation. This suggests that many of them believe that the pursuit of social justice need not be expressed in the form of volunteerism in a specific organisation, but as a lifestyle.

The second significant point is that while an overwhelming percentage of the respondents are pursuing social justice, they are of the view that their local church leaders' understanding and their churches' pursuit of social justice are subpar. Nineteen per cent of the respondents do not

---

[674] Terence Chong, "Megachurches in Singapore: The Faith of an Emergent Middle Class", *Pacific Affairs* 88.2 (June 2015): 215, p. 218; Terence Chong, Hui Yew-Foong, *Different Under God: A Survey of Church-going Protestants in Singapore* (Institute of Southeast Asian Studies, 2013).

> **There is a perception that our local church congregations do not understand social justice.**

think that their church leaders understand social justice. 45 per cent of the respondents think that their church is *not* doing enough regarding social justice. If indeed 81 per cent of the respondents think that their church leaders do understand social justice, why then do 45 per cent of the respondents think that their church is not doing enough regarding social justice? This raises the question of whether there is a lack of *willingness* on the part of church leaders or a lack of resources.

Third, there is a perception that our local church congregations do not understand social justice. Fifty-six per cent of respondents think that the majority of their church congregation *do not* understand social justice, and 34 per cent only slightly agree that the majority of their church congregation do understand it.

Fourth, there is a significant percentage of respondents who desire their local churches to support their social justice vocation or calling financially and non-financially (80 per cent). This is followed by another 40 per cent of the respondents who desire their local churches to support the social justice work of para-church or secular organisations.

Fifth, 44 per cent of the respondents' local churches have *not* had any sermon, workshop, discussion or ministry on social justice.

Sixth, many of the respondents are pessimistic about the Singapore Government's work in furthering the interests of the Singapore community (20 per cent disagreeing, and 39 per cent slightly agreeing, that the Singapore Government is furthering the interests of the Singapore community). It may be due to the fact that many of the respondents are keenly sensitised to social justice issues and thus may be more critical of the Government's work.

Seventh, many respondents believe that non-Christians perceive Christians negatively (41 per cent). This is similar to the results of a survey done in the US, which suggests that Christians and Christianity are indeed perceived by non-Christians with scepticism.[675] Both in Singapore (based on the results of this survey) and in the US, the view that Christians are "hypocritical" comes out tops.

D. Reflections and Lessons from the Survey

It appears from the above trends that there are Singapore Christians who are presently pursuing social justice and who feel discontented about their local churches in relation to this aspect of their faith. This empirical survey accords with my prior anecdotal observations about how many young adults in the Church today have felt frustrated, disappointed or disillusioned with what they perceive as their local churches' apathy towards social, economic and political issues which they feel are important to them and their faith. Biblical social justice is not even raised in many of their churches at all. Many perceive their church leaders and fellow church members as having little understanding about what the Bible says about social justice, and what they are doing in regard to social justice. And many of them feel disenchanted about a lack of support for their own social justice pursuits. I know of young adults who left, or thought about

---

675 David Kinnaman, Gabe Lyons, *unChristian, What a New Generation Really Thinks about Christianity and Why It Matters* (Baker Books, 2007).

leaving, their local churches because they felt that their church did not support or understand their social justice ministry.

If indeed one accepts that God is concerned about justice—including *social* justice; that God desires—*demands*—His Kingdom people to seek justice, then much more needs to be done in this department. This can be both a challenge and opportunity for the Singapore Church.

A Challenge to Church Leaders
Church leaders should actively grapple with the notion of biblical justice as a key aspect of the Christian faith which requires intentional discipleship. This requires church leaders to first investigate the claims of the Bible concerning social justice (much of which has been traversed in this book), and to *also* step out and immerse themselves in the work, ministry and experiences of various individuals, organisations and churches who are actively pursuing social justice. This is because understanding the demands of justice requires understanding that is not only theoretical or practical, but also emotional.

Next, church leaders should prayerfully consider what could be practically done in their churches to intentionally disciple their church members on biblical social justice. Clearly, there is a need for teaching about biblical social justice: Forty-six per cent of the respondents desire this in their local churches. Such teaching can be done over the pulpit or through special Bible study classes. It is important for churches to plan the topics and themes of their preaching and teaching in a way, and with the frequency, which emphasises different aspects of the Christian faith proportionate to their importance in the general scheme. Preaching too much about justice at the expense of the forgiveness of sins or preaching too much about sexual ethics at the expense of social holiness are examples of disproportionate emphasis.

Another aspect of intentional discipleship would be to explore ways to support church members who are already pursuing social justice. Interestingly, only 31 per cent of the respondents indicate that they desire their church to start specific cause-based or people-based social justice ministries. I would suggest that a primary means of discipleship in this area would be empowering individuals Christians to pursue justice rather than for the local church as an organisation to be undertaking justice programmes. This does not mean that churches should not undertake any activities. Rather, such activities should be merely a means to an end: To expose, empower and commission individual members to pursue social justice outside of the institutional church. The focus thereafter would then be to provide ways to support their social justice vocational calling.

Three key suggestions stand out in terms of local churches supporting the social justice ministries of their members.

The first is for local churches to support the social justice vocation or calling of their members. Forty-nine per cent of respondents expressed this desire. How can this be done? I suggest pastoral care, prayer support, holding special sessions where the member shares his justice ministry with others and church leaders commission and bless his ministry, and leaders (occasionally) participating in the ministry's activities. Such acts are not mere lip service but provide important encouragement and affirmation for the member.

The second suggestion is that local churches should consider partnering with, and supporting, para-church organisations in their social justice work (40 per cent of respondents affirmed this option). This would be resource-efficient for both the local church and the para-church organisation, since the local church need not duplicate the work already started by others who are 'specialists' and who have already been working the ground. Send cell groups of church members to volunteer with these para-church organisations. Commission particular individuals to explore meaningful partnerships: Consider what needs these para-church organisations have and how the local church can meet them. Besides para-church organisations, local churches should also partner with individual members to explore social enterprises and the Business as Missions (BAM) model[676] as platforms for pursuing holistic dignifying social justice. For example, in a recent local news incident, a restaurant customer told the restaurant owner to fire a dishwasher who had a genetic disorder (neurofibromatosis) causing him to have many benign tumours all over his body. The restaurant owner told the customer off. It was later reported in an interview with the restaurant owner, who chose to remain anonymous, that she hired people no one else would. This included a 27-year-old chef who weighed 156kg and who had been rejected 9 times prior in his applications to work at *zi char* kitchens because he was too big and would obstruct the kitchen space. The restaurant owner hired him and reconfigured her kitchen to accommodate him. Another staff, an 81-year-old lady who had various medical problems and thus frequently had to take off for medical appointments, similarly couldn't find work for 20 years prior to this restaurant owner approaching her to hire her when she noticed that the lady often sat at the hawker centre all day "doing nothing". Such an example illustrates the potentially powerful witness of Christian businesspersons in how they do business.[677]

The third key suggestion given by many respondents (40 per cent) is for the local church to *financially* support their individual social justice ministry, just like how many churches financially support "cross-cultural or

---

676 See C Neal Johnson, *Business as Mission: A Comprehensive Guide to Theory and Practice* (Downers Grove, Ill.: IVP Academic, 2009); Mats Tunehag, Wayne McGee and Josie Plummer, "Business as Mission", *Lausanne Occasional Paper (LOP)* No. 59 (2004), https://www.lausanne.org/docs/2004forum/LOP59_IG30.pdf.
677 See "Restaurant boss hires those no one will", *My Paper* (19 November 2015), http://mypaper.sg/top-stories/restaurant-boss-hires-those-no-one-will-20151119.

overseas missionaries". In several conversations I have had with different people, a sentiment is expressed that there is no difference between a missionary who *preaches* and *demonstrates* the gospel in a foreign land and a missionary who does the same in Singapore. It is commonly expressed that churches would readily label the former "missionaries" but the latter as merely doing "ordinary" evangelism. I have a few friends who have the privilege of church leadership who understand the importance of their social justice ministry *outside of the local church environment* and grant them the flexibility of using "work hours" as church staff to engage in their social justice ministry. However, this remains an anomaly rather than the norm. I'd suggest that church leaders should seriously rethink their pre-existing assumptions and paradigms about "paid ministry work".

Engage Your Local Church

If you are an individual Christian passionate about social justice, but perhaps feel disappointed about your local church leaders' and members' attitudes on social justice, I encourage you to stay on and persevere in transforming your church.

First, you must recognise that you are privileged to have the passion for social justice. You may feel like a salmon swimming upstream. Yet, that is the nature of being a pioneer and being counter-cultural. Pray for perseverance.

Second, you should engage your church leaders in understanding biblical social justice. Start by first obtaining a good grasp of the biblical narrative and exegesis of passages on biblical justice (I hope this book helps you!). In engaging your leaders, the theology you espouse must be thought through, well-informed and orthodox. It must not appear to come from sentimentality or some fashionable fad. Inform, and be accountable to, your church leaders about what you do in this department.

Invite them to your ministry. As a matter of wisdom, perhaps even be selective about whom you engage or ask *first*. Perhaps a particular elder whom you have a closer affinity with or a younger deacon whom you know to be more open-minded.

Third, engage in meaningful conversations with other church members about the topic. Talk about your own ministry. If asked further, talk about your theological convictions underpinning your ministry. Share with them Christian writings and perspectives on justice issues which are close to your heart.

Opportunity for Witness, Discipleship and Gospel

Embracing biblical social justice creates opportunities for the Singapore Church in terms of its witness to the world, discipleship of members and expression of the Gospel. Many respondents believe that non-Christians perceive Christians to be hypocritical. Based on anecdotal observations, I think many non-Christians perceive Christians as hypocritical because their 'niceness' is superficial. Often, non-Christians have the expectation that Christians should 'go the extra mile' or 'go deep' in caring for people, and spend more time and money on the needy. Also, similar to the findings in the survey on non-Christians' perceptions of Christians in the US,[678] many non-Christians hold the view that Christians behave 'nice' or show concern to others *only* to proselytise.

> **When we embrace biblical social justice, our expressions of it would necessarily be deep, genuine and winsome.**

A proper perspective of the Gospel of

---

[678] David Kinnaman, Gabe Lyons, *unChristian, What a New Generation Really Thinks about Christianity and Why It Matters* (Baker Books, 2007).

the Kingdom of God should mould our attitudes and lifestyles in a way that we express justice, mercy and love to others *not only* as a means to share the Gospel and disciple others, but *also* as a way of expressing our love and reciprocal faithfulness to God. When we embrace biblical social justice, our expressions of it would necessarily be deep, genuine and winsome. As apostle Peter urged his flock, we should do good so that the foolish and the persecutors will be silenced or won over.[679]

Deep and genuine justice-seeking enables us to build bridges for, and simultaneously engage in, disciple-making and expressing the Gospel. The starting point must be that such conduct are *per se* acts of love and faithfulness to God. For without love—for God and for others—we are nothing.[680]

E. Some Justice Issues in Singapore

As we pursue social justice, it is important to understand the local context and pray for wisdom to negotiate the local environment so as to go forth and meet people where they are. For Jesus is already there with those in need, tending to their wounds and wrongs, and "[i]f anyone serves [Him], he must follow [Jesus]; and where [Jesus is], there will [His] servant be also".[681]

Throughout this book, I have sought to raise pertinent examples, statistics, issues and anecdotes. However, these are non-exhaustive. People's needs are constantly in flux; so our just response must also be dynamic. For the same reason, I decided not to set out in chapter

---

679   1 Peter 2:12, 15.
680   1 Corinthians 13.
681   John 12:26.

and verse specific issues and needs. Nevertheless, I have set out in the additional materials on the book's website a list of social justice areas and issues or communities which I think are pertinent in the Singapore context and some organisations started by Christians serving those areas.[682]

F. Need for Catalyst and Community

We have considered that anecdotal and statistical evidence suggests that *the Singapore Church is presently lacking in sufficient emphasis on biblical social justice as an integral facet of God's Kingdom community, in terms of teaching, discipleship and action.* This may be a challenge and an opportunity for church leaders and members to critically examine their pre-existing assumptions and paradigms about biblical social justice.

For the above reason, a group of friends and I initiated in 2013 an informal community of Christians called Micah 6:8 Intersections. It was meant to be (i) a space for Jesus followers to explore what it means to seek justice and show mercy to the marginalised, needy and poor among us; (ii) a platform for Christ-led organisations and individuals to share about how God is empowering them to express the Micah Mandate in Micah 6:8; and (iii) a community for Jesus followers to worship, to connect, be equipped and be challenged about living out Micah 6:8.

Then in 2015, a few Christians and I got together and initiated a six-month long intentional gathering of Christian activists called TeamZero. The idea was that in the light of Singapore's Jubilee year (Singapore's 50th year of independence), we wanted to return to the ground zero of our faith and critically examine the convictions and theology

---

682   See book's website's section on "Some Justice Issues In Singapore".

underlying our praxis so that our praxis would be fundamentally shaped by the cognizance that we live in between two Jubilees, Jesus in His Incarnation being our first Jubilee, and Jesus' immanent return as our final Jubilee.

Since then, we at Micah 6:8 Intersections and TeamZero realised the need for a catalyst to ignite this movement of engaging local churches to reclaim biblical social justice, the need for a community of Christian justice practitioners and the need for a resource to help local churches and individuals figure their way around in pursuing social justice. In the light of that, my teammates and I have remoulded Micah 6:8 Intersections into **Micah Singapore,** the Singapore chapter of the international Micah Network.

Our vision is to see the Singapore Church embrace biblical social justice, as part of its integral mission, in faith, discipleship and witness. And our mission is to support local churches in embracing this challenge and opportunity of reclaiming biblical social justice. We believe that it is in and through community that we can achieve this. I hope that you, too, will share this same vision, join our community and play your part in pursuing this.

Chapter Summary

- Embracing biblical social justice creates opportunities for the Singapore Church in terms of its witness to the world, discipleship of members and expression of the Gospel.
- Based on the empirical survey, it appears the Singapore Church is presently lacking in sufficient emphasis on biblical social justice as an integral facet of God's Kingdom community, in terms of teaching, discipleship and action.
- There is especially a need for local churches to:
  - Disciple and teach about biblical social justice;
  - Support the ministry of church members who are already pursuing social justice; and
  - Partner with, and support, para-church organisations in their social justice work.
- Individual Christians should engage their local church leaders and fellow church members on biblical social justice.

Discussion Questions

1. How does your local church teach and disciple its members about biblical justice? What do you wish were different? How would you express this wish to your church leaders?
2. How would you engage church leaders and other members in your church on biblical justice?
3. What can you and/or your local faith community do to pursue biblical justice in your areas of influence, whether geographical or otherwise? How best should this be done in terms of organisation, structure and activities?

INTERVIEW: Eunice Lim

● ● ●

Eunice is a social worker by training who now serves full-time in her home church, Woodlands Evangelical Free Church. She previously spent seven years at the National Council of Social Service and continues to maintain close ties with the social service sector. She also serves actively at a ministry that seeks to bring healing, help and hope to the street ladies in Singapore's red light district.

Any given week or two has her spending time equipping and pouring into her young adult ministry leaders, engaging in pastoral ministry, reaching out to street ladies as well as the men who control or seek out these ladies, introducing ex-streetwalkers to Jesus and witnessing firsthand how He is pursuing them relentlessly, and challenging and training social service professionals to grow in competence, courage and creativity.

Eunice desires for her life and ministry to be characterised as one spent on comforting the disturbed and disturbing the comfortable, in response to a God who calls us to full-time devotion, not just full-time ministry.

1. Share with us your journey in your involvement with social justice.
I have always wanted to spend my life being a voice for the voiceless. But beyond that, I've never had a childhood ambition or known what I wanted to be or do with my life. So not too surprisingly, I ended up becoming a social worker.

I joined the National Council of Social Service (NCSS) upon graduation and spent seven years working on development, implementation and delivery of social services at a national level. It was a tremendous time of exposure and growth. However, no matter how 'shiny' my project assignments were, I kept being plagued with the feeling that all my efforts were but icing on the cake. While there's always more that can be done to improve social services, truth be told, much of our social service infrastructure is very much in place and I sensed that the Lord was calling me to move out to where the needs were still unmet.

I had no idea where or what that was, but after a long wrestle, I left NCSS. I had no clue where God would lead but it was clear He was asking me to leave by faith and to trust Him to open the next door. So I quit my job and took a six-month sabbatical to wait on Him—stepping away from work, ministry and everything else I had grown increasingly busy with.

Half of that time, I chose to spend away in the United States where I knew no one and had all the time in the world to hear from the Lord. Just one week before I flew off though, God spoke to me in a crystal clear voice that He wanted me in full-time ministry. That freaked me out because that was the last thing I wanted to do. The church was the last place in my mind to have unmet needs that I could work on or where I could serve the most marginalised and vulnerable. So with much fear and dread, I headed to the US, desperate to *really* hear from the Lord about why the call to full-time ministry and what that meant.

While in the US, I sought to volunteer in the kinds of places I had little or no exposure to in Singapore since I was still looking to find what it meant to meet unmet needs. So I volunteered to help out in shelters that housed and fed men with AIDS and homeless women. None of what I did (like mop the floor, disinfect the tables and chairs, chop tomatoes, etc.) felt vaguely important or felt like it was helping to shift the needle in any of the work with these communities. But every time I walked out from a five-hour shift in one of these shelters into the bitter cold winter, there was a strange warmth and fullness in my heart that was so unfamiliar and made so little sense.

It made me feel uncomfortable though. Because all that we did in these shelters—feeding and supporting people well regardless of their commitment to change or work on their issues—the opposite of much that I used to do at NCSS to ensure that social services were optimising resources to achieve clear outcomes. And as I struggled to reconcile how what felt so right seemed so wrong, God opened my eyes to see that what I was witnessing was extravagant grace being poured forth on undeserving individuals. This was the Gospel being lived out.

And suddenly, it made sense. There was a bottom tier of people who were still beyond the reach of professional social services who needed people who would literally handhold them and pursue them and relentlessly support them no matter how many times they failed and pushed us away. A bottom tier who had no personal incentive and motivation to change because they had never known life any other way and had no means to live any differently. And God convicted me strongly that when it came to journeying with these people often labelled as undeserving, unmotivated, ungrateful, etc., the uncomfortable conclusion was that this was precisely the role of the Church, not the Government, not social services. Because extravagant grace that is willing to take risks, be taken advantage of, and yet keep hoping and giving and pursuing is the heart of the Gospel and has been demonstrated in the life of Christ.

So I came back to Singapore with these convictions, but still no idea what full-time ministry in that context looked like. I felt torn because I felt such a burden to serve the marginalised but I could not see how this would be a full-time ministry position in my church or any church. Nonetheless, I came back and started looking for groups/agencies/people who did this kind of work with migrant workers, prostitutes, people struggling with LGBT issues, etc. My church graciously extended an invitation for me to intern for six months to explore whether God was calling me to full-time ministry in church or in a particular mercy ministry outside of church since I felt strongly about both despite the fact that they seemed to be mutually exclusive at that point.

Within my first month back from the US, a friend introduced me to a ministry that reached out to offer help, healing and hope to prostitutes. The minute I met with the co-founders and heard their vision and burden for the work, I knew this was it. I plugged in and started serving. Every time I spent time at this ministry, I was blown away. Every week I went, I would see or hear about a miracle in the life of one of the women or in the way the Lord was providing for the ministry. And for the first time in my life, I saw God working in such tangible, amazing ways not for a season but regularly! And it made me question, why was this not happening in my church?

The more I served in church and at this ministry to the women on the streets, the more it felt like I was toggling between two different screens. This ministry to the streetwalkers was so Spirit-led and so... unstructured. Church was so structured and so much less... dependent on the Spirit. And I was forced to ask, amidst all the structure, all the strategic planning, where is Jesus? So many of us are so comfortable in church and our friends and communities that we were content to focus on us and others like us. It struck me that if Jesus came to Singapore for a day, He would more likely be in the back alleys of Geylang seeking out the lost where they were, than in our boardroom meetings, or even in the evangelistic events we run in church for our friends. And so God allowed me to grow increasingly uncomfortable with the status quo I had grown up with in church, and I was forced to unlearn many things, and learn many new things about Him.

So three months in, when both church and this ministry I had been serving with asked me if I would join them on staff as a full-time ministry worker, I was torn. On the one hand, I knew that if I worked at ministry to street ladies, it'd be with likeminded, amazingly passionate people who made their life and ministry about serving the marginalised, which I craved to do. Yet, if I joined them, in all likelihood, my church would put me on stage, commission me, send me, and then forget about me (because I knew I was guilty of that when it came to other missionaries since out of sight meant out of mind too!).

If I stayed within the church though, I could be the "thorn in its flesh", constantly questioning why and what we were doing and teaching, instigating more to live lives of radical obedience, and hopefully have a role to play in challenging the status quo. Initially, there was some concern that I would take people away from the church to serve outside of it where my passions lay, but slowly, the leaders saw that those who went out to be a part of mercy and justice work returned recharged to serve in church or wherever they were called to, because there was a fresh appreciation of the Gospel, its power, and what it meant to be saved by grace for good works.

Eventually, after seeking God about where He wanted me to serve, I sensed His clear leading to serve full-time in my church. He showed me that as much as His heart is for the lost, His desire is also for His Church, that the Bride of Christ be perfected for His return and aroused from the stupor that I, too, had found myself in for much of my Christian life. I slowly sensed that He had allowed me to be exposed to the work amongst street ladies and other social justice ministries that I may mobilise more people to come and see His heart for the lost, to be awakened to the power of the Gospel, and that those of us within the church who are saved will see and savour this God who pursues His creation relentlessly, regardless of who we are.

So needless to say, a major part of this journey had to do with God redefining what I understood about worship and being awakened to the fullness of the Gospel. He knew that unless I was deeply convicted of my sin, I would engage in mercy and justice work with a sense of self-righteousness.

I remembered most clearly that on one of my first few prayer walks in Geylang as we were praying and reaching out to the streetwalkers, I felt put off by the men on the streets. I thought to myself, "These men are such scum. They're the reason these women are being sold on the streets." Then the Spirit convicted me and it felt like a punch in my stomach. He said "These men you think of as scum, well that's the same way I see you. Apart from Christ's blood that has been shed for you, you are just as filthy and despicable. There's no reason why I chose you other than grace, and I love them as much as I love you."

And so God continues to refine me and break me that I might be used in His hands for His work. It's humbling that while we are out ministering on the streets thinking that we are here to help these people, God uses what I see to convict me about my own sin and brokenness, His heart for His Church, and His love that pursues relentlessly the streetwalker, the Sunday church-goer and myself, a sinner.

So, I suppose I stumbled into social justice work. God had laid certain passions in my heart and granted me certain training and expertise. But ironically, He's had to purify and refine these passions, strip away what I thought would make for good skills in such work, and learn that any social justice work is all about God, done in His power, for His pleasure.

2. How should the Church relate to the social service sector?
Many of today's social services are backed or started by churches. And they do great work. Fei Yue Community Services or Care Corner, for example. You definitely need these well-run social services. In many instances, churches establish these organisations and fund them, but the running of the day-to-day services is handled by professionals, which is needful. But, it does not absolve the role of the church, by which I mean the individual members that make up the church.

There are different tiers in terms of individual church members' involvement. One can donate financially to these services, serve in the management committee or board, spend time reading to children from low-income families or playing basketball with at-risk youths. But we tend to stop there.

I think we're called to do more though. The Bible is instructive about people mostly at the margins. And light is the brightest in the darkest places. If we are all content to be playing in a safe zone where, to be honest, any good citizen of this land can and should do, then what's distinctive about our Christian witness?

Let me give you an example. Recently, Speaker of Parliament Halimah Yacob commented on the transvestite prostitutes in one of the parks in Woodlands. The Government's response was that it would provide more policing and get rid of the problem. But this pushes the prostitutes yet further to the margins. I wondered, is the church rejoicing at this news, relieved that these prostitutes are being gotten rid of, or is the church asking what she can do to reach them? It's obviously a complicated, messy issue, but I think it's in these dark, messy places where the church has the greatest impact. We need to go to where the church is not usually seen.

Don't get me wrong—there's a time and space for church members to give money, serve on committees, etc. But there is so much more. Jesus came and went out of His way to seek out and be with the sinner and the sick. I believe if we want to be like Christ in every way, it necessarily involves getting our hands dirty and going where conventional human wisdom or structures or services aren't enough to fix problems.

You can say I am idealistic or ignorant, but I really think that where social services are limited because the type of care or work is too costly, where time and relationships and trust are needed to be forged, where we have to move beyond our comfort zone not to help fix someone but to show them the love of Christ, where change is unlikely or super hard to come by through behaviour modification alone without the transforming power of the Gospel, that's where the church needs to be. But people are so reluctant to go there because it's costly.

3. How should the Church help, urge, prod, enable, the ordinary church member to pursue social justice in this way?

Think of it in terms of awareness, acceptance and action.

Raising awareness by opening up conversations about where the needs are is one way. Many people have no idea we have local prostitutes, for example. But awareness of needs is just one bit of the equation. Beyond hearing, they need to see. But seeing is also not enough. It's through meaningful interaction that we move towards acceptance of people vastly different from us. And as we learn to accept and love them the way Christ does, we move towards healthy action. I say healthy because if we act on a worldly sense of injustice, it feeds our ego. But action that does not seek to fix but to love and restore; and done *with* those we are trying to help, not just *for* them, is often far more dignifying and honouring to the people we're serving and to God.

So I would say get out of your comfort zone, go see, allow your heart to be broken, ask the Lord where and what He wants you to do, and do it. I am heartened to see how many churches and especially youth/young adult groups are now exposing their people to various mercy and justice ministries and I am excited to see how God is moving.

And then there are also instances where people in church are already passionate about such things, but do not seem to find the church open or much interested in social justice. Often, these are young people who are exposed to such work through school and their friends and they begin to question why their church does not seem to care or even understand what is happening outside its walls. If we do not listen and journey with these young people, we risk losing them. If we lose the young people to other churches, that's not so bad. But if they leave the faith entirely because they cannot reconcile the chasm they see between what the Bible says and what the Church is, then I think that is really something we need to sit up and deal with.

Personally, I'm thankful that I got pointed to TeamZero, which is a community that encourages and facilitates deep theological reflection by individuals committed to following Jesus and who are ready and willing to engage in praxis. Being involved in Team Zero gave me a safe space to question, find answers to and learn with others with similar passions and interests across denominations, vocations and ages. So while individual churches may not be ready to start their own social justice ministry arms, encouraging those with such interests to be in community with others and giving them space to learn and experiment is often helpful. In fact, it is probably a better idea for churches wanting to get involved in social justice ministry to learn from others already engaged in such work.

4. Are you saying that churches should mobilise their members to go out to work with organisations and ministries that are already out there doing good work, and not start their own justice and mercy ministries or programmes?

In terms of social services, I personally do not think churches should start new services. There are already so many in existence. If they really feel led and want to provide social services, they definitely should do their due diligence and find out where the needs are greatest, not just act on areas where they think there are needs. In all honesty, starting a new social service arm is not the best way to meet social needs because it requires extensive expertise and resources. But a lot of churches want to have their own social arm to call their own and I would ask why. We could well be more effective as a Body of Christ if we gave resources to an existing agency doing the work and pointed our people to serve with them rather than start your own.

All the more so when it comes to social justice work with groups such as with migrants, sex workers, I would say go to existing organisations. Partner them. Learn. Understudy. The ugly way of saying it is, if it's for your vainglory or one person's heartfelt passion, it will fail. The church does not necessarily have the expertise. Go to where people have expertise. That is the beauty of it. It is not about my church or your church. It is about the larger church community. One of the things I really appreciate about the ministry I serve in that reaches out to streetwalkers is how at our prayer walks, there can be people from 18 different churches from seven denominations but we all go out under Christ's banner to seek and save the lost. No one can claim to own this ministry. It is the Lord's and we His people are all a part of it.

5. For churches, perhaps there's a sense of a need for KPIs.
Yes that's true, but I suppose it begs the question of what the biblical basis for that is. There can be no selfish pride in this work. It's not about who started it, who accomplished what, who saw this prostitute come to faith, etc. In Geylang, because of the number of groups that are now going out for prayer walks, the pimps see us collectively as the "Hallelujah People" and I think that is great! It is not which church or group is best known on the streets. It is about whether people on the streets know that Jesus is seeking them out.

I will always remember how, when one of the co-founders of the ministry to the street ladies was asked how she felt about more and more groups going out to the streets for prayer walks and whether it was too much or encroaching in what they were doing, she said, "No! The more the better! If we can have groups go out to pray every single night of the week, how much light we would bring into this dark place!" So I definitely feel that the more we do together, the more we serve each other's needs, the more God is glorified. I like, too, how this ministry to street ladies gladly offers its premise to other groups that do similar work as itself. It recognises that God has blessed them with a premise not for their work solely, but for Kingdom work. That our churches would have the same openness, generosity and eagerness to partner each other for God's glory!

6. From my survey, a number of people say, I want my church to support my social justice vocation or calling. How do you think churches should support their vocation or calling?
There are a lot of ways. Church leadership can get behind it. It can be reflected in the church budget. It can be preached from the pulpit. Small groups can begin going to serve. But for a lot of churches where that is not the DNA, the next best thing is to give space. Giving them space to

do these things. That's where it's hard. Because if you have a not so open-minded pastor, they will be thinking, "Why do you do these things?" But where pastors go and see, have conversations with them, that is one key way they can support individuals passionate about social justice. Young people need the space to go and try.

I was most thankful when my church said to me, take your internship time and spend it 50-50, half in church and half of the time, you go out and explore these ministries that God has given you a burden for. I was amazed. That's very generous, giving me the space when there are so many needs in church. I suppose the issue is what kind of support do you need?

So while I am now full-time on staff with my church and about 10 to 15 per cent of my time is spent working with the street ladies and their children, so much of my conversations in church centre on the ministry in Geylang to help them expand their worldview and to provide a different perspective. Slowly, people who catch the vision come. Young people come. Leaders come. After a year of serving at this ministry to streetwalkers, I got the chance to share about this ministry with the entire congregation because the leaders now see that besides sending people overseas, there is an entire mission field in Geylang. And God's heart is as much for the people right here as it is for those far, far away.

Yet, I also think it is different between big and small churches. I was speaking at a youth camp of a small church recently and the pastor who was there caught the vision immediately as it was something that God had been laying on his heart for awhile now. He immediately mobilised the leaders to come join us for the prayer walks and started preaching about it in his sermons. So in a small church, it is much faster. It definitely takes more time in a large church since there are so many more ministries, layers, considerations, etc. But it is okay. It is about catching God's heart.

And nobody should dictate that there is only one social justice ministry everyone must be involved in just because God laid it on his or her heart. It is not about you. I do not believe there is just one ministry God has called the whole church to since God has given us different gifts, talents, passions and experiences. In my church, there are multiple justice and mercy ministries. We have a prison in-care and after-care ministry, we reach out to the poor and needy around us, some of us go to Geylang, etc., and I think that is great!

I think God wants us to see His heart and respond as He leads. And that will likely take time, patience, much sacrifice, community, faithful preaching of His Word, and all the gifts that God has given us.

7. What other thoughts do you have on this topic?

It is a conversation which cannot be had without the Gospel. It is easy to get caught up in the action. Without centering on the Gospel, it is easy to get married to your cause. Centering on the Gospel means anytime God says change direction, you drop it. Because it is about God doing it, not how much or what I have invested to see change or for the people we serve. That is why it is hard for professional organisations doing it. Or churches for that matter that feel they must have five-year roadmaps, etc. It is also very anti-Singaporean because it is anti-pragmatic. So more than just finding a balance between planning and moving with the Spirit, I think it is about constantly keeping focused on the Gospel, what it calls us to pick up and put down, and where it takes us to the glory and praise of God.

This work also calls for wisdom, clarity and integrity. It requires that I be clear about my role in different platforms. For example, when I train and teach social service professionals, I share snippets about the work we do with the local street ladies and how we work with their families to highlight how as social workers, we must be mindful of cultural and sub-cultural differences to work effectively with our clients. However, it is not always appropriate to share that much of what we do since we primarily bath our desire to see not just their lives change but for them to have eternal life, in worship and prayer. Conversely, although this ministry I serve with wanted me to join them in the capacity of a social worker to some of the ladies we worked with, I decided against it since my burden in working with these ladies is that they may know Christ, that I may teach, share, show and talk about Him in and through all I do, and since I want to be true to the ethics of the social work profession, I chose not to relate to them as their social worker but as a befriender and mentor. So it is important to be clear and wise about our roles in relation to those we serve. They often need professional social services AND much spiritual, emotional and other forms of support. So we need to each work in our areas of strengths, passions and expertise, abide by the structures, play creatively in the space, but always keep our integrity.

8. What's the point of all these things that you are doing?

It is about reconciling people to Christ. No matter how far off they are. People, policy makers, ask what is your agenda? We *buay paiseh* one. To let people know they are made in the image of God. That God is pursuing them. That God is pouring on them extravagant grace. That's how we earn the right to do this.

I have learnt that we are most effective at social justice work when we have been emptied of our sense of self, ambition, and all that makes us feel secure. I realised that if any of the ladies I work with were to turn around and ask me what I had given up for the sake of the Gospel since we asked them to give up their life on the streets to come, taste and see that the Lord is good, I have to be certain that Christ was my soul's satisfaction.

And when He is, then He often challenges us to give up things that used to satisfy us or give us a sense of security, that we may constantly test, taste and see that He is good. And then that comes forth powerfully and sincerely to the ladies who are learning about who Christ is from what they see of us and our relationship with Him. And that is why I believe that apart from worship and prayer, social justice work in itself can be very much about self if it is not from Him, through Him, and for His glory alone.

One of the areas of tensions in working with the marginalised and voiceless is to do with respecting their beliefs and religious backgrounds and not being overbearing with ours, especially since we are in a position of power and in control of the resources and the help they need from us. Yet, we want to be completely upfront and uninhibited in saying that we do desire that they come to the saving knowledge of Jesus Christ. I have learnt that it's a genuine love and concern for their wellbeing that melts down these barriers.

I remember how one of the street ladies we worked with insisted that her son not join the other kids for devotions although he could join in for all other activities. We respected her decision although we were saddened. After awhile though, she fell so behind on her nursery school fees in the religious institution her son attended that she had to pull him out of school. Desiring that he return to school, we gave her a list of all nurseries around the area and asked her to call and enquire which one would give her a kinder rate given her financial situation. Finally, she chose to enrol her son in a nursery run by a church. When we went with her to enrol him into school, we made sure she understood that it was a Christian-run nursery started by a church that would have devotions daily. She said she knew and when asked why she allowed her son to attend this school of all other schools, she simply said "It's the only place where the

Principal spoke to me with respect and was willing to charge me so little and let him enrol so soon."

So where our words and testimony may have its limits, our showing of extravagant love and grace have none. And it is by these actions and reflections of Christ that the hardest heart will see Christ. So social justice work is not just for those at the frontlines but for every Christian who is called to do justice, love kindness, and walk humbly before our God (Micah 6:8).

When there is complete allegiance to justice work, there is abundance. When you have nothing of your own, you will have everything. And you are just writing on your Father's cheque. And the people will see it. It is your greatest credibility. Not what we do, but Who we belong to and how He calls us to live our lives for Him and others around us.

10

Journey's End— Or What's the Point of All This?

> ... We shall not cease from exploration
> And the end of all our exploring
> Will be to arrive where we started
> And know the place for the first time.
> Through the unknown, unremembered gate
> When the last of earth left to discover
> Is that which was the beginning;
> At the source of the longest river
> The voice of the hidden waterfall
> And the children in the apple-tree
>
> Not known, because not looked for
> But heard, half-heard, in the stillness
> Between two waves of the sea.
> Quick now, here, now, always—
> A condition of complete simplicity
> (Costing not less than everything)
> And all shall be well and
> All manner of thing shall be well
> When the tongues of flames are in-folded
> Into the crowned knot of fire
> And the fire and the rose are one.
>
> —TS Eliot, "Little Gidding" (1942)

A. Returning to the First Things

I began this book by talking about the stirrings of a journey which I embarked on to understand what Jesus had meant by the Great Commission to "make disciples... teaching them to observe all [Jesus had] commanded" and to "proclaim the gospel". I explored what God's Word says about "justice". The journey led me to many places—both physical and metaphysical—and to meet many people—from the past and from the present. The journey led me to do things I never imagined I could have done, to experience things which were never within my mental horizon. At the present conclusion of—perhaps more a pause in—this journey, I have arrived at where I started. But as it has been said, "you cannot step twice into the same stream".[683] It is thus an appropriate time for me to attempt to pull the different strands explored in this book together. Here I return to the 'first things'.

Beginning with the Beginning, God created the universe as good, beautiful and pleasing. All of creation was in harmony with their Creator. When the Fall happened—whether or not it was divinely intended—all that was good, beautiful and pleasing became shameful. All relationships ruptured—between God and humanity, between humans, and between humanity and creation. Ergo, the consequences of the Fall pervading all of humanity and all of history; consequences including injustice, suffering, brokenness, shame and guilt.

Yet, God has always desired for His people to live in justice, mercy, righteousness and faithfulness in all their relationships. This was constantly expressed through different means, but always through God's divine revelation to, and in relationship with, His people. The history of God's people as recorded in the biblical narrative is marked by failure after failure to live up to this demand. God's Kingdom was in ruins because His people rejected Him as King. Yet, humanity had always sought for themselves kingdoms and kings. God's people had to constantly negotiate between the earthly kingdoms and kings they were subjected to, and the Kingdom of God they truly, ultimately belonged to. Yet, God did not leave His people without hope. In prophecy after prophecy, God promised a King who would establish His Kingdom perfectly and eternally.

---

683 Plato, *Cratylus*, 402a.

At the divinely appointed time, the one true King of God's Kingdom arrived. The Gospel of the Kingdom of God is the good news that Jesus is the King of God's Kingdom and that He has arrived to establish this Kingdom. Jesus inaugurated a new form of God's Kingdom through the Cross, rather than wielding any earthly form of power. This reveals the ethos of God's Kingdom: Humble suffering service rather than power and coercion.

The entrance to God's Kingdom is at the Cross of the King. By God's grace, anyone can have faith in Jesus and enter the Kingdom. This is the New Covenant open to all. By grace, those who are citizens of God's Kingdom, while also living as resident aliens and exilic sojourners in their earthly kingdoms, are able to live justly, love mercy, walk humbly in righteousness and serve God with faithfulness.

At the right time, the King of Kings will return to bring to fruition perfect justice, love and righteousness throughout the world. The world will then return to the Edenic state of *shalom* in a new heavenly city. Everything will be transformed. Everything will be renewed. Stumps will give life. Ashes will turn into beauty. Ruins will turn into glory.

That is the Gospel which God's Kingdom people are to proclaim and demonstrate as worship unto God. They are to live out the teachings of Christ, including all He had taught about justice, mercy and righteousness. Such justice, mercy and righteousness are to be our expression of covenantal faithfulness in response to God's own covenantal faithfulness to us.

That is the Micah Mandate. That is *God's justice demand*. Such justice, mercy and righteousness have a predominantly *social* aspect because they concern what is good and right in the relationships between God and humanity, between humans, and between creation and humanity. The failure to live these out is sin. Yet, as New Covenant people, our sins have been forgiven by grace in Jesus. We are then justified by grace to be just. *The justice demand has been fulfilled to become our grace-fuelled justice response.*

Through the prism of the New Covenant, justice, mercy and righteousness are refracted into the ethics of love and good works. The primary, though not exclusive, locus of our lives' expression of this ethic—the ethic of love as justice, mercy and righteousness—is the Church, the community of God's Kingdom people on earth. The Church is also the means by which we express, proclaim and demonstrate the Gospel of God's Kingdom. The organic Church, each individual believer playing different roles within her, is to be faithful to this calling in accordance with the leading of God through His Holy Spirit. *In summary, justice, as an expression of the Greatest Commandments, is integral to the life of a Jesus disciple; disciples are to make disciples and to express the Gospel of the Kingdom of God pursuant to the Great Commission.*

What then is *justice*? The social aspect of justice or "social justice" as gleaned from God's Word is God's especial concern for the socially, economically and politically marginalised to be included into His community. Such inclusion may be through social, economic and political means. This may take the form of provision, empowerment, deliverance or establishing just institutions. This may be at personal, developmental or systemic levels. Biblical justice is always pursued justly and in accordance with what is morally good; it resists exploitation; it is generous; it is dignifying and responsible; it is relational and grounded in empathy; it seeks to restore and reconcile; it delivers people from oppression; it involves responsible

> **The justice demand has been fulfilled to become our grace-fuelled response.**

stewardship, especially of creation; it requires practical wisdom and virtue to be sought from God.

These spiritual truths must challenge our lives, our orientation, our paradigms, our behaviour and our communities. We must critically examine whether we are actively or unintentionally buttressing societies, systems or institutions of exclusion rather than inclusion, of division rather than harmony, of unfairness rather than equity, of oppression rather than freedom, of violence rather than peace, of injustice rather than justice.

Yet, biblical social justice is glaringly missing from the Singapore Church's vocabulary, pulpits and praxis. A generation of church members are beginning to question this absence and feel disenchanted with the status quo. *The Singapore Church must reclaim biblical social justice as an integral facet of living the Gospel and manifesting God's Kingdom.* This is a challenge and an opportunity for the Singapore Church in this generation to faithfully pursue Christ's Great Commission and Greatest Commandments.

B. The End and Always is Being with

What is the point of all our justice-seeking? Is it not futile if in the end, our goal is not to build a Christian Kingdom on earth (as I have briefly discussed in Chapter 8)? In a conversation I had with a friend, he expressed to me a sense of meaninglessness in the social justice ministry he and several others had been involved in for a few years, befriending needy families in York Hill. "My aunt asked me, what's the objective of whatever I was doing. I thought hard about it. And I could not answer." He then compared his ministry with that of another friend's, which he felt was clear in its goals: To develop literacy in its beneficiaries. Indeed, what is the end point of all our endeavour on earth? Even if we were able to successfully develop literacy among low-income children, or promote social economic flourishing among the poor, or include the marginalised at the fringes of society into the mainstream, *so what?*

In response to my friend, I asked, "What's man's chief end?"

He said, "Well, the Westminster Shorter Catechism says, to glorify God and enjoy Him forever."

"Exactly," I said.

"What?"

"Revelation 21 says that at the end, God will dwell with us, and we will be his people, and *God himself will be with us*."

"So, what are you saying?"

"If the end point is to *be with* God and have God *be with* us, shouldn't that be our present purpose as well? As between God and us, and as between others and us? Your ministry of befriending; it's doing exactly that. Being with people. And who knows—God may through that bring them to be with Him."

That conversation sharpened my own perspective of what I was supposed to be doing on earth. If indeed the perfected Kingdom of God in the New Heavens and the New Earth, in the Holy City, is a place of *being with one another*, a place where we would literally 'hang out', then it must be right that our present lives should have a shadow of that state. *The end is the always*. The end begins in the present.

In John 17:3, Jesus said that eternal life is "that they know you, the only true God, and Jesus Christ whom you have sent." Eternal life does not begin upon mortal death. Instead, eternal life begins now. Eternal life is to know God. Eternal life is being with God. Another friend of mine used to have difficulty with the idea of an eternity in heaven. The concept of eternity was in itself a terrifying one for him. And the often-caricatured picture of heaven as endless kneeling and singing worship songs did not exactly help. A couple of us were just 'chilling' together at a *kopitiam* over *kopi peng* after church service on Sunday talking about this. So I told him, what if heaven is just the extended freedom of being able to do this? Just hanging out together in the presence of God and one another. It was a comforting thought for him, as it is for me. Transposing backwards from the end to the present, it follows for me that the joy of *being with* people within a community of grace and love is both our present and final purpose.

A grace community cannot possibly be a community of love, a community of *shalom*, without justice. Imagine—if it is at all possible—that God's community of saints in heaven does not treat one another with justice. It would not—could not—be God's community.

This is of fundamental importance regarding how we should live in this age on earth. If the 'end' is the 'always', and if the Kingdom of God in the New Heaven and the New Earth is supposed to manifest in the present age through God's Kingdom community, i.e., the Church today, then our living out of the Gospel of God's Kingdom, our proclamation and demonstration of the Kingdom, must begin *today*. Our lives must be one continuous unbroken line extending heavenward. The point of all our justice-seeking today is to manifest God's Kingdom in the present so that all may know and pursue His Kingdom for eternity. And if the end point of justice-seeking is egalitarian participation in God's community, i.e., being with one another, then every moment of "being with" people is itself part of just living, and every justice pursuit must involve "being with" people.

> **A grace community cannot possibly be a community of love, a community of shalom, without justice.**

C. The Joy of the Just

Yet, pursuing social justice entails suffering, sacrifice and disappointments. People who pursue justice risk being persecuted. A Christian activist friend sent me a BBC news report which inspired her.[684] The report was about an Indian Christian John Dayal who left a career in journalism to investigate human rights abuses, including violence against ethnic and religious minorities, especially persecuted Christians in India. His activism resulted in him being a target of extremist Hindu nationalists' ridicule and death threats. One of the Beatitudes in Jesus' Sermon on the Mount goes: "Blessed are those who are persecuted for righteousness' sake, for theirs is the kingdom of heaven."[685] Indeed, while there may be persecution for pursuing righteousness and justice, God guarantees them the Kingdom of Heaven.

Living a life of justice necessarily entails sacrifice. It means generously giving from what we have laboured to earn. Our sinful flesh may say, "This is my hard-earned money!" But the Spirit will remind us, do not cling on to money but be content with what we have, because our loving Heavenly Father will never leave or forsake us.[686] Living justly means giving up our privileges to what the world will offer us as a matter of entitlement, so that we may do right by others. Again, our sinful flesh may say, "But this is what I deserve," or "This is what I need"! But the Spirit will remind us, seek first the Kingdom of God and His righteousness, and all these things, God will add to you.[687] Our sinful flesh may say, "But that is too inconvenient." The Spirit will say, if you try to save, preserve, make easy, convenience

---

684 "Viewpoint: The depressing reality of being trolled", *BBC* (18 September 2015), http://www.bbc.com/news/world-asia-india-34266119.
685 Matthew 5:10.
686 Hebrews 13:5.
687 Matthew 6:33.

your life, you will lose it; whoever loses his life for Jesus' sake will find his life.[688] And the Spirit will say, if you purport to serve Jesus, you must follow Him, and where Jesus is, there will His servant be also; are you where Jesus is?[689]

But if we expect to actually achieve the eradication of poverty, injustice, oppression, suffering, marginalisation and indeed all wrongs, on earth through our efforts, we will be sorely disappointed. If we expect to even achieve anything to any degree at all, we will be just as disappointed. For there will never cease to be poor in the land.[690] Because sin will not be wholly eradicated until the Final Day.

So what is the point? I think the point of our faith expressing itself in love and justice is relationships; it is about being with people. And in these things, there will be joy.

Amidst poverty, there can be joy. Because blessed are the poor, theirs is the Kingdom of God.[691] Amidst suffering, there can be joy.[692] Amidst the troubles, there will be comfort.[693] From grief, there will be joy.[694] This joy and comfort come from God out of His grace and always through relationships, through people being with one another, through love. And that is why social justice is so important. Social justice is about bringing every person who was once outside of community into a community of grace. Through this, all of us may be with one another and with God. And in that, there will be joy.[695] As Pope Francis wrote, "[t]o be evangelizers of souls, we need to develop a spiritual taste for

---

688   Matthew 16:24-26.
689   John 12:26.
690   Deuteronomy 15:11.
691   Luke 2:20.
692   1 Peter 4:12-19; Romans 5:1-5.
693   2 Corinthians 1:3.
694   Jeremiah 31:33; John 16:20.
695   Psalm 21:6.

being close to people's lives and to discover that this is itself a source of greater joy".[696]

I think we would be hard pressed to find anyone who would disagree that a universal intrinsic desire of humanity is to have happiness. The important question is: How do we obtain happiness? The wise Teacher in Ecclesiastes similarly concludes "that there is nothing better for [humanity] than to be joyful and to do good as long as they live".[697] But do not miss the deep insight revealed in that observation. There is a necessary relationship between *joy* and *doing good*. The ancient wisdom literature texts inform us that "[w]hen justice is done, it is a joy to the righteous but terror to evildoers"[698] and "[t]he hope of the righteous brings joy, but the expectation of the wicked will perish".[699] Indeed, the Kingdom of God is about righteousness, peace and *joy* in the Holy Spirit.[700] The one who serves God as a good and faithful servant will "enter into the joy of [his] master".[701] Jesus declared to His disciples that if they keep His commandments, they will abide in His love, and by this, Jesus' *joy* may be in them and their *joy* will be full.[702] The apostle Paul wrote in agony to his flock that he had worked for their joy because their joy was his joy.[703] The apostle John wrote of his joy being complete by his writing to his flock in order that they may have fellowship with him and with God.[704] When Jesus' 72 disciples returned from preaching the Gospel of the Kingdom

---

696 Apostolic Exhortation *Evangelii Gaudium* Of The Holy Father Francis (2013) at para. 268.
697 Ecclesiastes 3:12.
698 Proverbs 21:15.
699 Proverbs 10:28.
700 Romans 14:17.
701 Matthew 25:21.
702 John 15:7-11.
703 2 Corinthians 1:24; 2:3; 7:4; Philippians 1:25; 1 Thessalonians 2:19-20; Philemon 7.
704 1 John 1:1-4.

of God, they returned with joy (notwithstanding that we have no idea whether anyone believed in their Gospel).[705]

The profound law of God's Kingdom is thus: *As you seek the joy of others, you will receive joy.* As you give, you will receive. As you die, you will live. As you seek justice for others, you will have joy. As you live a life of justice, you will have joy. This is the joy of the Gospel.[706]

The joy of the Gospel is the joy that is founded on the firm conviction that we are loved by a God who is also the sovereign Lord over human history and over the whole universe.[707] The joy of the Gospel is founded on the spiritual truth that the Christian faith is both very hard and very easy: God asks for all of us, but also offers all we ever need.[708]

Here, I have come to a point of my journey where I pause and admit that, living a life of justice, mercy and righteousness has not been easy. In truth, each day is a struggle. It is a struggle to live justly especially when it calls for serving the unlovable. But such encounters remind me that I am myself unlovable before God. It is only by His grace that I am embraced into His love, His family, His Kingdom. Each day's struggle reminds me that I need the grace of God in Christ, who is my perfectly just, merciful and righteous King, and who judges me not on my failings but His victory. And that gives me assurance and joy. Here, I wish you joy.

> **As you live a life of justice, you will have joy. This is the joy of the Gospel.**

---

705 Luke 10:17.
706 Apostolic Exhortation *Evangelii Gaudium* Of The Holy Father Francis (2013).
707 1 John 4:19. Revelation 11:15.
708 Matthew 11:30; 2 Corinthians 12:9; CS Lewis, *Mere Christianity* (Harper Collins, 2001) at 196-198. Apostolic Exhortation *Evangelii Gaudium* Of The Holy Father Francis (2013) at para. 12.

I pray that you may be convicted by the Gospel of this mighty but also tender King.

May you always experience the profound joy of the Gospel, *the joy of the just.*

***

Thank you for journeying with me thus far. As mentioned in the first chapter, this book can only be a small part of a lifelong process of seeking God's calling on your life in relation to pursuing justice and mercy. When I first started, I was lost and lonely. But I found community. And it was in and through community that I discerned God's leading.

I hope that you will give me, and others who share the same burden as I, the privilege of sharing your faith journey in the pursuit of justice together with our Micah Singapore community. Please write to me at thejusticedemand@gmail.com or visit the book's website at <http://www.ronaldjjwong.com/the-justice-demand/> to connect with and join our community. Together, we can journey in pursuing God's work of justice in His Kingdom.

GRACEW♥RKS

Graceworks is a publishing and training consultancy based in Singapore dedicated to promoting relational transformation in church and society, and seeing lives transformed through books that present truth for life.

Our publications can be found on
www.graceworks.com.sg/store
and at major online book retailers.

Get in touch with us at enquiries@graceworks.com.sg
or follow us @GraceworksSG.

www.ingramcontent.com/pod-product-compliance
Lightning Source LLC
LaVergne TN
LVHW010306070526
838199LV00065B/5463